To Liz
Let me be your
guide to the
place I call
home.

Cheers,

Debbie Giuquinda

Cover design by Linda Pierro, Flint Media

Editor: Keidi Keating

Photos by Debbie Gioquindo

Interior Layout by Christi Koehl

IBSN: 978-0-9981540-0-8

E-Book IBSN: 978-0-9981540-1-5

Library of Congress Control Number: 2017900223

Published by Million Dollar Sips LLC
www.milliondollarsips.com

DEDICATIONS

This book is dedicated to the many wineries, breweries, distilleries and cideries in the Hudson Valley who opened up their cellars to me, and spent time talking to me, keeping me updated and welcoming me into their tasting rooms.

To the members of Hudson Valley Tourism who have shown me through the many years what a great region we live in and who always have their doors open to me.

To my husband, Paul, thank you for encouraging me and never doubting what I can accomplish. For allowing me to be 'locked in my office' and always having a glass of wine waiting for me when I come out. I love you and couldn't have done this without you and your unconditional love and support.

Tapping the Hudson Valley

by Debbie Gioquindo

TABLE OF CONTENTS

About the Author

A true apostle for the Hudson Valley wine region, Debbie Gioquindo grew up in the Hudson Valley and made it her home raising her two children in LaGrange.

If you would have asked Debbie when she was in college whether she even liked wine, she would have said no. In the late 1990's, when her husband was told by his doctor to lay off the hard liquor and drink beer or wine, that changed Debbie's mind about wine. Out went Paul's scotch and Debbie's vodka. They went to the liquor store and brought home a bottle of Rioja, a bright young red that exemplified the beginning of a fun and educational journey with wine.

Debbie knew her family had some kind of wine history but it didn't become clear until recently. Her family dates back to the 1700's in Tapolca, Hungary where they were wine merchants and vineyard owners. They had immigrated to the region from the Rhine, bringing their grapevines. The family was very instrumental in the European wine trade.

Debbie began educating herself about wine, and in 2006 she began her blog "Hudson Valley Wine Goddess." Her intention was to share her knowledge and journey with her followers. In 2010, she received her Certified Specialist of Wine designation from the Society of Wine Educators, and in 2011 she became a Wine Location Specialist in Port and Champagne. In 2015, she was ranked #38 in the Excel Wines "Top 100 Most Influential Wine Bloggers."

Growing up in the Hudson Valley, Debbie had a career in marketing and travel. She worked in various local media outlets and owned a travel agency "Personal Touch Travel and Exclusive Wine Vacations." She became a Certified Travel Counselor in 1997. Her love of wine and experience in marketing and travel led her to become the marketing director for the Shawangunk Wine Trail.

Raising the awareness for the wine trail and the region, Debbie was responsible for the regional branding initiative put forth by the New York Wine and Grape Foundation for regional branding and she launched Hudson Valley Wine Country. It has been said by many winery owners that Debbie was responsible for putting the Hudson Valley Wine Region on the map.

In 2008, Debbie was named Chairperson of the Hudson Valley Wine Competition. To bring more awareness to the wines of the region she moved the competition in 2010 to the Hudson Valley Wine and Food Festival and included spirits. It was then renamed "The Hudson Valley Wine and Spirits Competition," and it includes wines, spirits, and ciders produced in the Hudson Valley. When the wine competition concludes, you can find Debbie giving wine seminars at the festival.

Debbie had a dream of producing a wine of her own, and in 2011 that dream came true when she partnered with author Keryl Pesce via a Twitter post and launched Happy Bitch Wines. The name coming from Pesce's well-read and much enjoyed book of same name.

Debbie also is a contributing writer for *Hudson Valley Wine Magazine.*

When not writing about wine, Debbie enjoys traveling, cooking, downhill skiing, and spending time with her family, her husband, two children and her loving 11 year old Boykin Spaniel, Summer.

Introduction

Whether you are a local or a visitor, I hope you use this book to navigate the region, taste through it, and see the many sites the Hudson Valley has to offer.

I happened upon wine by accident. I didn't realize I lived in the oldest wine region in America. I immersed myself with the wine and history of the region in the past twelve or so years, and not only has the number of wineries, breweries, cideries and distilleries increased, but the beverages being produced are award winning. Just like my children, I have an emotional connection to the region and I am so proud of the quality of the craft beverages being produced and the richness of the region's history.

When I owned my travel agency I planned many itineraries for people traveling through the Hudson Valley. When I worked with the Shawangunk Wine Trail, I helped customers plan their winery route during the trail events and for their weekend visit.

Today, social media makes it easy for people to contact me and ask for suggestions on where to taste and eat, and what to see in the Valley. That is what prompted me to realize that I should share this information with you.

I grew up in the Hudson Valley, have raised my children here, traveled the routes, tasted the beverages, and stopped and admired the gardens and historical sites. It's a very special place and is getting better known by people who seek out good food, wine and other artisanal beverages.

One thing I urge you to do when you are out tasting is to TRY different things, whether it's wine, cider, beer or spirits. Get outside your comfort zone and you might be pleasantly surprised at what you find. It's okay if you don't like it. You won't hurt anyone's feelings, as every palate is different. Believe me, my husband and I don't always agree.

Many of the wines in the region are produced in small case production, which means, if you like it, purchase it. Don't wait to come back a different day, or go home and decide to order it online (then you have to pay for shipping). Chances are it might be sold out. Once sold out, you're out of luck. If you truly like the wine, purchase at least two bottles: one for now and one for later.

Remember, when you are out tasting, it's the only time you can try before you buy. When you get home, share your wine and experience with your friends.

Cheers,
Debbie Gioquindo, CTC, CSW, WLS
www.hudsonvalleywinegoddess.com

A BRIEF HISTORY OF
HUDSON VALLEY CRAFT
BEVERAGES

1677

French Huguenots planted the first vines in New Paltz, New York.

1804

Robert A. Underhill purchased 250 acres on Croton Point for farming. Over the next twenty years he experimented with cross-breeding native and European vines and created grapes that would be hardy enough to survive the cold climate of the East. His vineyard was the first large vineyard in the country.

1816

Jean Jacques purchased a farm in the Hudson Valley and began planting grapes. In 1837, Jacques Brothers Winery was established. Today this winery is known as Brotherhood Winery, the oldest continuously operated winery in America.

1845

William Cornell established a vineyard near Clintondale in Ulster County

1877

Andrew Caywood began his vineyard experimenting with hybrid grapes at what is Benmarl Winery

1976

New York Governor Hugh Carey signed the Farm Winery Bill making it affordable for the smaller winery to receive a winery license.

2007

New York Farm Distillery Act passed letting farms become distilleries and open tasting room to tourists

2012

New York Governor Andrew M. Cuomo signed the Farm Brewing Law

2013

New York Governor Andrew M. Cuomo signed the Farm Cider Bill.

Today, the Hudson Valley has become a craft beverage mecca with wineries, distilleries, cideries, breweries, and a region full of history spanning 144 miles from Albany to Yonkers.

A BRIEF HISTORY OF
HUDSON VALLEY WINE TRAILS

EARLY1980

Hudson River Wine Council was
formed. Consisted of all the
Hudson Valley Wineries

EARLY 1990

Jack Ransom of Rivendell Winery
formed a wine trail that included:
Rivendell, Adair, Baldwin, Brimstone,
Magnanini, and Walker Valley. That
was the beginning of The
Shawangunk Wine Trail.

EARLY 1990

Dutchess Wine Trail formed.

2009

Berkshire Beverage Trail founded
in 2009 by Sue Goold Miller of
Brookview Station Winery and
Carlo and Dominique DeVito of
Hudson Chatham Winery.

Hudson Valley Terroir

The Hudson Valley wine region is a very geological complex region. With
180 degree days and 3000 hours of sunlight, the Hudson Valley has a
longer growing season. The steep Palisades are an important conduit of
maritime air the region receives. The Hudson River is also a tidal estuary
where the sea water meets the fresh water keeping the climate
temperate and serving as a conduit for maritime breezes from the south.

The ground consists of deposits of shale, slate, schist and limestone
known as the Taconic Province.

Enjoying Your Day Out Tasting

Some of the tasting rooms in the region are close together, while others are a fifteen to twenty minute drive apart. You will find tasting rooms of all sizes and shapes. Some are large and spacious with the feeling you are in the Loire Valley, while others are much smaller with a homey feeling. Regardless of the size, they all have one thing in common and that is to educate you, tell the story of the winery, brewery, distillery, the winemaker, the brewmaster, the distiller, and their libations. In many instances the owner, winemaker, distiller or brewmaster will be speaking with you.

Before heading out for the day or weekend consider these things you need to know to make the most of your visit.

Many of the larger wineries are open all year-round but may only be open on the weekends during the off season, November through March. If you are planning to visit in the winter check the operating hours in advance of your visit. If a tasting room is closed for the season, don't hesitate to contact them as many will take appointments.

Most tasting rooms are open from April through New Year's Eve. Peak season runs from May through October, with mid-September to the end of October being the busiest period. In November and December expect weekend hours, or by appointment if visiting mid-week.

Personally, I think the best time to visit the tasting rooms is June to August. The tasting rooms won't be as packed as they are in the fall when everyone is trying to take advantage of the changing of the leaves and harvest. Weekdays are less crowded than weekends.

Here's an insider tip: Travel in a group may get you unique experiences. Groups of of eight people or more, must call ahead and make reservations. Many tasting rooms have private areas for groups. In addition, your group tasting can be enhanced with special pairings if planned ahead of time. If it is busy and your group shows up without an appointment they may well turn you away.

You will incur fees in the tasting room ranging from $8 to $13 depending on the establishment. Wineries will give you a list to choose from. Make sure you read the descriptions and mark off what you want to taste. Each tasting usually consists of at least five selections. In breweries you can get flights of their beers. This is the time to taste whatever you like and go outside your comfort zone. Promise to try at least one selection you wouldn't normally try, regardless of whether it's a wine, beer, cider or a distilled spirit. This is the time to do it! This small sample will give you an affordable way to try something new and different. Open your taste buds and enhance your palate!

Don't be afraid to share a tasting, especially if you are the driver. It is perfectly acceptable to spit! Don't be embarrassed or ashamed to use that spit bucket, as that is what it is there for. If there isn't a bucket in front of you, and you have a mouth full, point at it and someone will pass it down. Don't feel obligated to drink the entire pour. Just dump it in the bucket. Nobody's feelings will be hurt.

When tasting wine, you will usually taste white before red, dry before sweet with dessert, and late harvest wines last. You can rinse your glass between tastings with the water on the table. Some may feel that the water will dilute the next tasting and insist on you rinsing your glass with a small amount of the wine you will be tasting next. Make sure if you taste red and then go to a white, you do rinse thoroughly. The white selection should be white and not rosé.

The crackers that the winery provides are to cleanse your palate in between each taste. They are not meant for you to snack on the entire time, so save some for the next person. Remember, you have snacks in the car.

If you really like a wine and are thinking of purchasing a bottle or two, it's okay to ask for a second tasting. Make sure you tell them that is the objective.

Remember, you are under no obligation to purchase in the tasting room. But if you do like the wine, cider, beer or spirit, purchase at least a bottle of it. Many of the wines, ciders, and spirits are produced in small quantities, fifty to two hundred case production. Once you get home and decide you want a particular bottle, they could be sold out. Many of the products aren't distributed, so you won't be able to find it in your local wine shop. The last thing you want to do is incur UPS charges if you order online. Many wineries offer case discounts or multi bottle discounts when purchasing.

If you are really impressed with the wines at the winery, check whether they have a wine club. That is a great way to enjoy the wines throughout the year. Wine clubs all have different structures; some are quarterly, some are twice a year, some are referred to as a case club, and based on how many cases you purchase.

A few things to remember before signing on that dotted line for the wine club is to make sure you really like the wine. If you live a good distance away and know you can't pick up a bottle at your wine store that's a good reason to join. Double check on shipping and make sure the winery can ship to your state. Interstate shipping laws don't allow all wineries to ship to all states. Read the fine print. See how long the commitment is for the wine club. Some might be a year. Remember membership has its privileges and there are usually complimentary tastings and special events held throughout the year.

Going out tasting for a day or weekend can be overwhelming. How will you remember that wine you liked so much? Don't be afraid to take a picture of the bottle or record your notes on your phone. You might even want to use an app like Delectable, Cellar Tracker or Vivino to record your tasting notes.

Many of the wineries, distilleries, cideries, and breweries are family and pet friendly. Before you go, make sure to find out. You don't want someone to have to wait in the parking lot with your puppy while everyone else is inside tasting. If you bring your children, make sure they are well behaved and you look after them. When my kids were aged six and eight we went to a tasting room in Virginia and did the tour. There was one other couple with us and they were much older and gave us a look to kill. How could we bring our kids with us? At the conclusion of the tour the owner asked if we had any questions. At this point my son raised his hand and asked, "How do you know when the grapes are ready to pick?" That was a turning point with this other couple. The owner said that was a great question and answered it. While we were at the tasting bar, my kids sat at a table and played cards. The couple who was ready to kill us for spoiling their afternoon by bringing our kids along, now became our good friends for the afternoon and everyone had an enjoyable time. My point is to make sure your kids are well behaved. Engage your children, wine making, brewing and distilling offers science education. Don't forget to bring snacks for the kids. When they see adults cleansing their palate with crackers they might get hungry.

Day Out Tasting Check List

Eat a Good Breakfast

Pack a Picnic
Make sure to include lots of water and snacks .

Empty Cooler
This is for your wine purchases. You don't want the wine to spoil in the hot car.

Don't Wear
Aftershave, cologne, perfume, use chapstick or lipstick. It will interfere with the taste and aroma of what's in the glass.

No Gum or Coffee
It will kill your palate and spoil your experience.

How To Use This Book

Planning a travel itinerary for a day or weekend can be nerve wracking and overwhelming, especially if you don't know the area or the right routes to take. Then there is the question of where to eat and where to stay.

Through my twenty years of planning itineraries for people in countries outside of the United States and wine regions in California and New York, it's my pleasure to put together itineraries for you in my backyard. Itineraries I have traveled many times. Wineries, breweries, cideries, and distilleries I've tasted at, restaurants I've eaten in, sites I've visited, and accommodations I've put people up in.

Use this book as a guide. Some itineraries are long and you might not get through it all in one day depending on how long you stay at each place. Or you might have no interest in going to some of the mentioned stops, and that's okay. I've included lodging at the end of each itinerary in case you don't want to drive all the way home after a day out.

The itineraries are structured so you can maximize your time from where you enter the Hudson Valley until you have to go home. I tried to include a mix of things to do with each itinerary. If you have more time to spend in the region, you can link the different itineraries together. I wanted to give you a good variety yet not overload you.

I have designed the itineraries with the four entry points into the Hudson Valley (Albany, Harriman, Newburgh & Millbrook) within each of the designated focus areas, wineries, breweries, and sightseeing. You will find distilleries and cideries mixed in on all itineraries. We call the Hudson River 'the great divide' because everyone seems to stay on their own side. Many of the multi-day itineraries have you crossing the river to get a well-rounded experience of the different personalities each side holds. You'll see what I mean.

Travelers from New York City, and Connecticut can enter the region from the Taconic Parkway or the two various New York State Thruway points. It's important to look at the itineraries to decide your entrance: Harriman or Newburgh.

Coming from New Jersey and Pennsylvania you will want to enter through either the Harriman Interchange to Route 17 or Newburgh exit off I84.

If you are coming from Massachusetts, Vermont, New Hampshire or Western New York you can enter through the Albany region or head south on the Thruway or Taconic Parkway to any of the entry points.

The itineraries are very packed and I know you won't be interested in making every stop. Make sure you read the descriptions and plan for what interests you. If you want to include something on the three-day itinerary during the one-day trip and it's not too out of the way, then go for it.

I do want to stress the fact that reservations are needed. If you think you are going to come in the fall and stumble upon a hotel room, think again. There are certain times of the year where occupancy rates are very high. May is one such month because of the various college graduations. Restaurant reservations are the same way. To be on the safe side, always make reservations.

Although this book is designed with the assumption you have a car, you can also reach the region by rail. Metro North Railroad (http://www.mta.info/mnr) runs from Grand Central Station to Beacon or Poughkeepsie and the eastern part of the county, Pawling and Dover Plains. On the western side of the river, Metro North is served by New Jersey Transit (http://www.njtransit.com/) from Hoboken to Harriman and Middletown. You can plan a day trip by taking the train up and arranging a car service and provide them with your pre-planned itinerary.

There are many car services available. Here are a few, but make sure you do your research:

Mahogany Ridge Transportation 845.724.4403
The Little Wine Bus 917.414.7947
The Little Beer Bus 917.414.7947
All Transportation Network 845.565.2306
West Point Tours 845.446.4724
Visconti 845.562.4040
Hudson Valley Craft Beer Tours 845.478.5118

Grape Varietals Grown in the Region

Seyval Blanc – French American hybrid grape cross between S.5656 and Rayon d'Or. Heavy producing white. Most widely planted white grape in the Hudson Valley. Produced dry it is similar to a Sauvignon Blanc. Flavors of green apple, pineapple, lemon, and grapefruit.

Baco Noir – French American hybrid grape cross between Folle Blanche, Grand Glabre, and V. riparia ordinair. Produces medium bodied, deeply tinted red wine with high acid levels and lots of berry, plum fruit, cedar tobacco, leather, and chocolate. It can have herbal notes of black pepper, licorice, and cinnamon.

Chardonnay – French Vinifera grape. Aromas of green apple, melon, and pear. Can be barrel aged or aged in stainless steel. Most widely planted vinifera grape in the Hudson Valley.

Cabernet Franc – Red vinifera grape best suited for growing in the Hudson Valley. Produces a wine with soft tannins, flavors of cranberry, tea, tobacco, mushroom, strawberry with a peppery nose. Hudson Valley's signature grape.

Pinot Noir – Light to medium bodied red wine with aromas of cherry, raspberries, strawberry, and some earthy tones.

Gamay Noir – French vinifera grape dating back to the fifteenth century. Light bodied acidic red wine that is a clone of Pinot Noir. Produces a wine with elements of blackcurrant, raspberry, and cranberry.

Vignoles – French American hybird. A cross between S.6905 and a Pinot Noir. White wine that can be made into a dry wine or late harvest wine. Floral aromas and fruity flavors of pineapple, green apple, grapefruit, bananas, peach, apricots, and tropical fruit.

Riesling – A crisp white wine characterized by mineral and slate flavors with fruit notes of peaches and apricots when fully ripened. It will also have characteristics of honeysuckle, jasmine, and petrol when well-aged.

Gewurztraminer – White wine with spicy characteristics, and floral aspects of lychee on the bouquet.

Vidal – French hybrid cross of St. Emilion x Rayon d'Or. High acidity white wine, clean citrus flavors of pineapple, lemon, and grapefruit. Can be made bone dry, barrel-aged or as an ice wine. Produces a good balanced wine that's paired well with seafood and poultry.

Frontenac – Named after a village in Minnesota, Frontenac is a Minnesota hybrid cross of MN 89 Riparia and Landot 4511. Very high in acidity. Flavors of black cherry and plum.

Traminette – A cross between Gewurztraminer and the French-American varietal Johannes, this grape is hardy and has good resistance to fungus. The taste is similar to a Gewurztraminer with its lychee and spicy characteristics.

DeChaunac – A hardy French-American hybrid grape cross of S.5163 and S. 793 which can withstand some of the harshest winters. Wines produced from this grape can be very inky in color and are medium body. You'll find flavors of leather, cinnamon, earthy notes, and dark berry.

Hudson Valley Cabernet Franc Coalition

As I am writing this first edition of this book I was honored to participate in a Hudson Valley Cabernet Franc tasting. I have to admit, Cabernet Franc is one of my favorite varietals, especially the ones that hail from the east coast cool climates. I love the black pepper spice on the finish, and that it's not a fruit bomb. It's elegant and exciting.

The Hudson Valley grape growers, winemakers and researchers from Cornell University, have been conducting extensive research on the Cabernet Franc grape. After many years of research, they found that Cabernet Franc really thrives in the Hudson Valley and they have designated it their "Flagship Wine."

The Hudson Valley Cabernet Franc Coalition was founded in the spring 2016 by Doug and MaryEllen Glorie, owners of Glorie Farm Winery, along with Linda Pierro and Robert Bedford of *Hudson Valley Wine Magazine*. The coalition consists of about two dozen area winemakers and grape growers who have committed to putting Cabernet Franc in the forefront of the region, supporting it with ongoing discussions and research on how and where it grows best. Most of all, to plant more.

One of the reasons Cabernet Franc grows so well in the Hudson Valley is that it can handle the cold weather. Cabernet Franc can handle temperatures below zero, usually to about minus nine, and there have been times in the Hudson Valley when it really does get that cold.

Hudson Valley grape growers have found through research with

Cornell that managing the grape canopy and getting rid of some leaves early enhances the grape to ripen accordingly. Allowing the sun to reach the grapes during verasion has eliminated the methoxypyrines (green pepper, vegetal notes) that were found in the wine. This is a key to producing a great Cabernet Franc.

What can you expect from Hudson Valley Cabernet Franc? Expressions of violets, raspberry, strawberry, blackberry, tea, tannins, oak, and closing with a gentle burst of black pepper.

Hudson Valley

Wineries

Day Tripping

Southern Tip of the Shawangunk Wine Trail

One-Day Itinerary

Suggested Stops

Palaia Winery • Brotherhood Winery • Orange County Distillery
• Warwick Valley Winery & Black Dirt Distillery • Clearview
Vineyard • Applewood Winery & Naked Flock Cider

Suggested Dining

Vinum Café • Iron Forge Inn

Suggested Lodging

Anton's on the Lake

Traveling on the New York State Thruway entering the region at the Harriman Interchange, Woodbury Toll. From the toll booth take the NY-17 ramp to NY-32 Suffern/Newburgh. Turn right onto NY-17 N/ Averill Avenue and keep left to NY-32 N. Driving time: 15 minutes.

PALAIA WINERY

10 Sweet Clover Road | Highland Mills, NY | 10930
845.928.5384 | http://www.palaiavineyards.com/

Take a trip back to the seventies where it was all about peace, love, and rock- n -roll. That is the vibe at Palaia Winery. In the year 2000, Jan and her husband Joe purchased a 200-year-old cow farm "The Seaman Homestead at Sweet Clover Farm" and planted 1500 vines. Built in the early 1800's the homestead now sits on thirty-two acres of what is left from the tract of land purchased from Aaron Burr in 1784. In 1888, the barn was added to the property and today it is home to the winery and tasting room. Their wines range from dry to sweet. They have music every weekend and a kickass outdoor stage venue that rocks in the summer months.

Take a left onto NY-32. Take a slight left onto Pleasant Hill Road. Turn left onto Orrs Mills Road then a slight left onto NY-94. Turn right onto Brotherhood Plaza Dr. Driving time: 15 minutes.

BROTHERHOOD "AMERICA'S OLDEST" WINERY
100 Brotherhood Plaza Drive | Washingtonville NY | 10992
845.496.3661 | http://www.brotherhood-winery.com/

Brotherhood is the oldest continuously operating winery in America, and a visit here is full of history of winemaking in the Hudson Valley and the country. It was started by John Jaques a cobbler who moved to a small town called Little York, which is now Washingtonville, New York in 1810. The first vintage Brotherhood produced was in 1839, the same year construction of the underground cellar began. Today you can tour the underground cellar, which has become a museum, and relive the history of Brotherhood. On display are artifacts dating back to the 1800's along with the history, the people, the vintage labels, and more. You will get a sense of how important Brotherhood was not only to the Hudson Valley, but to wine tourism as an industry. Taste their B Sparkling, a great inexpensive sparkling wine. If you like it sweet, try the Carpe Diem Spumante. One of the favorites around the holiday time is their Holiday Spiced Wine.

VINUM CAFÉ
84 Brotherhood Plaza Dr | Washingtonville, NY | 10992
845.496.9001 | http://vinumcafe.com/

Located on the site of Brotherhood Winery, Vinum Café occupies the ground floor of the original winery building built in 1839. Depending on time, you can dine in the café or restaurant. Both offer a nice variety ranging from soup to crab cakes, seafood choices, and steaks. Weather permitting you can sit outside and enjoy the historic scenery. If you would like to bring in a bottle of wine, there is a $10 corkage fee. Reservations are recommended for groups of eight or more.

Go South on Brotherhood Plaza Drive and take NY 94 West toward Goshen. Take a left onto Maloney Lane. Driving time: 25 minutes

ORANGE COUNTY DISTILLERY
19 Maloney Lane | Goshen, NY | 10924
845.651.2929 | http://orangecountydistillery.com/

(Note: Their second location at The Cocktail Room at Brown Barn Farms is closed Monday through Wednesday. Directions to the Brown Barn from the Distillery will be below.)

Orange County Distillery is a farm to bottle craft distillery. They grow it and they distill it. What began in 2014 with six thousand sugar beets sitting in John Glebocki's warehouse (he's a fifth generation farmer) has turned out to be a business for friends John Glebocki and Bryan Ensall. Those sugar beets became vodka and the rest is history. They produce gin, whiskey, and vodka. If you have never visited the distillery before I suggest you do so to see how they make the spirits, and see the farm where everything is grown. Afterwards, visit the Cocktail Room at Brown Barn Farms, sit down, relax, listen to music, and enjoy a cocktail made with their spirits.

Three miles from the distillery to the Cocktail Room at Brown Barn Farms. Turn left onto Pulaski Hwy, left onto Cross Rd and left onto Maple Avenue. It will be on your right. Driving time: 5 minutes

COCKTAIL ROOM AT BROWN BARN FARMS
286 Maple Avenue | New Hampton, NY | 10958
845.347.2077 | http://orangecountydistillery.com/

This is the tasting room for Orange County Distillery. Here you can bring a picnic lunch and eat in the tasting room. They feature all their spirits and cocktails along with New York produced beer, cider, wine, and other spirits.

Directions from the Distillery – turn right onto Pulaski Highway. Turn left onto Mt Eve Rd. Turn right onto Little York Road. Winery will be on your left. Driving time: 10 minutes

Directions from Cocktail Room – turn right onto Cross Road. Turn right onto Pulaski Highway. Turn left onto Mt Eve Rd. Turn right onto Little York Road. Winery will be on your left. Driving time: 14 minutes.

WARWICK VALLEY WINERY & BLACK DIRT DISTILLERY

114 Little York Road | Warwick, New York | 10990
845.258.4858 | http://wvwinery.com/
http://blackdirtdistillery.com/

Set on an apple orchard purchased in 1989, Warwick Valley Winery & Distillery has created wine and other fruit based alcoholic beverages since 1994. Their Doc's Hard Apple Ciders won many awards. In 2001, they were awarded a New York State grant to create a fruit distillery and became New York's first fruit micro distillery. Black Dirt Distilling LLC was formed in 2012 to meet the demand of their renowned Black Dirt Bourbon and Black Dirt Apple Jack. Don't forget to try Warwick Gin. During the Fall you can go apple picking. They also offer dining at their Pané Cafe/Black Dirt Grill. Tours of the distillery are by appointment only.

Turn left onto Little York Road. Turn left onto Pine Island Turnpike. Turn left onto NY-17A W / NY-94 E (Maple Avenue) Left onto Clearview Lane. Winery will be on the left. Driving time: 15 minutes.

CLEARVIEW VINEYARD

35 Clearview Lane | Warwick, NY | 10990
845.651.2838 | http://clearviewvineyard.com

Frank and Karen Graessle decided they needed a change so they picked up and moved to Warwick, New York in 2004. They purchased a farm that Karen always wanted and in the spring of 2007 their first vines were planted. Their first commercial vintage was released in 2009. Grown on their estate are Cayuga White, NY81, Seyval Blanc, Traminette, and Vidal Blanc, along with Baco Noir, Cabernet Franc, and Noriet. Their bestselling wine at the winery is Noriet and it won a Gold Medal in the 2015 Hudson Valley Wine & Spirits Competition.

Head East on Clearview Lane towards NY-94. Turn right onto NY-17A W / NY-94 W. Sharp left onto East Ridge Road. Right onto 4 Corners Road. Winery will be on your right. Driving time: 5 minutes.

APPLEWOOD WINERY & NAKED FLOCK CIDER
82 4 Corners Road | Warwick, NY | 10990
845.988.9292 | http://www.applewoodwinery.com/

Jonathan and Michelle Hull started Applewood Winery in 1993. It sits on a 120-acre farm full of apple trees. Applewood's wines are produced from New York State grapes along with grapes from their own vineyard and fruit from their orchards. Jonathan, having always produced a cider, decided to take his cider production to the next level and launched "Naked Flock Cider." Their Original Cider is fermented with champagne yeast and sweetened with a touch of local honey. They produce three varieties of cider that are made with Hudson Valley Apples. Keeping on the apple theme, Applewood also produces an apple based gin and vodka. Taste it all in their tasting room. During the Fall you can also pick apples from the orchard.

Turn left onto 4 Corners Road. Turn right onto Kings Highway. Turn left onto Wisner Road. Turn left onto Lower Wisner Road and right onto Iron Forge Road. Driving time: 10 minutes.

IRON FORGE INN
38 Iron Forge Road | Warwick NY | 10990
845.986.3411 | http://www.ironforgeinn.com/

Located at the foot of Mount Peter, the Inn is located on the site of an historic forge in a revolutionary era home that was built in

1760. A graduate of the Culinary Institute of America, chef/owner Erik Johansen changes the menu with the seasons and focuses on local ingredients. Feeling good, try their four or seven course tasting menu. Small plates and big ones too are served in the Tap Room. Try Crispy Pork Belly or Crispy Duck Breast with creamy Bleu Spätzle and Zucchini. A $15 corkage fee applies if you choose to bring your own wine.

Go southwest on Forge Road towards 17-A. Turn left onto 17-A E. Keep right and continue on Windermere Avenue. Turn left onto Waterstone Road. Driving time: 10 minutes.

ANTON'S ON THE LAKE
7 Waterstone Road | Greenwood Lake NY | 10925
845.477.0010 | http://www.antonsonthelake.com/

This waterfront bed and breakfast with country charm is an excellent place to end your day. Feather beds will lull you to sleep and you will be bright and fresh in the morning to hike the Appalachian Trail or one of the many parks that surround the area. The rooms are clean and spacious. A breakfast basket is delivered to your room each morning filled with muffins, yogurt, and coffee.

Weekend Rendezvous

Southern and Middle Shawangunk Wine Trail

Three-Day Itinerary

Suggested Stops

Palaia Winery • Brotherhood Winery • Orange County Distillery • Bellvale Creamery Warwick Valley Winery & Black Dirt Distillery • Clearview Vineyard • Applewood Winery & Naked Flock Cider • Brunel & Rafael Winery • Benmarl Winery • Stoutridge Winery

Suggested Dining

Limoncello at the Orange Inn • Elsie's • Pané Café • Painter's Restaurant • Hudson Street Café Jones Farm • Cosimo's Brick Oven

Suggested Lodging

Comfort Inn & Suites • Caldwell House • Hampton Inn

Traveling on the New York State Thruway entering the region at the Harriman Interchange, Woodbury Toll and take NY-17W. Get off at Exit 125 NY-17M E/South Street. Turn left onto NY-17M / Chester Avenue. Turn right onto South Street and left onto S Church Street.

Friday

GOSHEN FARMERS MARKET

Main Street and South Church Street | Goshen, NY | 10924
845.294.7741 | http://goshennychamber.com/goshenfarmersmarket2015/

Located at the Village Square the market is on Fridays from the end of May through October from 10 a.m.to 5 p.m. Their mission is to promote local and regional agriculture and to ensure a supply of fresh local produce for their community. It's a great place to begin your tour with local products. Try and get a good parking space and walk to dinner afterwards.

Take Main Street (207) east for two miles. Restaurant will be on the left.

LIMONCELLO AT THE ORANGE INN
159 Main Street | Goshen, NY | 10924
845.294.1880 | http://limoncelloatorangeinn.com/

Located in an old Inn dating back to 1790, they specialize in Northern Italian cuisine with an international twist. Dine in one of their three dining rooms. They have an extensive wine list to choose from and their menu selections will please all palates. Corkage fee is $15 if you bring your own bottle.

Take Main Street (207) and make a left onto Greenwich Avenue. Turn right onto Hatfield Lane. Turn right onto Policy Highway and right onto US-6 E. Hotel will be on the right. Driving time: 5 minutes.

COMFORT INN & SUITES
20 Hatfield Lane | Goshen, NY | 10924
845.637.2476 | http://www.choicehotels.com

This Comfort Inn is centrally located, close to I84 and Rt 17, restaurants and shopping, and it is smoke free. It has a fitness center so you can work out in the morning before heading out to taste for the day, or you can take a swim in their outdoor pool. There is free high-speed internet access throughout the hotel. They also offer a complimentary hot breakfast in the morning. Rooms come with coffee maker, refrigerator, TV, hair dryer, and iron.

Saturday

Head southeast on Hatfield Lane and turn left onto Greenwich Avenue. Turn left onto New Street and right onto W. Main Street. Driving time: 5 minutes.

ELSIE'S
128 W. Main Street | Goshen, NY | 10924
845.294.5765

Elsie's is a small luncheonette located on Main Street. It's typical small town charm. Open from 6 a.m. to 2 p.m, it's a great place for breakfast or lunch. All food is cooked to order. They have fabulous pancakes, so try their blueberry or pumpkin cinnamon when in season.

Head west on W. Main Street toward New Street. Turn left onto New Street. Turn right on first cross street onto Greenwich Avenue. Merge onto US-6E / NY-17 E to exit 126 NY 94/Chester/Florida. Turn left onto NY 94 E. Turn right onto second cross street Brookside Avenue. Turn right onto County Rd. 13/Kings Highway. Driving time: 15 minutes.

SUGAR LOAF ART & CRAFT VILLAGE
1371 Kings Hwy | Chester, NY | 10918
http://www.sugarloafnewyork.com/fun/

As I traveled the Shawangunk Wine Trail I always ended up driving through Sugar Loaf and stopped each time, especially during the holidays. This is a small community of independent artists. They have beautiful art galleries, craft and jewelry shops, and more. You might even check the schedule at the Sugar Loaf Performing Arts Center and catch a show or play while in town. Since the stores are all independent the hours vary, but they are all open on the weekends. You must stop as you're driving through!

Stay left on Kings Highway. Take a right onto Ridge road and a left onto 4 Corners Road. Winery entrance is on left. Driving time: 5 minutes.

APPLEWOOD WINERY & NAKED FLOCK CIDER
82 4 Corners Road | Warwick, NY | 10990
845.988.9292 | http://www.applewoodwinery.com/

Jonathan and Michelle Hull started Applewood Winery in 1993. It sits on a 120-acre farm full of apple trees. Applewood's wines are produced from New York State grapes along with grapes from their own vineyard and fruit from their orchards. Jonathan, having always produced a cider, decided to take his cider production to the next level and launched "Naked Flock Cider." Their Original Cider is fermented with champagne yeast and sweetened with a touch of local honey. They produce three varieties of cider that are made with Hudson Valley Apples. Keeping on the apple theme, Applewood also produces an apple based gin and vodka. Taste it all in their tasting room. During the Fall you can also pick apples from the orchard.

Turn right onto 4 Corners Road. Take a left onto Ridge Road E. Turn right onto Minturn Road. Turn left onto 17A E / NY 94 W. Turn right onto Clearview Lane. Driving time:10 minutes.

CLEARVIEW VINEYARD
35 Clearview Lane | Warwick, NY | 10990
845.651.2838 | http://clearviewvineyard.com

Frank and Karen Graessle decided they needed a change so they picked up and moved to Warwick, New York in 2004. They purchased a farm that Karen always wanted and in the spring of 2007 their first vines were planted. Their first commercial vintage was released in 2009. Grown on their estate are Cayuga White, NY81, Seyval Blanc, Traminette, and Vidal Blanc, along with Baco Noir, Cabernet Franc, and Noriet. Their bestselling wine at the winery is Noriet and it won a Gold Medal in the 2015 Hudson Valley Wine & Spirits Competition.

Turn right onto NY 17A E / NY-94W. Turn right onto Grand Street. Turns into Pine Island Turnpike. Turn right onto Little York Road. Driving time: 15 minutes.

PANÉ CAFE/BLACK DIRT GRILL
114 Little York Road | Warwick, New York | 10990
845.258.4858 | http://wvwinery.com/pane/

Pané Cafe located at Warwick Valley Winery serves fresh pizzas, sandwiches, and salads. Try their Sausage and Sage Pizza, Porchetta Sandwich or Strawberry and Pistachio Salad. The Black Dirt Grill menu is available May through October and features items such as Grilled Main Lobster or Slow Cooked Brisket on Brioche. Grab a bottle of wine or cider and eat outside and enjoy the view.

WARWICK VALLEY WINERY & BLACK DIRT DISTILLERY
114 Little York Road | Warwick, New York | 10990
845.258.4858 | http://wvwinery.com/
http://blackdirtdistillery.com/

Set on an apple orchard purchased in 1989, Warwick Valley Winery & Distillery has created wine and other fruit based alcoholic beverages since 1994. Their Doc's Hard Apple Ciders won many awards. In 2001, they were awarded a New York State grant to create a fruit distillery and became New York's first fruit micro distillery. Black Dirt Distilling LLC was formed in 2012 to meet the demand of their renowned Black Dirt Bourbon and Black Dirt Apple Jack. Don't forget to try Warwick Gin. During the Fall you can go apple picking. They also offer dining at their Pané Cafe/ Black Dirt Grill. Tours of the distillery are by appointment only.

Head south on Little York Road towards Pine Drive. Turn left onto Pine Island Turnpike. Continue straight onto County Road 1A. Take a slight left onto NY 94E. Turn right onto 17A Galloway Road. Driving time: 15 minutes.

BELLVALE CREAMERY
1390 NY-17A | Warwick, NY | 10990
845.988.1818 | http://bellvalefarms.com/

If you like ice cream this is a must stop. The Wisner family began their dairy farm in 1818 and opened the creamery in 2003. All their ice cream is homemade. On any given day you will be able to select from twenty flavors that rotate and can be seasonal. Choose from flavors such as Black Dirt Blast, which is chocolate coffee ice cream with fudge and toffee pieces, or Maple Cinnamon made with real maple syrup and fresh ground cinnamon. If you want to take a tour of the farm it is only one mile away from the creamery at 75 Bellvale Lakes Road.

Take 17A West (It becomes Pumpkin Hill Road, Upper Wisner Road, Wisner Road). Turn left onto Kings Highway, turn right onto Ackerman Road, turn right onto 17A W/NY-94E, turn left onto Meadow Road, and continue onto Pumpkin Swamp Road. Turn right onto Pulaski Highway, left onto Maloney Lane. Driving time: 20 minutes.

ORANGE COUNTY DISTILLERY
19 Maloney Lane | Goshen, NY | 10924
845.651.2929 | http://orangecountydistillery.com/

(Note: Their second location at The Cocktail Room at Brown Barn Farms is closed Monday through Wednesday. Directions to the Brown Barn from the Distillery will be below.)

Orange County Distillery is a farm to bottle craft distillery. They grow it and they distill it. What began in 2014 with six thousand sugar beets sitting in John Glebocki's warehouse (he's a fifth generation farmer) has turned out to be a business for friends John Glebocki and Bryan Ensall. Those sugar beets became vodka and the rest is history. They produce gin, whiskey, and vodka. If you have never visited the distillery before I suggest you do so to see how they make the spirits, and then you can see the farm where everything is grown. Afterwards, visit the Cocktail Room at Brown Barn Farms, sit down, relax, listen to music, and enjoy a cocktail made with their spirits.

Three miles from the distillery. Turn left onto Pulaski Hwy, left onto Cross Rd, and left onto Maple Avenue. It will be on your right. Driving time: 5 minutes

COCKTAIL ROOM AT BROWN BARN FARMS
286 Maple Avenue | New Hampton, NY | 10958
845.347.2077 | http://orangecountydistillery.com/

This is the tasting room for Orange County Distillery. Here you can bring a picnic lunch and eat in the tasting room. They feature all their spirits and cocktails along with New York produced beer, cider, wine, and other spirits.

Directions from the Cocktail Room: Take Maple Avenue turn right onto Police Highway, turn right onto Hatfield Lane, turn left onto Greenwich Avenue, (Greenwich Avenue turns right and becomes Main Street and Rt 207). Turn right onto Sarah Wells Trail (NY-207), right onto NY-208, turn left onto Main Street, and left onto Brotherhood Plaza. Driving time: 25 minutes.

BROTHERHOOD
"AMERICA'S OLDEST" WINERY
100 Brotherhood Plaza Drive | Washingtonville NY | 10992
845.496.3661 | http://www.brotherhood-winery.com/

Brotherhood is the oldest continuously operating winery in America, and a visit here is full of history of winemaking in the Hudson Valley and the country. It was started by John Jaques a cobbler who moved to a small town called Little York, which is now Washingtonville, New York in 1810. The first vintage Brotherhood produced was in 1839, the same year construction of the underground cellar began. Today you can tour the underground cellar, which has become a museum, and relive the history of Brotherhood. On display are artifacts dating back to the 1800's along with the history, the people, the vintage labels, and more. You will get a sense of how important Brotherhood was not only to the Hudson Valley, but to wine tourism as an industry. Taste their B Sparkling, a great inexpensive sparkling wine. If you like it sweet, try the Carpe Diem Spumante. One of the favorites around the holiday time is their Holiday Spiced Wine.

Head north on Brotherhood Plaza Drive towards Ahern Blvd. Turn right on Ahern Blvd, turn left onto NY94-E. Keep right onto Orrs Mills Road. Turn right onto NY-32, turn left onto Quaker Avenue. At the traffic circle take the third exit Chadeayne Circle, continue onto Main Street. Turn right onto Hudson Street. Driving time: 15 minutes.

PAINTER'S RESTAURANT
266 Hudson Street | Cornwall-on-Hudson, NY 12520
845.534.2109 | http://painters-restaurant.com

Housed in what was formerly the Cornwall Inn, Painter's offers an eclectic menu of Italian, Mexican, and American fare, practically anything your palate desires. The menu changes seasonally and they offer daily specials on the blackboard. Choose from over one hundred beers from around the world and a nice wine list. Should you choose to bring your own bottle the corkage fee is $25. There is a very casual atmosphere in here so get cozy and relax at the end of the day. Make sure you check out the artwork displayed from local artists. If you like a piece, you can also purchase it.

Head west on Hudson Street, take a slight left onto Main Street and continue onto Quaker Avenue. At the traffic circle take the second exit and stay on Quaker Avenue. Turn right onto NY-32, turn left onto Orrs Mills Rd. Driving time: 10 minutes.

CALDWELL HOUSE
25 Orrs Mill Road | Salisbury Mills, NY | 12577
845.496.2954 | http://www.caldwellhouse.com/

Caldwell House is a historic bed and breakfast that dates back to1802. Beautifully restored, today the inn looks the same as when the house first opened. You will relax in luxury as each room is individually climate controlled, and you'll have a Smart HDTV that includes access to Direct TV, Netflix, Hulu+ and free WiFi. Some rooms have a jacuzzi or their own fireplace. In the morning, you will be served a full three-course homemade breakfast featuring items from local farms.

Sunday

Head east on Orrs Mills Road. Take Quaker Avenue to Main Street (at traffic circle) and take a slight right onto Hudson Street. Driving time: 15 minutes.

HUDSON STREET CAFÉ
237 Hudson Street | Cornwall- on-Hudson NY | 12520
845.534.2450 | http://www.hudsonstreetcafe.com/home

Serving breakfast, lunch, and brunch with a choice of indoor or outdoor seating (of course weather permitting). Their menu changes seasonally with fresh and locally grown ingredients. They also offer items for those with gluten, dairy, and other food allergies as well as selections for vegetarians and vegans.

Head northeast on Main Street and take a slight right onto Hudson Street. Stay on Hudson Street and turn right onto Mountain Road. Driving time:10 minutes.

HIKE THE CROW'S NEST
Mountain Road | Intersection of US9W, NY 293 | Cornwall-on-Hudson, NY | http://snip.ly/40ty5

First off, wear sneakers or hiking shoes, no flip flops or heels. You are going to have magnificent views of the Hudson Valley. The Howell Trail (blue trail) is 3.6 miles and involves some intermediate hiking but once you get to the top the effort is well worth it! On the way down you'll go across a small bridge over a stream. If it has rained, be careful as it can be slippery. There are other trails available that are shorter like the Bobcat Trail .4 miles (white trail) or the Bluebird Trail .6 miles. (blue and red trail)

Head south on Mountain Road and turn right onto US 9W N. Turn right toward Angola Road (follow signs) then left onto Angola Road. Driving time: 5 minutes.

JONES FARM
190 Angola Road | Cornwall, NY | 12518
845.534.4445 | http://www.jonesfarminc.com/

After the hike, you will have worked up an appetite so a stop at Jones Farm is perfect. As you enter the farm, watch out for livestock wandering around. When entering the barn house - bakery & gift shop your mouth will begin to water simply as a result of the delicious smell of the baked goods. The country store is the place to shop for local produce, eggs, honey, gourmet foods, and more. They have daily specials for breakfast and lunch. Then wander over to the old dairy barn that has been converted to a large gift shop. It's a great place to look for a unique gift that you will not find anywhere else. Just when you thought you were done, stop at the Art Gallery where the walls are covered with original oils, pastels and watercolors, unique prints of the Hudson Valley and West Point, and local photography.

Take Angola Road to US-9W N and take a slight right onto River Road. (If you miss it don't worry, just stay on US-9W – this is a shortcut). Take a right onto Balmville Road, which will merge with US-9W N. Turn left onto Lattintown Road (at Stewarts) and turn right to stay on Lattintown Road. Winery entrance is on Lattintown Road. There will be a sign.

BRUNEL & RAFAEL WINERY
180 South Street | Marlboro, NY | 12542
845.306.5450 | http://www.brunelandrafael.com/

This is one of the newest wineries to the area and it is located in a century old home. Entering the house, the tasting will take place in what was once the old living and dining room. Enjoy their hometown hospitality. They focus exclusively on dry wines, but plan on introducing a sweet wine to their portfolio in the future.

Head south on South Street. Turn right onto Rosa Drive and right onto Highland Avenue. Driving time: 5 minutes.

BENMARL WINERY
156 Highland Avenue | Marlboro, NY | 12542
845.236.4265 | www.benmarl.com

Benmarl Winery sits on the oldest continuously planted vineyard in the United States, Slate Hill Vineyard, home to New York's

Farm Winery License #1. Located on thirty-seven scenic acres overlooking the Hudson River and Berkshire Mountains with a kickass view for great picture taking. This historic winery was purchased by artist Mark Miller from Andrew J. Caywood, an early American viticulturist in 1957, and in 2006 it was purchased by Victor Spaccarelli who fulfilled his lifelong dream of owning a vineyard. Victor's son Matt is the General Manager and winemaker focusing on producing small batch wines that capture the unique terroir of the vineyard. In addition, Matt and his partner Casey have produced a line of wines, Fjord Vineyards from very small estate grown acre lots and small batches sourced regionally. At the time of writing this, Fjord tasting room was open on sporadic days and times. Ask for directions to their Ridge Road tasting room from the Benmarl staff, and if you visit, make sure to try their award winning Albariño.

Go right onto Highland Avenue and right onto Western Avenue. Go left onto White Street and left onto Prospect Street. Turn left onto Ann Kaley Lane. Driving time: 5 minutes.

STOUTRIDGE VINEYARD
10 Ann Kaley Lane | Marlboro, NY | 12542
845.236.7620 | http://www.stoutridge.com/

Stoutridge Vineyard sits on the site of a historic homestead farm, which has had vineyards planted since the early 1800's and a commercial winery from 1880-1910. In the early 1940's the farm was confiscated by the U.S. Government for operating an illegal still. In 2001, Stephen Osborn and his wife Kimberly Wagner purchased the farm and restored it, replanted the vineyard, restored the farmhouse, and the constructed a state-of-the-art winery utilizing 'gravity flow' design built directly on the original winery site. Stephen is the winemaker and uses no chemicals in his winemaking process. Their focus is on showing people how older wine can be stable without chemical additions and taste better as they age. Look for their distillery coming on line focusing on whiskey.

From Ann Kaley Lane turn right onto Prospect Street. Go right onto

White Street, and left onto Western Avenue to US-9W S. Just past the Quick Chek turn left onto Albany Post Road and turn left onto Balmville Road and at the end of the road turn left onto River Road. Continue onto Blooming Grove Turnpike and the entrance to US-9W S is right there on the left. Get on US-9W S. Take the Quaker Avenue exit. Turn left onto Quaker Avenue and follow signs to NY- 32 S. Turn left onto NY-32 S and right onto Sweet Clover Road. Driving time: 30 minutes.

PALAIA WINERY

10 Sweet Clover Road | Highland Mills, NY | 10930
845.928.5384 | http://www.palaiavineyards.com/

Take a trip back to the seventies where it was all about peace, love, and rock- n -roll. That is the vibe at Palaia Winery. In the year 2000, Jan and her husband Joe purchased a 200-year-old cow farm "The Seaman Homestead at Sweet Clover Farm" and planted 1500 vines. Built in the early 1800's the homestead now sits on thirty-two acres of what is left from the tract of land purchased from Aaron Burr in 1784. In 1888, the barn was added to the property and today it is home to the winery and tasting room. Their wines range from dry to sweet. They have music every weekend and a kickass outdoor stage venue that rocks in the summer months.

Turn right onto NY-32 S. Driving time: 10 minutes.

COSIMO'S BRICK OVEN – WOODBURY

100 NY-32 | Central Valley, NY | 10917
845.928.8265 | http://cosimosgroup.com/woodbury

At the end of the day, step into Tuscany at Cosimo's. The open floor plan with vaulted ceilings makes it a perfect venue to stop for dinner. Try the wood fired pizzas as they are wonderful. If you aren't in the mood for pizza choose from their wide variety of specialties, such as Blackened Steak Salad, Grilled Chicken Penne, or Wood Fired Snapper. There is an entree for everyone. The corkage fee is $15 if you bring your own bottle.

Head southwest on NY-32 S. Continue on Averill Avenue. Turn left onto Centre Drive just after the RT- 17 interchange.

HAMPTON INN – WOODBURY
60 Centre Drive | Central Valley, NY | 10917
845.782.9600 | http://snip.ly/esr45

Relax and unwind in this 136-room hotel. Enjoy views of the mountains, free Wi-Fi, a gym/fitness center and an indoor pool. The hotel is close to major routes and walking distance to Woodbury Commons for your outlet shopping.

Day Tripping

The Hudson-Berkshire Beverage Trail

One-Day Itinerary

Suggested Stops
Brookview Station Winery • Harvest Spirits • Chatham Berry Farm • Chatham Brewery • Hudson-Chatham Winery • Tousey Winery • Hudson Valley Distillers • Clermont Vineyards

Dining Suggestions
The Shakin Bacon • Swoon Kitchen

Lodging Suggestions
WM Farmer & Sons

Entering from Albany via the New York State Thruway or I 90 to I787 to exit 3 and merge onto US-20/US-9 across the Dunn Memorial Bridge. Turn left on to Broadway.

THE SHAKIN BACON
138 Broadway | Rensselaer, NY | 12144
518.977.3602 | http://theshakinbacon.com/

Begin your day with some bacon and a great breakfast! We all like bacon and this bacon is caramelized with a hint of maple. You will find unique breakfasts choice including Cinnamon Roll Pancakes with candied walnuts or how about S'mores pancakes! There are a good variation of omelets and egg sandwiches. The Starvin Marvin should get you through the day with three eggs, caramelized bacon, handmade roasted sausage links, and cheese on a toasted hero (sub) roll. There is outdoor seating for when the weather is nice.

Head southwest on Academy Street towards Columbia Street. Follow 9-J to Stony Point Road. Turn left onto Stony Point Road, turn left onto Western Road, turn left onto NY-150N, and left onto Brookview Station Road. Driving time: 15 minutes

BROOKVIEW STATION WINERY
1297 Brookview Station Road | Castleton, NY 12033
518.732.7317 | http://www.brookviewstationwinery.com/

Located at Goold Orchard, Brookview Station Winery opened in 2006 when third generation owner Sue Goold Miller and her husband Ed began making wine. Brookview Station is named after the small train station where Sue's grandparents arrived. Their wine names are train themed. Try their award-winning Whistle Stop White, a semi-dry apple wine. They also produce three hard apple ciders. Look around their store and pick up one of their fresh baked pies and cider donuts. In the Fall take an hour or two to go apple picking.

Head southwest on Brookview Station Road and continue straight onto Simons Road. Turn left onto Maple Hill Road. Turn right onto US 9 South. Harvest Spirits will be on your left. Driving time: 15 minutes.

HARVEST SPIRITS
3074 US Route 9 | Valatie, NY | 12184
518.758.1776 | http://www.harvestspirits.com/

Harvest Spirits is located at Golden Harvest Farms, where fifteen varieties of apples are grown on two 100 acre orchards. Derek Grout is a third-generation apple farmer turned distiller. Known for their Core Vodka, made from their apples, it's a must-try and as smooth as can be. All you need is to shake it up on some ice and serve. Their range of spirits include vodka, applejack, brandy, and whiskey.

Head south on Route 9. At the traffic circle take the third exit and stay on Route 9. Turn left onto Main Street and then right onto NY

203 S. The farm will be on your left. Driving time: 10 minutes.

THE CHATHAM BERRY FARM
2304 NY-203 | Chatham NY | 12037
518.392.4609 | http://thechathamberryfarm.com/

In season stop here to pick your own berries, and off season stop to get greens from their greenhouse. Their store carries produce and products from other local Hudson Valley vendors. You'll find fresh veggies, gluten-free products, local free-range eggs, dairy products and freshly baked goods from their kitchen.

Head east on NY-203 S and turn left onto Hudson Avenue and turn into Main Street. Driving time: 5 minutes

CHATHAM BREWERY
59 Main Street | Chatham, NY | 12037
518.697.0202 | http://www.chathambrewing.com/

When I first visited Chatham Brewery we tasted beers in an alley from a tapped keg. They have come a long way from that back alley, the tasting room now located on Main Street with fourteen ales and lagers on tap along with seasonal offerings and a menu to pair it all with. Large picture windows offer views of Main Street and the small town action. One of their most popular beers is the Farmer's Daughter Rye IPA made with rye malt from neighboring distillery Hillrock in Ancram, New York. Order that beer with your grass-fed burger. Their buns and greens are sourced from local farmers, plus anything else available locally.

Head southwest on Main Street and it will turn into NY 66 S. Driving time: 10 minutes.

HUDSON-CHATHAM WINERY
1900 NY-66 | Ghent, NY | 12075
518.392.9463 | http://www.hudsonchathamwinery.com/

Authors and book publishers turned winery owners, Carlo and

Dominique DeVito, purchased their farm in 2006. Their winemaker Steve Casscles strives for great quality and known for his Baco Noir. Taste and compare their Casscles Vineyard Block 3 North Creek Vineyard, Fieldstone and Old Vines Mason Place Vineyards Pultney Farms Baco Noir. Under the Paperbirch label is their small production of artisanal ports, sherries, and other dessert wines. New products include an entire line of balsamic-styled vinegars and a cognac-style brandy to be released in the not too distant future. Grab a bottle, have a picnic, and enjoy the views.

Head southwest on N-66. Turn left onto NY-9H S and continue on US 9S. Driving time: 25 minutes.

TOUSEY WINERY
1774 US 9 | Germantown, NY | 12526
518.567.5462 | http://www.touseywinery.com/

When Kimberly and Ben Peacock moved back to the states from Europe they joined forces with Kimberly's Dad, Ray Tousey, to realize Ray's dream of turning their grounds into a vineyard and winery. Ben was a former assistant at the Houses of Parliament in London who embraced this life changing position with open arms. They are a diamond in the ruff. Try their Riesling, Pinot Noir, and Queen of Clermont. New is their Blanc de Blanc sparkling wine. Check out the Scarlet Tiger label, a series of wines which tells a story about a missing tiger. As you walk into the tasting room you will see the empty cage. The Queen of Clermont is the only one who knows where the tiger is and each of the other varietals are supporting characters in this epic story. Each vintage is a different part of the story, so start collecting the bottles.

Take a left out of Tousey and go just down the road. Driving time: 3 minutes.

HUDSON VALLEY DISTILLERS
1727 US 9 | Germantown NY | 12526
518.537.6820 | http://www.hudsonvalleydistillers.com/

Meet Chris and Tom, childhood friends who always knew they wanted to do something together. The plan was that when Tom retired from the Coast Guard they would partner in a second career. Together they purchased a small apple farm that was once owned by Chancellor Robert Livingston, an author of the Declaration of Independence and who administered the oath of office to George Washington. They converted the 170-year-old barn into the distillery. Make sure you take the distillery tour and meet Jethro, Bonita, and Arenda who produce small-batch artisanal vodka, applejack, fruit brandies, and whiskey using ingredients sourced locally, within five miles. The outbuilding next to the distillery houses their cocktail bar where you can have creative cocktails made with their spirits.

Head south on US 9 turn right onto Lasher Road then turn right onto NY 9G North. Turn right onto County Route 6. Driving time: 5 minutes.

CLERMONT VINEYARDS
241 County Route 6 | Clermont, NY | 12526
845.663.6611 | http://clermontvineyards.com/

More than a decade ago Tony transformed a former dairy farm into a vineyard and winery. Wine is produced in the traditional Portuguese fashion from grapes grown on their seven acres of land. The renovated barn that houses the winery and tasting room has floor to ceiling windows with spectacular views of the Catskills. Grab a bottle and sit on the deck and watch the sunset. They are open Friday and Saturday until sunset and Sunday until 5 p.m. April through December.

Head west on County Route 6 and turn right onto NY-9G N. Turn right onto Warren Street. Swoon Kitchen will be on your left. Driving time: 20 minutes.

SWOON KITCHEN
340 Warren Street | Hudson, NY | 12534
518.822.8938 | http://www.swoonkitchenbar.com/

This is a true example of New York City meets Hudson Valley. Chef Jeff Gimmel and his wife Nina Bachinski-Gimmel, who worked as a chef and pastry chef in New York City, moved to the Hudson Valley and opened Swoon Kitchen. They use locally-sourced items that give variety to the menu, which changes daily. They offer an extensive wine list to satisfy all palates. Bring your wallet because dinner and drinks can be pricey.

Head northwest on Warren Street and turn left onto S Front Street. Driving time: 10 minutes.

WM FARMER AND SONS
20 S. Front Street | Hudson, NY | 12534
518.828.1635 | http://www.wmfarmerandsons.com/

You'll find comfortable and eclectic rooms in this historic boarding house in downtown Hudson. You'll be surrounded by great hospitality, history, and warmth from the moment you make the reservation. Each of ten rooms each with their own personality. Enjoy a night cap in the Barroom downstairs. It is in a very convenient location, walking distance to local shops, galleries, and antique stores.

Weekend Rendezvous

Capital Region to Mid-Hudson Valley

Three-Day Itinerary

Suggested Stops

Nine Pin Cider Works • Albany Institute of Art • Brookview Station Winery • Hudson-Chatham Winery • Olana State Historic Site • Clermont Vineyard • Tousey Winery • Hudson Valley Distillers • Old Rhinebeck Aerodrome • Millbrook Vineyards & Winery • Clinton Vineyards

Suggested Dining

New World Bistro • Iron Gate Café • Mexican Radio • Licks Ice Cream • Gigi Trattoria • Bread Alone • Another Fork in the Road • Aurelia

Suggested Lodging

Albany Thruway Courtyard by Marriott • Beekman Arms • Wing Castle Bed and Breakfast

Friday

Traveling on the New York State Thruway entering the region at Albany, New York to I-787 to exit 4 towards US-9/US-20 W. Merge onto Quay Street. Quay Street to Colonie Street to right onto Erie Blvd. Left onto N Ferry Street and right onto Broadway. Driving time: 15 minutes.

NINE PIN CIDER WORKS

929 Broadway | Albany, NY | 12207
518.449.9999 | http://www.ninepincider.com

All it took was a sample of local hard cider and Alejandro was hooked. Nine Pin Cider was New York's first farm cidery, and in 2013 Alejandro's cider won a gold medal at the Great Lakes International Cider Competition. The tasting room is located in downtown Albany, in an old warehouse. Alejandro makes cider from apples sourced from the Capital Region, Hudson Valley, and his family farm. Signature is their flagship cider using apples from Samascott Orchards. You will find a selection of seven ciders to taste and they rotate depending on production.

Head southwest on Broadway and turn left onto North Ferry Street which becomes Water Street to Route 9. Get on I-787 South to Hurlbut Street. Turn right onto Hurlbut Street, and then right onto Delaware Avenue. Driving time: 10 minutes.

NEW WORLD BISTRO BAR
300 Delaware Avenue | Albany, NY | 12209
518.694.0520 | http://newworldbistrobar.com/

You will always have a good time at one of Ric Orlando's restaurants (his other is in Saugerties). You might remember Ric as he appeared on the Food Network's show "Chopped" but I've known him since before these shows were around. The atmosphere in his restaurants is lively. Most of his ingredients are regional, organic, and sustainable. A must-try is his Blackened String Beans as a starter. His menu is pretty extensive so you will be sure to find something to please your palate. You will be able to pair a nice New York wine, beer or cocktail made with regional spirits with your meal. There's a $10 corkage fee should you wish to bring your own wine.

Head southwest on Delaware Avenue, turn right onto St. James Place, and left onto Hackett Blvd. Turn right onto S. Manning Blvd and turn left onto Washington Avenue. Driving time: 15 minutes.

ALBANY THRUWAY COURTYARD
BY MARRIOTT
1455 Washington Avenue | Albany, NY | 12206
518.435-1600 | http://www.marriott.com/hotels/travel/albws-courtyard-albany-thruway/

Located close to the University of Albany and many sites in the Capital District, guest rooms are nicely appointed. There is a small gym to workout in before you begin the day, and free Wi-Fi.

Saturday

Head northwest on Washington Avenue and turn right onto I-90 E. Take exit 6 towards Henry Johnson Blvd. Keep right at the fork and follow signs for US-9S/Arbor Hill and merge onto US-9 S. Turn left onto Clinton Avenue, right onto Lark Street, and left onto Washington Avenue. Driving time:10 minutes.

IRON GATE CAFE
182A Washington Avenue | Albany, NY | 12210
518.445.3555 | http://www.irongatecafe.com/home

Begin your day with a hipster vibe and a full belly. Enjoy breakfast inside or outdoors on their garden patio. Specials are made and updated daily. Try their Cider Belly Sliders – two grilled Cider Belly donuts stuffed with scrambled eggs, cheddar cheese and bacon, or their Stuffed French Toast. Don't worry if you are vegan as they offer a Vegan Tofu Scramble and other vegan selections. You might want to pick up a salad or sandwich to go. Now you are ready for a day of wine tasting.

No need to move the car, the Institute of History and Art is .1 tenth mile down the road. This makes a nice walk after breakfast.

ALBANY INSTITUTE OF HISTORY AND ART
125 Washington Avenue | Albany, NY | 12210
518.463.4478 | http://www.albanyinstitute.org/

The Albany Institute of History and Art is dedicated to collecting, preserving, and promoting interest in the history art and culture of Albany and the Upper Hudson Valley region. Ongoing exhibits include works by the Hudson River School, and an Ancient Egypt exhibit about mummies. Learn about the people who shaped Albany.

Head northwest on Washington Ave towards Dove St. Turn left at the first cross street onto Dove Street. Turn left onto Hamilton Street and left onto Swan Street. Turn right onto S. Mall Arterial. Continue onto Dunn Memorial Bridge to Columbia Street. Take a slight right onto NY-9J/South Street. Turn left onto Stony Point Road, left onto Western Road. Turn left onto NY-150 and left onto Brookview Station Road. Driving time: 20 minutes.

BROOKVIEW STATION WINERY
1297 Brookview Station Road | Castleton, NY 12033
518.732.7317 | http://www.brookviewstationwinery.com/

Located at Goold Orchard, Brookview Station Winery opened in 2006 when third generation owner Sue Goold Miller and her husband Ed began making wine. Brookview Station is named after the small train station where Sue's grandparents arrived. Their wine names are train themed. Try their award-winning Whistle Stop White, a semi-dry apple wine. They also produce three hard apple ciders. Look around their store and pick up one of their fresh baked pies and cider donuts. In the Fall take an hour or two to go apple picking.

Head southwest on Brookview Station Road and continue straight onto Simons Road. Turn left onto Maple Hill Road. Turn right onto US 9 South. Harvest Spirits will be on your left. Driving time: 15 minutes.

HARVEST SPIRITS
3074 US Route 9 | Valatie, NY | 12184
518.758.1776 | http://www.harvestspirits.com/

Harvest Spirits is located at Golden Harvest Farms, where fifteen varieties of apples are grown on two 100 acre orchards. Derek Grout is a third-generation apple farmer turned distiller. Known for their Core Vodka, made from their apples, it's a must-try and as smooth as can be. All you need is to shake it up on some ice and serve. Their range of spirits include vodka, applejack, brandy, and whiskey.

Head south on US 9. At the traffic circle take the second left onto NY 9H S. Turn right onto Hudson Avenue and left onto Hudson Avenue. Turn right at the first cross street onto Mile Hill Road. Mill Hill Road turns into Church Street. Turn right onto NY 66. Driving time: 15 minutes.

HUDSON-CHATHAM WINERY
1900 NY-66 | Ghent, NY | 12075
518.392.9463 | http://www.hudsonchathamwinery.com/

Authors and book publishers turned winery owners, Carlo and Dominique DeVito, purchased their farm in 2006. Their winemaker Steve Casscles strives for great quality and known for his Baco Noir. Taste and compare their Casscles Vineyard Block 3 North Creek Vineyard, Fieldstone and Old Vines Mason Place Vineyards Pultney Farms Baco Noir. Under the Paperbirch label is their small production of artisanal ports, sherries, and other dessert wines. New products include an entire line of balsamic-styled vinegars and a cognac-style brandy to be released in the not too distant future. Grab a bottle, have a picnic, and enjoy the views.

Head Southwest on NY66. Continue straight onto Columbia Street. Turn left onto Park Place and right onto Warren Street. Driving time: 15 minutes.

MEXICAN RADIO
537 Warren Street | Hudson NY |12534
518.828.7770 | http://mexrad.com/

If you love Mexican food or you're simply in the mood for it, this is the place. They offer a $12 lunch, which is a great value. They are gluten free as well as vegan friendly. Don't forget to try one of their margaritas. If you bring your own wine the corkage fee is $25. After lunch you might want to walk and check out the antique shops along Hudson Street and head to Licks for some ice cream.

Take a walk on Warren Street to Licks. Walking time: 5 minutes.

LICKS – ICE CREAM
253 Warren Street | Hudson NY | 12534
518.828.7254 | http://www.lickhudson.com/

While walking down Hudson Street stop in at Licks for some delicious ice cream. They source their ice cream locally from Jane's (http://janesicecream.com/), which makes their ice cream in small batches from a recipe that has been handed down through the generations. A must-stop if you're an ice cream lover!

Warren Street turn left onto NY23 B / NY 9G S. Left onto Olana State Historic Site. Driving time: 15 minutes

OLANA STATE HISTORIC SITE
5720 Route 9G | Hudson NY | 12534
518.828.0135 | http://www.olana.org/

This is the home and estate of Hudson River School painter Frederic Church. This 250-acre estate is open year round. You'll find hiking, picnicking, and there is also a pond for kayaking and fishing. Tour the main house and see the mixture of Victorian architecture and Middle Eastern motifs.

South on NY 9G turn left onto County Route 6. Driving time: 15 minutes

CLERMONT VINEYARDS
241 County Route 6 | Clermont, NY | 12526
845.663.6611 | http://clermontvineyards.com/

More than a decade ago Tony transformed a former dairy farm into a vineyard and winery. Wine is produced in the traditional Portuguese fashion from grapes grown on their seven acres of land. The renovated barn that houses the winery and tasting room has floor to ceiling windows with spectacular views of the Catskills. Grab a bottle and sit on the deck and watch the sunset. They are open Friday and Saturday until sunset and Sunday until 5 p.m.

April through December.

Head east on County Route 6. Turn left onto US 9 North. Tousey will be right there on the right. Driving time: 8 minutes.

TOUSEY WINERY
1774 US 9 | Germantown, NY | 12526
518.567.5462 | http://www.touseywinery.com/

When Kimberly and Ben Peacock moved back to the states from Europe they joined forces with Kimberly's Dad, Ray Tousey, to realize Ray's dream of turning their grounds into a vineyard and winery. Ben was a former assistant at the Houses of Parliament in London who embraced this life changing position with open arms. They are a diamond in the ruff. Try their Riesling, Pinot Noir, and Queen of Clermont. New is their Blanc de Blanc sparkling wine. Check out the Scarlet Tiger label, a series of wines which tells a story about a missing tiger. As you walk into the tasting room you will see the empty cage. The Queen of Clermont is the only one who knows where the tiger is and each of the other varietals are supporting characters in this epic story. Each vintage is a different part of the story, so start collecting the bottles.

Take a left out of Tousey and go just down the road. Driving time: 3 minutes.

HUDSON VALLEY DISTILLERS
1727 US 9 | Germantown NY | 12526
914.537.6820 | http://www.hudsonvalleydistillers.com/

Meet Chris and Tom, childhood friends who always knew they wanted to do something together. The plan was that when Tom retired from the Coast Guard they would partner in a second career. Together they purchased a small apple farm that was once owned by Chancellor Robert Livingston, an author of the Declaration of Independence and who administered the oath of office to George Washington. They converted the 170-year-old barn into the distillery. Make sure you take the distillery tour and meet Jethro,

Bonita, and Arenda who produce small-batch artisanal vodka, applejack, fruit brandies, and whiskey using ingredients sourced locally, within five miles. The outbuilding next to the distillery houses their cocktail bar where you can have creative cocktails made with their spirits.

Head south on Route 9 to Rhinebeck. Rt 9 is Montgomery Street. Destination will be on the left. Driving time 20 minutes.

GIGI TRATTORIA
6422 Montgomery Street | Rhinebeck, NY | 12572
845.876.1007 | http://www.gigihudsonvalley.com/

Good times and good food, chef, dietitian, restauranteur and author Laura Pensiero doesn't disappoint. She was one of the first in the area to source the bulk of her ingredients directly from local farmers. Gigi's focus is on a Mediterranean style of cooking with whatever foods are in season. Get a taste of the local artisanal cheese with a Cheese Plate or try her Skizza's for an appetizer or a meal. You can't go wrong. The place does get hopping, so if you have to wait, order a cocktail at the bar. During the busy season Gigi also offers patio dining. If you bring your own bottle of wine the corkage fee is $15.

Head south on Route 9 and Beekman Arms is on the right. (Route 9 turns into Mill Street). You might want to check into the Beekman Arms first and walk up to Gigi's

BEEKMAN ARMS
6387 Mill Street | Rhinebeck, NY | 12572
845.876.7077 | http://www.beekmandelamaterinn.com/
beekmanarms.htm

You'll find history at the Beekman Arms, America's oldest continuously operated hotel. Many famous people have slept here. President Franklin Delano Roosevelt concluded his campaign for governor and President, talking from the front porch. The main house might be old and historic, but all rooms have a private bath, TV, phone, and a decanter of sherry. The Guest House is a comfortable motel type accommodation located behind the main inn. These rooms have air conditioning and refrigerators and they are pet friendly. Other accommodations are also in "The Old Firehouse," which was the original firehouse to the village of Rhinebeck. If you have a group, The Townsend House will accommodate you in four large King size bedrooms with gas fireplaces.

Located across the street from the Beekman Arms.

GRAND CRU BEER & CHEESE MARKET
6384 Mill Street | Rhinebeck, NY | 12572
845.876.6992 | http://grandcrurhinebeck.com/

Mingle with the locals at Grand Cru, located just across the street from the Beekman Arms. This hidden gem has the largest collection of craft beer anywhere. Grand Cru is not only a bar but also a bottle shop, so you can mix and match your six-pack to go. With sixteen beers on tap curated personally by Rod the owner, you'll find a mix of local and not so local craft beers. They also have a liquor license and serve wine by the glass. Although they don't have a kitchen, they have a great selection of local artisan cheeses and charcuterie plates to start or end your evening. Don't forget to take in the local artwork that decorates the tasting room. Artwork changes monthly. Here you'll find great conversation, and tips on what to do next.

Sunday

Cross the street and stroll down East Market Street to Bread Alone and the Farmers Market.

BREAD ALONE
45 East Market Street | Rhinebeck, NY | 12572
845.657.3328 | http://www.breadalone.com/rhinebeck/

Can you say fresh certified organic bread? Each delicious slice of the many varieties of bread you will have with your breakfast or lunch is certified organic bread, freshly baked each day. Stop in for a great breakfast and try their Sourdough French Toast made with their San Francisco sourdough, cinnamon butter and maple syrup, or their Parmesan and Veggie, which is scrambled eggs, cauliflower, onion, arugula pesto, on an organic baguette. Don't forget to get a sandwich to go for lunch too.

Just to the left of Bread Alone in the parking lot you will find the farmers market.

RHINEBECK FARMERS MARKET

61 East Market Street | Rhinebeck, NY | 12572
http://www.rhinebeckfarmersmarket.com/

Just past Bread Alone in the parking lot is the Rhinebeck Farmers Market, which is one of the best farmer's markets on Sundays. You will find items from local beers, distilled spirits, wines, local fruit and vegetables, local grass-fed beef, chickens, local cheese, Foie Gras, and more.

Head west on East Market Street towards Mill Street. Turn right onto Montgomery Street (US 9) Turn right onto Stone Church Road. Driving time: 10 minutes.

OLD RHINEBECK AERODROME

42 Stone Church Road | Rhinebeck, NY | 12572
845.752.3200 | http://www.oldrhinebeck.org/

Old Rhinebeck Aerodrome is a living museum of antique aircrafts from the Pioneer, World War 1 and Lindbergh eras. Relive the early years of aviation during their air shows. Their museum holds aircrafts like the original Aeromarine AKL-26, original Curtiss Wright Junior CW-1, original Albree Pigeon, Fraser Pursuit, and the original Bleriot XI. Not to miss for the aviation history buff.

Head east on Stone Church Road, continue onto Oriole Mills Road. Turn left onto Old Rock City Road and then merge onto NY-308 E. Then merge onto NY 199 E. Driving time: 10 minutes.

ANOTHER FORK IN THE ROAD
1215 Route 199 | Red Hook, NY | 12571
845.758.6676

I can't tell you how many times I've eaten here and seen the changes. This was our go-to brunch restaurant after cutting down our Christmas tree at Battenfeld's. Now called "Another Fork in the Road" their slogan is "Three Meals a Day, The Local Way." Their eclectic new American style menu is always evolving using local produce and the food is created fresh every day. From small plates to sandwiches, you will always find something good to eat.

Head South on NY-199 to the Taconic State Parkway South. Take the Taconic South and turn right onto Willow Lane (look for the sign). Turn left onto Clinton Corners Schultzville Road. Driving time: 15 minutes

CLINTON VINEYARDS
450 Clinton Corners Schultzville Road | Clinton Corners, NY | 12514
845.266.5372 | http://clintonvineyards.com/

Clinton Vineyards was established in 1976 when Ben Feder, a Bronx born book designer and artist purchased the property and turned the dairy farm into a beautiful vineyard and winery. He was inspired by the vineyards and wineries he loved in the French countryside. Celebrate with their estate bottled sparkling wines or their estate bottle Seyval. Make sure you try their famous Cassis too. You will find Clinton Vineyards to be small and intimate and most likely have a tasting with Ben's wife Phyllis who runs the vineyard/winery today.

Take Clinton Corners Schultzville Road and make a right onto Salt Point Turnpike. Turn left onto Clinton Corners Road, and left onto NY-82 N. Turn right onto Shunpike and left onto Wing Road. Driving time: 15 minutes.

MILLBROOK VINEYARDS & WINERY
26 Wing Road | Millbrook, NY | 12545
845.677.8383 | http://www.millbrookwine.com/

Known as the "Flagship Winery of the Hudson Valley" John Dyson purchased the 130-acre Wing Dairy Farm in 1982, his first vineyard and winemaking venture with his brother-in-law and General Manager David Bova. Winemaker John Graziano has been with them since the beginning crafting amazing award-winning wines. Try their Proprietor's Special Reserve Cabernet Franc, Block Five East Pinot Noir, and their Tocai Friulano. Grab a bite to eat at their Vineyard Café and enjoy a bottle on the grounds or in the new Four Season room overlooking the vineyard. The views are spectacular! The Millbrook portfolio goes beyond the Hudson Valley as they own Williams Selyem in Sonoma, CA, Villa Pillo, Tuscany, Italy, and Pebble Ridge Vineyards in the North Central Coast in CA. Some of these wines are available for purchase in the tasting room.

Turn left onto Wing Road from the winery and a right onto Shunpike, left onto Valley Farm Road, left onto Sharon Turnpike, right onto Franklin Avenue. Driving time: 10 minutes.

AURELIA
3299 Franklin Avenue | Millbrook, NY | 12545
845.677.4720 | http://aureliarestaurant.com

Dine outdoors on the terrace or inside on Mediterranean influenced cuisine. You will find dishes made with meat and poultry sourced from local Hudson Valley farms. They serve homemade ravioli and gnocchi with fresh soups and seasonal salads. Try their Seared Duck Breast with macerated figs, roasted potatoes, friseé, and truffle salad or their Stuffed Poblano Pepper with quinoa, mustard greens, charred corn, and soffrito. If you bring your own wine the corkage fee is $20.

Take Franklin Street east to US-44 E. Turn left onto Bangall Road. Driving time: 10 minutes.

WING CASTLE BED & BREAKFAST
717 Bangall Road | Millbrook, NY | 12545
845.677.9085 | http://www.wingscastle.com/

With views overlooking Millbrook Winery (no relation to the winery), Storm King and the Catskill Mountain ranges, Wing's Castle is a fifteen century country castle designed using 80 percent of recycled materials salvaged from antique buildings. This is the dream of Peter Wing and his wife, Toni Ann. If you ever had a dream about sleeping in the dungeon or tower room, this is the B&B for you to spend the night. Each of the rooms features a private bath and Wi-Fi.

Day Tripping

Northern Shawangunk Wine Trail

One-Day Itinerary

Suggested Stops

Brunel & Rafael Winery • Stoutridge Vineyard • Glorie Farm Winery • Nostrano Vineyards Bad Seed Cider • Adair Vineyards • Adams Fairacre Farms • Benmarl Winery

Suggested Dining

Alexis Diner • Raccoon Salon • Gunk House

Suggested Lodging

Moondance Ridge Bed & Breakfast

Traveling North on the New York State Thruway exit at Newburgh exit 17. Keep right as you exit the Thruway and follow signs for the Tandem Area. Turn right toward Stewart Ave and continue on Stewart Avenue and turn right onto NY-300. Adams will be on your left. Driving time: 5 minutes.

ADAMS FAIRACRE FARMS

1240 Route 300 | Newburgh, NY | 12550
845.569.0303 | http://adamsfarms.com/

Adams has been around for a long time. What began as a farm stand in Poughkeepsie now has four locations throughout the Hudson Valley. It's my favorite store! Adams is the best place for local products, such as My Brother Bobby's Salsa, Sprout Creek Farm, Coach Farm, and many other local cheeses, bakery items, fresh bread, jam, and more. Stop here and pick up some cheese, bread, fruit, dips, and cold cuts for your picnic needs. The wineries on this itinerary offer some wonderful picnic areas and views.

Get on I-84 heading East and get off at Route 9W Newburgh, the last exit before toll. Take a left at the traffic light onto Route 9W and diner is on your left. Driving time: 5 minutes.

ALEXIS DINER
5023 Route 9W | Newburgh, NY | 12550
845.565.1400 | http://www.thealexisdiner.com/

This is a great place to stop for a quick breakfast before you set out wine tasting. It's your classic Greek diner. Get your eggs, omelets, and other classic breakfast food and pastries.

North on US-9W. Turn left onto Lattintown Road. Winery entrance is on Lattintown Road by the intersection of South Street. Driving time: 10 minutes

BRUNEL & RAFAEL WINERY
180 South Street | Marlboro, NY | 12542
845.306.5450 | http://www.brunelandrafael.com/

This is one of the newest wineries to the area and it is located in a century old home. Entering the house, the tasting will take place in what was once the old living and dining room. Enjoy their hometown hospitality. They focus exclusively on dry wines, but plan on introducing a sweet wine to their portfolio in the future.

Head south on South Street. Turn right onto Rosa Drive and right onto Highland Avenue. Driving time: 5 minutes.

BENMARL WINERY
156 Highland Avenue | Marlboro, NY | 12542
845.236.4265 | www.benmarl.com

Benmarl Winery sits on the oldest continuously planted vineyard in the United States, Slate Hill Vineyard, home to New York's Farm Winery License #1. Located on thirty-seven scenic acres overlooking the Hudson River and Berkshire Mountains with a kickass view for great picture taking. This historic winery was purchased by artist Mark Miller from Andrew J. Caywood, an early American viticulturist in 1957, and in 2006 it was purchased by Victor Spaccarelli who fulfilled his lifelong dream of owning a vineyard. Victor's son Matt is the General Manager and winemaker focusing on producing small batch wines that capture the unique terroir of the vineyard. In addition, Matt and his partner Casey have produced a line of wines, Fjord Vineyards from very small estate grown acre lots and small batches sourced regionally. At the time of writing this, Fjord tasting room was open on sporadic days and times. Ask for directions to their Ridge Road tasting room from the Benmarl staff, and if you visit, make sure to try their award winning Albariño.

Go right onto Highland Avenue and right onto Western Avenue. Go left onto White Street and left onto Prospect Street. Turn left onto Ann Kaley Lane. Driving time: 5 minutes.

Right onto Highland Avenue and right onto Western Avenue. Left onto White Street and left onto Prospect Street. Turn left onto Ann Kaley Lane. Driving time: 5 minutes.

STOUTRIDGE VINEYARD
10 Ann Kaley Lane | Marlboro, NY | 12542
845.236.7620 | http://www.stoutridge.com/

Stoutridge Vineyard sits on the site of a historic homestead farm, which has had vineyards planted since the early 1800's and a commercial winery from 1880-1910. In the early 1940's the farm was confiscated by the U.S. Government for operating an illegal still. In 2001, Stephen Osborn and his wife Kimberly Wagner purchased the farm and restored it, replanted the vineyard, restored the farmhouse, and the constructed a state-of-the-art winery utilizing 'gravity flow' design built directly on the original winery site. Stephen is the winemaker and uses no chemicals in his winemaking process. Their focus is on showing people how older wine can be stable without chemical additions and taste better as they age. Look for their distillery coming on line focusing on whiskey.

Right onto Prospect Street, right onto White Street, and left onto Western Avenue. Look for parking as Raccoon Saloon is across the street on 9W. Driving time: 3 minutes.

RACCOON SALOON
1330 Route 9W | Marlboro, NY | 12542
845.236.7872 | http://www.raccoonsaloonmarlboro.com/

You will feel like you are entering an old saloon from the Wild West. Ask for a seat by the window overlooking the ravine and waterfalls, which flows into a "sucker hole" and various small pools before ending up in the Hudson River. They have great burgers here served with their homemade ketchup. No outside beverages are allowed, so save that wine for the hotel room.

Take Western Avenue, turn right onto Lattintown Road, turn left onto Mount Zion Road, left onto Truncali Drive to Mountain Road. Driving time: 10 minutes.

GLORIE FARM WINERY
40 Mountain Road | Marlboro, NY | 12542
845.236.3265 | http://gloriewine.com/

Housed in a 1913 barn near the top of Mt. Zion Mountain, Doug and MaryEllen Glorie opened Glorie Farm Winery in 2004. Glorie has one of the best growing sites for Cabernet Franc and his is a must-try. They offer more than eighteen wines to taste. From serious wines, such as their Seyval, Synergy and award winning Cabernet Franc, their cider, Mutiny, to seasonal wines like Rumple Pumpkin, which they release in the Fall. If you have it in you, hike to the top of the vineyard behind the tasting room and catch the spectacular view of the valley.

Head back on Truncali Drive to Mt Zion Road. Turn left on Mt Zion Road, left onto Lattintown Road, feft onto Gala Lane. Go all the way up the hill and the tasting room is at the top. Driving time: 10 minutes.

NOSTRANO VINEYARDS

14 Gala Lane | Milton, NY | 12547
845.795.5473 | http://nostranovineyards.com/

In 1943 Joseph and Ben Trapani established J&B Trapani Fruit Growers on 120 acres of land in Milton. They grew grapes, apples, pears, raspberries, currants, and cherries. Today fourth generation Nick Bozzo has repurposed some of the land of the family farm to growing grapes. He ripped up old apple trees that were being abandoned and planted Riesling, Cabernet Franc, Baco Noir, Frontenac, Pinot Noir, and table grapes. You will pass some of these vineyards on the way up the big hill to the tasting room. Grab a bottle, sit on the outdoor couches, and enjoy the view.

Left onto Lattintown Road. Turn right onto Milton Turnpike, left onto Milton Cross Road. Left onto Baileys Gap Road. Driving time: 5 minutes.

BAD SEED CIDER

43 Baileys Gap Road | Highland, NY | 12528
845.236.0956 | http://www.badseedhardcider.com/

There are two orchards I go apple picking at in the Hudson Valley and Wilklow Orchards is one of them. I've followed sixth generation apple farmer Albert through all the family newsletters from when he was a little kid. Albert and his friend Devin grew up together and in 2011 they put together their savings and turned their hobby into a reality for the love of cider. It's their pastime, their passion, their life, and is shows through the quality of their cider. The base of their cider comes from three apples: Winesap, Ida Red, and Empire. Then they mix in some Northern Spy, Braeburn, Pink Lady, and others. Their main ciders are a dry cider based on a French cider almost like a cider champagne, very crisp. Belgian Abby Cider has sour apple tones and yeasty characters. For people who like Belgian sours, Bourbon Barrel Cider is a dry cider aged in bourbon barrel for eight weeks and it picks up some oak and smoke and rounds out some of the acidity in the apples. It's more of a still cider. If you visit in the fall, try their Apple Pie Dry, it's the best apple pie you'll drink.

Take a right onto Baileys Gap Road and turn left onto US-44 W. Turn right onto South Ohioville Road and left onto Allhusen Road. Driving time: 10 minutes.

ADAIR VINEYARDS
52 Allhusen Road | New Paltz, NY | 12561
845.255.1377 | http://www.adairwine.com/

A visit to Adair Vineyards is a visit to a National Historic dairy barn over two hundred years old, set against the Shawangunk Mountains. The hayloft tasting room combined with the picturesque picnic grounds, garden, and the vineyards from which their wines are crafted, make a wonderful tasting experience. Try their new line of Kir's made with local Hudson Valley fruit. Currently there are four different kinds: Nectarine, Blackcurrant, Peach, and Peachberry. Back by popular demand is their Solitary Oak a Vidal, Seyval, and Vignoles blend made like a Pouilly Fume style. All wine made at Adair are made from 100 percent local Hudson Valley grapes and fruit. They are pet friendly.

Right out of parking lot onto Allhusen Road. Right onto S Ohioville Road and left onto US-44 E. Turn left onto Clintondale Road/South Street. Driving time: 5 minutes

GUNK HAUS
387 South Street | Highland, NY | 12528
845.883.0866 | http://www.gunkhaus.com/

After a day of wine tasting sit down for some German food and a beer with great mountain views. If the weather is nice, sit outside and take in the scenery. All dishes are prepared from scratch and where possible from local ingredients. Try their Smoked Whitefish Crostini served on a pretzel crostini. You will find typical German entreés, such as Chicken Schnitzel and German Short Ribs, and some innovative dishes like Currywurst, which is smoked beef sausage with Haus-made curry catsup on a pretzel roll. The corkage fee is $21 if you bring your own wine.

Head north on South Street and turn left onto NY-299 W. Turn right onto New Paltz Bypass/ N Putt Corners Road and left onto Shivertown Road. Driving time: 10 minutes.

MOONDANCE RIDGE BED & BREAKFAST
55 Shivertown Road | New Paltz, NY | 12561
845.255.4161 | http://moondanceridge.com/

Set in a 1900's Craftsman-style house with beautiful views of the Catskill, with guestrooms that feature a Hollywood's Golden Era themed decor and provide flat-screens and whirlpool tubs, along with sitting areas with electric fireplaces. A three-course breakfast made with home grown herbs and local produce is served in the morning. Coffee and tea are stocked in a guest fridge and fresh baked cookies are available in the afternoon. There are private walking paths, a pond with waterfall, and a seven-circuit labyrinth and gardens.

Weekend Rendezvous

Northern Shawangunk Wine Trail

Three-Day Itinerary

Suggested Stop

Motorcyclepedia • Stoutridge Vineyards • Benmarl Winery • Brunel & Rafael Winery • Stoutridge Vineyard • Glorie Farm Winery • Bad Seed Cider • Adair Vineyards • Tuthilltown Spirits Distillery • Minnewaska State Park Preserve • Baldwin Vineyards • Christopher Jacobs Winery at Pennings Vineyards • Angry Orchard Cider • Robibero Family Vineyards • Whitecliff Vineyard & Winery • Yard Owl Brewery • Kettleborough Cider House

Suggested Dining

Newburgh Waterfront • Frida's Bakery • Perch Restaurant • Tuthill House at the Mill • The Village Tea Room • Liquid Merchantile • Mountain Brauhause

Suggested Lodging

4 Points by Sheraton at Stewart Airport • Minnewaska Lodge

Travel North on the New York State Thruway and exit at Newburgh, exit 17. Stay in the right lane as you exit and head towards I-84 E. Get on I-84 E and get off at exit 8 for NY-52 Walden. Turn right onto S Plank Road and right onto Dupont Avenue. Dupont Avenue becomes Wisner. Turn left onto Little Britain Road and right onto Cerone Place. Turn right onto Lake Drive and right onto Lake Street. Driving time: 15 minutes.

Friday

MOTORCYCLEPEDIA

250 Lake Street | Newburgh, NY | 12550
845.569.9065 | http://www.motorcyclepediamuseum.org/

Motorcyclepedia is a motorcycle enthusiast's paradise with over 450 American motorcycles mainly from the first half of the twentieth century. Gerald A. Doering a motorcycle enthusiast collected Indian motorcycles from 1901-1953. His son Ted also shared in his passion for motorcycles, and in 1971 they began a wholesale motorcycle parts business. With the success of the business they expanded their motorcycle collection. In 2011, they opened Motorcyclepedia "A Family's Attic Full of Motorcycles" featuring more than 400 motorcycles. Along with the motorcycles you will find photographs, posters, memorabilia, machinery, and other items related to bikes.

Head Northeast on Lake Street and turn right onto Washington Street. At the end of the road turn left onto Water Street and turn right onto 4ᵗʰ Street and this will take you to Front Street. Driving time: 5 minutes.

NEWBURGH WATERFRONT
Front Street | Newburgh, NY | 12550
http://www.ribworks.com/ http://www.blu-pointe.com/
http://cena2000.com/ http://www.therivergrill.com/

Choose from a variety of restaurants and sit on the banks of the Hudson River enjoying the view of Mt. Beacon and watch the boats on the river. Restaurants vary from Billy Joe's Ribworks, Blu-Pointe, The River Grill, Cena 2000, and many more. Take a walk along the water, look at the menus, take in the vibe, and enjoy.

Get back up to Water Street and take that to RT 9W. Turn right onto 9W and get in the left hand lane to get onto I84-W. Get off at Exit 6 and take a right. Lakeside Drive is on the right at the Diner. Driving time: 10 minutes.

4 POINTS BY SHERATON
AT STEWART AIRPORT
5 Lakeside Road | Newburgh, NY | 12550
845.567.0567 | http://www.starwoodhotels.com/

This property is fairly new and centrally located right off I-84. Rooms are nicely appointed in a contemporary style. There is free wireless internet and each room has a mini refrigerator and a 50-inch flat screen TV. There is a restaurant and bar just off the lobby, and the hotel has a small workout room.

Saturday

Left onto NY17-K and left onto I-84 E. Get off at exit 10 (last exit before toll) and take a left onto US-9W N. Turn right onto James Road and right onto S Road. Turn left to stay on S Road and turn left onto Main Street. Parking is in back.

FRIDA'S BAKERY
26 Main Street | Milton, NY | 12547
845.795.5550 | http://www.fridasbakeryny.com/

Located in the sleepy town of Milton, a town time forgot. Park in the back of the building and take the elevator to the second floor (which is on street level). The menus are on the counter to the left. Make sure you look at the specials, and if they have the Funky Grilled Cheese for breakfast get it, it's awesome! You can also build your own breakfast sandwich or burrito. If you have a sweet tooth, it is a bakery so enjoy. (Look for the free samples by the cashier.)

Take S Road Southwest and turn right onto Willow Tree Road. Be careful crossing Rt 9W as the market is on the other side.

HEART OF THE HUDSON VALLEY FARMER'S MARKET
Cluett Schantz Park | 1801-1805 Route 9W | Milton, NY | 12547
http://www.hhvfarmersmarket.com/

This farmers market opens at the end of June and runs through mid-October from 9 a.m. to 2 p.m. Make sure you check the website for dates. You will find a large selection of Hudson Valley items from baked goods, pickles, jams, maple syrup to farm fresh veggies and fruits. Pick up something for lunch as the wineries of the day have beautiful picnic areas.

Turn left onto 9W-South. Take a right onto Western Avenue and a slight left onto Lattintown Road. Winery entrance is on Lattintown Road.

BRUNEL & RAFAEL WINERY
180 South Street | Marlboro, NY | 12542
845.306.5450 | http://www.brunelandrafael.com/

This is one of the newest wineries to the area and it is located in a century old home. Entering the house, the tasting will take place in what was once the old living and dining room. Enjoy their hometown hospitality. They focus exclusively on dry wines, but plan on introducing a sweet wine to their portfolio in the future.

Left onto Lattintown Road. Slight right onto Plattekill Road that turns into Western Avenue. Turn left onto White Street, left onto Prospect Street and left onto Ann Kaley Lane. Driving time: 5 minutes

STOUTRIDGE VINEYARD
10 Ann Kaley Lane | Marlboro, NY | 12542
845.236.7620 | http://www.stoutridge.com/

Stoutridge Vineyard sits on the site of a historic homestead farm, which has had vineyards planted since the early 1800's and a commercial winery from 1880-1910. In the early 1940's the farm was confiscated by the U.S. Government for operating an illegal still. In 2001, Stephen Osborn and his wife Kimberly Wagner purchased the farm and restored it, replanted the vineyard, restored the farmhouse, and the constructed a state-of-the-art winery utilizing 'gravity flow' design built directly on the original winery site. Stephen is the winemaker and uses no chemicals in his winemaking process. Their focus is on showing people how older wine can be stable without chemical additions and taste better as they age. Look for their distillery coming on line focusing on whiskey.

Turn right onto Prospect Street, right onto White Street, right onto Western Avenue and left onto Highland Avenue. Driving time: 5 minutes.

BENMARL WINERY
156 Highland Avenue | Marlboro, NY | 12542
845.236.4265 | www.benmarl.com

Benmarl Winery sits on the oldest continuously planted vineyard in the United States, Slate Hill Vineyard, home to New York's Farm Winery License #1. Located on thirty-seven scenic acres overlooking the Hudson River and Berkshire Mountains with a kickass view for great picture taking. This historic winery was purchased by artist Mark Miller from Andrew J. Caywood, an early American viticulturist in 1957, and in 2006 it was purchased by Victor Spaccarelli who fulfilled his lifelong dream of owning a vineyard. Victor's son Matt is the General Manager and winemaker focusing on producing small batch wines that capture the unique terroir of the vineyard. In addition, Matt and his partner Casey have produced a line of wines, Fjord Vineyards from very small estate grown acre lots and small batches sourced regionally. At the time of writing this, Fjord tasting room was open on sporadic days and times. Ask for directions to their Ridge Road tasting room from the Benmarl staff, and if you visit, make sure to try their award winning Albariño.

Right onto Highland Avenue, right onto Western Avenue and right onto King Street. Driving time: 5 minutes.

PERCH RESTAURANT
1 King Street | Marlboro, NY | 12542
845.236.3663 | http://www.perchmarlboro.com/

Owned by the same people of Cathryn's Tuscan Grill in Cold Spring, Perch offers globally inspired food and they source their ingredients locally. The beer and wine list highlights the great craft beverages the Hudson Valley offers. Try their Pork Belly Tacos, Pappardelle Pasta with Pulled Rabbit Meat, Seedless Grape and White Truffle Oil or their Grilled Cheese Panini with Irish Cheddar, onions and Hudson Valley Homestead Mustard. Want to bring in a bottle? Their corkage fee is $15.

Depending on where you parked, you want to head back up Western Avenue as if going back to Benmarl. Continue on Western at end of road take a left onto Ridge Road and a right onto Lattintown Road. Take a left onto Mt. Zion Road, left onto Truncali Drive to Mountain Road. Driving time: 10 minutes.

GLORIE FARM WINERY
40 Mountain Road | Marlboro, NY | 12542
845.236.3265 | http://gloriewine.com/

Housed in a 1913 barn near the top of Mt. Zion Mountain, Doug and MaryEllen Glorie opened Glorie Farm Winery in 2004. Glorie has one of the best growing sites for Cabernet Franc and his is a must-try. They offer more than eighteen wines to taste. From serious wines, such as their Seyval, Synergy and award winning Cabernet Franc, their cider, Mutiny, to seasonal wines like Rumple Pumpkin, which they release in the Fall. If you have it in you, hike to the top of the vineyard behind the tasting room and catch the spectacular view of the valley.

Go back down Truncali Drive, turn right onto Mt. Zion Road and left onto Lattintown Road. Turn left onto Gala Lane. Driving time: 10 minutes.

NOSTRANO VINEYARDS
14 Gala Lane | Milton, NY | 12547
845.795.5473 | http://nostranovineyards.com/

In 1943, Joseph and Ben Trapani established J&B Trapani Fruit Growers on 120 acres of land in Milton. They grew grapes, apples, pears, raspberries, currants, and cherries. Today fourth generation Nick Bozzo has repurposed some of the land of the family farm to growing grapes. He ripped up old apple trees that were being abandoned and planted Riesling, Cabernet Franc, Baco Noir, Frontenac, Pinot Noir, and table grapes. You will pass some of these vineyards on the way up the big hill to the tasting room. Grab a bottle, sit on the outdoor couches, and enjoy the view.

Turn left onto Lattintown Road. When road ends, right onto Milton Turnpike, left onto Milton Cross Road, left onto Baileys Gap Road. Driving time: 5 minutes.

BAD SEED CIDER
43 Baileys Gap Road | Highland, NY | 12528
845.236.0956 | http://www.badseedhardcider.com/

There are two orchards I go apple picking at in the Hudson Valley and Wilklow Orchards is one of them. I've followed sixth generation apple farmer Albert through all the family newsletters from when he was a little kid. Albert and his friend Devin grew up together and in 2011 they put together their savings and turned their hobby into a reality for the love of cider. It's their pastime, their passion, their life, and is shows through the quality of their cider. The base of their cider comes from three apples, Winesap, Ida Red, and Empire. Then they mix in some Northern Spy, Braeburn, Pink Lady, and others. Their main ciders are a dry cider based on a French cider almost like a cider champagne, very crisp. Belgian Abby Cider has sour apple tones and yeasty characters. For people who like Belgian sours, Bourbon Barrel Cider is a dry cider aged in bourbon barrel for eight weeks and it picks up some oak and smoke and rounds out some of the acidity in the apples. It's more of a still cider. If you visit in the fall, try their Apple Pie Dry, it's the best apple pie you'll drink.

Take a right onto Baileys Gap Road and turn left onto US-44 W. Turn right onto South Ohioville Road and left onto Allhusen Road. Driving time: 10 minutes.

ADAIR VINEYARDS
52 Allhusen Road | New Paltz, NY | 12561
845.255.1377 | http://www.adairwine.com/

A visit to Adair Vineyards is a visit to a National Historic dairy barn over two hundred years old, set against the Shawangunk Mountains. The hayloft tasting room combined with the picturesque picnic grounds, garden, and the vineyards from which their wines are crafted, make a wonderful tasting experience. Try their new line of Kir's made with local Hudson Valley fruit. Currently there are four different kinds: Nectarine, Blackcurrant, Peach, and Peachberry. Back by popular demand is their Solitary Oak a Vidal, Seyval, and Vignoles blend made like a Pouilly Fume style. All wine made at Adair are made from 100 percent local Hudson Valley grapes and fruit. They are pet friendly.

Take a left out of the parking lot onto Allhusen Road. At end of road take a left onto Route 32. At traffic light take a right onto Route 44. Turn left onto Albany Post Road and right onto Tuthilltown Road and left onto Grist Mill Lane. Driving time: 15 minutes.

TUTHILLTOWN SPIRITS DISTILLERY
14 Grist Mill Lane | Gardiner, NY | 12525
845.255.1527 | http://www.tuthilltown.com/

Tuthilltown is New York's first whiskey distiller since prohibition. When arriving at Tuthilltown, it will remind you of the Wild West. See how they transformed the historic 220 year old Tuthilltown Gristmill granaries into a micro-distillery. In 2005 they began producing small batch spirits. Their Hudson Baby Bourbon was the first Bourbon made in New York since prohibition. Try their line of Whiskey's ranging from Corn, Four Grain, Rye, Maple Cask Rye, Single Malt, and their Baby Bourbon. Their spirits include: Indigenous Wheat Vodka, and Indigenous Apple Vodka which is made with Hudson Valley apples, and their Half Moon Gin which is an 80 percent wheat based spirit and 20 percent apple based with eight botanicals. They also have a line of bitters that were created in their basement, hence the name "Basement Bitters" that are barrel aged and excellent for whiskey cocktails.

Located on the Tuthilltown compound.

TUTHILL HOUSE AT THE MILL

20 Grist Mill Lane | Gardiner, NY | 12525
845.255.4151 | http://www.tuthillhouse.com/

The Tuthill House Gristmill is the oldest continuously operated water powered gristmill in New York State and on the National Register of Historic Places. You get that historic feel the minute you walk in. Start your experience with a cocktail from Patrick, the best mixologist around! They make their own tinctures, which adds a wonderful pizzazz to their cocktails. Many of their cocktails are made from local spirits and they have a great local wine and beer list. Their menu offers a nice variety for the carnivore to the vegetarian. Corkage fee is $20

Turn right onto Tuthilltown Road and left onto Albany Post Road and a left onto Route 55. Lodge will be on your left. Driving time: 10 minutes.

MINNEWASKA LODGE

3116 US-44 | Gardiner, NY | 12525
845.255.1110 | http://www.minnewaskalodge.com/

You will have that true "lodge" experience surrounded by 25,000 acres of Minnewaska State Park. The twenty-six nicely appointed guest rooms will make you nice and comfy for your stay. Some of the rooms have private balconies, others have cathedral ceilings, and all have views of the mountains or the forest. Enjoy their complementary coffee and tea bar with freshly baked cookies all day. Complimentary Wi-Fi, a small workout room and complimentary continental breakfast is provided.

Sunday

Left onto NY 44/55 and a right onto NY-299 E. Turn right onto Plattekill Avenue. Driving time: 15 minutes.

THE VILLAGE TEAROOM
10 Plattekill Avenue | New Paltz, NY | 12561
845.255.3434 | http://www.thevillagetearoom.com/

Located in the heart of the Village of New Paltz, The Village Tearoom is housed in the old "A. Schoomaker Tailor Shop," built in 1883. Agnes Devereux's menu uses the finest local ingredients sourced from local farms in New Paltz and the surrounding area. Enjoy a nice breakfast with items such as Potato Pancakes, Gravlax Sandwich, and House Made Granola.

From Plattekill Avenue, turn right onto Main Street NY-299. Continue straight and the farmer's market will be on your left. Driving time: 5 minutes.

NEW PALTZ FARMER'S MARKET
257 Main Street | New Paltz, NY | 12561
http://www.newpaltzfarmersmarket.com/

Stop by the New Paltz Farmer's Market after breakfast and get some of the bounty the Hudson Valley offers. It is open from June to November, 10 a.m. to 3 p.m.

Head northwest on NY-299/Main Street. Turn right onto US-44. The road gets windy. Park and the entrance is on the left. Driving time: 20 minutes.

MINNEWASKA STATE PARK PRESERVE
5281 Route 44/55 | Kerhonkson, NY | 12446
845.255.0752 | http://www.nysparks.com/parks/127/details.aspx

When I was a teenager, we would go up to "Lake Minnewaska," as it was called then, to hike, canoe, and cliff jump. Cliff House Hotel was up there which burned down in late 1978. I have memories of the ruins while making my way to the lake. Today those ruins are gone and the area is owned by the New York State. There is a $10 vehicle fee to get in. Please get there early as the parking lots fill up fast. You can take a short hike of .7 mile or a longer one of 4.3 miles. Make sure you dress appropriately and wear your hiking shoes or sneakers, and also bring water and a camera with you. The views and scenery will be breathtaking.

Follow US44-55 right into Gardiner. Driving time: 20 minutes.

LIQUID MERCANTILE
128 Main Street | Gardiner, NY | 12525
845.633.8764 | http://www.gardinerliquidmercantile.com/

Gardiner is home to many farms and craft beverage producers. Stop in the Liquid Mercantile for a quick bite to eat. Owned by Gable Erenzo, former Chief Distiller at Tuthilltown Spirits Distillery, Gabe opened the Gardiner Mercantile as a retail outlet for his nano-distillery and has plans to develop it as a hub for all the farm beverages and food produced within 20 miles of the village of Gardiner. Grab a small plate full of local flavor. The Liquid Mercantile captures the quaintness of the small town. Should you want to bring your own bottle of wine their corkage fee is $25.

Head west on US 44-55 and turn left onto Bruynswick Road. Turn left onto Bruyn Turnpike/Wallkill Avenue and right onto Hardenburgh Road. Winery will be on the left. Driving time: 15 minutes.

BALDWIN VINEYARDS
176 Hardenburgh Road | Pine Bush, NY | 12566
845.744.2226 | http://baldwinvineyards.com/

In 1982, Jack and Pat Baldwin sold their home in New Jersey and purchased the 37-acre Hardenburgh Estate that included the 200-year-old stone home and an 18,000 square foot outbuilding. Today, that outbuilding is the winery and tasting room with their daughter Wendy and husband Alex at the helm. They are known for their awarding Strawberry wine. On selected weekends they have a Strawberry Chocolate and Wine Festival pairing their wines with chocolate and strawberry desserts.

Turn right out of the winery towards Riverside Drive. Left onto Cooper Road and left onto Bruynswick Road. Right onto NY-52 and left onto Burlingham Road. Turn left onto Shawangunk Lake Road and right onto Crawford Street. Driving time: 10 minutes.

CHRISTOPHER JACOBS WINERY AT PENNINGS VINEYARDS
320 Crawford St | Pine Bush, NY | 12566
845.728.8066 | http://www.christopherjacobswinery.com/

In 2006, Monica and Christopher planted their first block of grapes branching off and leading a new generation of Pennings farmers into the wine industry. Take the 30-minute tour of the vineyard when available led by Monica or Christopher. If you are traveling with a group and would like a tour, reservations are recommended. Taste three of their wines and a white Sangria, and enjoy the views of the valley in their outdoor tasting room. Try their award winning Appleoosa made with fruit predominantly from Pennings Orchards. They are keeping it all in the family.

Continue on Crawford Street towards Howard Seeley Road. Turn left onto County Road 48 to County Route 17. Right onto NY-52 E and Left onto Albany Post Road. Angry Orchard is on the corner with a big red barn. Driving time: 15 minutes.

ANGRY ORCHARD CIDER
2241 Albany Post Road | Walden, NY | 12586
http://angryorchard.com/

Look for the red barn on the corner. This facility was opened up by Angry Orchard Cider to be used for research and development. It is a state-of-the-art facility on a 60-acre farm. You will learn everything about apples – how apples are grown and how cider is made. The farm itself dates back to the 1700's with it becoming a full-time orchard around the 1950's. You will be able to taste ciders created just for this local market that may eventually become available across the country, as well as new and old ciders in the tasting room. The interactive Visitor's Center will give you a lesson on the history and heritage of cider making.

Head north on Albany Post Road. At the bend stay to the right and continue on Albany Post Road. Robibero will be on the left. Driving time: 10 minutes.

ROBIBERO FAMILY VINEYARDS
714 Albany Post Road | New Paltz, NY | 12561
845.255.9463 | http://rnywine.com/

We all have big dreams when we are kids and Harry Robibero dreamed of following his grandfather's footsteps and owning a winery. That dream became reality in 2003 when he and his wife Carole purchased the 42 acres of land that Rivendell Winery sat on. Luck had it that in 2007 Rivendell went out of business and Harry and Carole revealed their plans for their winery, Robibero Family Vineyards. Today their daughter Tiffany runs the winery. It's a true family destination. You will always find a Robibero family member behind the tasting bar. They have a great fire pit and bouncy house for kids at their events. They are dog friendly. Their most popular wines are their Rabbits Foot and 87 North. You will always find new wines on their tasting menu as they are constantly experimenting and changing things up. Come for a taste and stay for a bottle on their beautiful deck or around the fire pit.

Right onto Albany Post Road. At fork stay to the left. Turn right onto McKinstry Road. Winery will be on the left. Driving time: 5 minutes.

WHITECLIFF VINEYARD & WINERY
331 McKinstry Road | Gardiner, NY | 12525
845.255.4613 | http://www.whitecliffwine.com

Michael Migliore is a pioneer in the Hudson Valley winemaking scene. He has lived on his 70-acre farm winery since 1975 and the vineyard is one of the largest vineyards in the Hudson Valley dedicated to producing quality wines. In 2011, Whitecliff expanded their operations and built a geo-thermal winery. They offer tours of the winery at designated times in the fall or by appointment. Their most popular wine is Awosting White, which is a blend of Seyval and Vignoles. Their Sky Island is a Bordeaux style blend and they have wines for all palates, dry, semi-sweet, port style, and sparkling. Have a glass or bottle on their porch with a view of the white cliffs of the Shawangunk Ridge.

Take a right out of the winery onto McKinstry Road. Turn left onto Albany Post Road (US 44/55) Turn left onto Dusinberre Road. Left onto Steves Lane and left onto Osprey Lane. Yes, you are in an industrial park. Driving time: 5 minutes.

YARD OWL BREWERY
19 Osprey Lane | Gardiner, NY | 12525
845.633.8576 | http://www.yardowlcraftbrewery.com/

James and Kristop were friends for twenty years. James knew brewing, and Kristop who was and still is a local winemaker with various wineries in the Hudson Valley, understood fermentation. Two friends who liked to drink the same beers put their skills together in the backyard shed two years before moving to the facility they are in now. The Yard Owl name comes from the parliament of owls living in James's backyard and in keeping with the backyard theme, Yard Owl was the name they decided on. They brew all Belgium style ales except for their IPA, which is Belgium yeast strain with American hops brewed in the traditional Belgium fashion. Their brews are dry and aren't overly hoppy.

Head towards Steves Lane when you come out of the brewery. Turn left onto Dusinberre Road and right onto Phillies Bridge Road. Left onto NY-208 N. Driving time: 5 minutes.

KETTLEBOROUGH CIDER HOUSE
277 State Route 208 | New Paltz, NY | 12561
845.255.7717 | http://www.kettleboroughciderhouse.com/

The Dressel family has been growing apples in the Hudson Valley since 1923. After graduating from Cornell University in 2007, Tim

Dressel began making cider with the apples from the family farm. They have sixteen European varieties and four heirloom American varieties planted, a total of twenty varieties devoted entirely to cider production. They produce a nice variety of cider. Their tasting room is open on Saturday and Sunday during the season.

Head northeast on NY-208. Turn left onto Main Street (NY-299). Restaurant is at intersection of NY-299 and US 44/55. Driving time: 10 minutes.

MOUNTAIN BRAUHAUS RESTAURANT
3132 US-44 | Gardiner, NY | 12525
845.255.9766 http://www.mountainbrauhaus.com/

After a long day of tasting, sit down German style. Owned by the same family since 1917, you will get the German vibe the minute you walk in. Start with the Bavarian Pretzel with two Mustards and warm Smoke Gouda and Horseradish dip. You'll find your Bratwurst and Kraut, and Wiener Schnitzel on the menu but if you feel like a burger, they have those too. Corkage fee is $10 if you bring your own bottle.

Turn left onto US-44 and the lodge is on the right.

MINNEWASKA LODGE
3116 US-44 | Gardiner, NY | 12525
845.255.1110 | http://www.minnewaskalodge.com/

You will have that true "lodge" experience surrounded by 25,000 acres of Minnewaska State Park. The twenty-six nicely appointed guest rooms will make you nice and comfy for your stay. Some of the rooms have private balconies, others have cathedral ceilings, and all have views of the mountains or the forest. Enjoy their complementary coffee and tea bar with freshly baked cookies all day. Complimentary Wi-Fi, a small workout room and complimentary continental breakfast is provided.

Day Tripping

Dutchess Wine Trail and Beyond

One-Day Itinerary

Suggested Stops

Innisfree Gardens • Millbrook Vineyards & Winery • Clinton
Vineyards • Taconic Distillery • Dutch's Spirits • Hillrock Distillery

Suggested Dining

Vineyard Grille at Millbrook Winery • The Stissing House

Suggested Lodging

Beekman Arms

*Traveling on the Taconic State Parkway Millbrook, NY off Taconic
State Parkway. Take the US-44 exit toward Poughkeepsie/Millbrook
and take a right onto US-44 E. Turn right onto South Road and
right onto Tyrrel Road. Driving time: 5 minutes.*

INNISFREE GARDENS

362 Tyrrel Road | Millbrook, NY | 12545
845.677.8000 | http://www.innisfreegarden.org/

Noted as one of the world's ten best gardens, this 150-acre Asian
inspired garden was once the summer home of Walter and Marion
Beck. The gardens consist of streams, waterfalls, terraces, rocks,
plants and a 40-acre glacial lake. It is one of the undiscovered
treasures in the Hudson Valley. Innisfree is open seasonally from
May through mid-October, Wednesday through Friday 10 a.m. to 4
p.m. and weekends from 11 a.m. to 5 p.m. It will take approximately
ninety minutes to tour the gardens.

*Head north on Tyrrel Road and turn left onto South Road and left
onto US-44 W. Right onto NY-82 N. Right onto Shunpike and left
onto Wing Road. Winery is on the right. Driving time: 15 minutes.*

MILLBROOK VINEYARDS & WINERY
26 Wing Road | Millbrook, NY | 12545
845.677.8383 | http://www.millbrookwine.com/

Known as the "Flagship Winery of the Hudson Valley," John Dyson purchased the 130-acre Wing Dairy Farm in 1982, his first vineyard and winemaking venture with his brother-in-law and General Manager David Bova. Winemaker John Graziano has been with them since the beginning, crafting amazing award-winning wines. Try their Proprietor's Special Reserve Cabernet Franc, Block Five East Pinot Noir, and their Tocai Friulano. Grab a bite to eat at their Vineyard Café and enjoy a bottle on the grounds or in the new Four Season room overlooking the vineyard. The views are spectacular! The Millbrook portfolio goes beyond the Hudson Valley as they own Williams Selyem in Sonoma, CA, Villa Pillo, Tuscany, Italy, and Pebble Ridge Vineyards in the North Central Coast in CA. Some of these wines are available for purchase in the tasting room.

Located on the grounds of Millbrook Vineyards & Winery.

VINEYARD GRILLE AT MILLBROOK WINERY
26 Wing Road | Millbrook, NY | 12545
845.677.8383 | http://www.millbrookwine.com/

Open Memorial Day through late October and run by Slammin' Salmon in Millbrook. Enjoy a burger, sandwich or salad and sit among the vines with a bottle of wine.

Take a left out of winery onto Wing Road and a right onto Shunpike. Left onto NY-82 S. Turn right onto Hibernia Road then right onto Clinton Corners Road. Bear slight right onto NY-115 (Salt Point Turnpike) as road bends take a left onto Clinton Corners Schultzville Road. Winery will be on your left. Driving time:15 minutes.

CLINTON VINEYARDS
450 Clinton Corners Schultzville Road | Clinton Corners, NY | 12514
845.266.5372 | http://clintonvineyards.com/

Clinton Vineyards was established in 1976 when Ben Feder, a Bronx born book designer and artist purchased the property and turned the dairy farm into a beautiful vineyard and winery. He was inspired by the vineyards and wineries he loved in the French countryside. Celebrate with their estate bottled sparkling wines or their estate bottle Seyval. Make sure you try their famous Cassis too. You will find Clinton Vineyards to be small and intimate and most likely have a tasting with Ben's wife Phyllis who runs the vineyard/winery today.

Take a right onto Clinton Corners Schultzville Road from the winery. Turn left onto NY-115 (Salt Point Turnpike) continue straight onto Market Lane. Turn right onto Hicks Lane, and turn right onto Bulls Head Road. Turn left onto Bowen Road. Driving time: 10 minutes.

TACONIC DISTILLERY
179 Bowen Road | Stanfordville, NY | 12581
845.393.4583 | http://www.taconicdistillery.com/

In 2010, the Coughlin family purchased 113 acres of an old beef farm called Laufred Farms and renamed it Rolling Hills Farm. When you pull up to the distillery you will be in awe of its beauty with the rolling hills. Paul is an avid outdoorsman and bourbon aficionado. Grab a taste of their Dutchess Private Reserve, Barrel Strength, Founder's Rye Whiskey or Rolling Hills Rum. Take time to stroll through the grounds and enjoy the view.

Head south on Bowen Road and turn left onto Bulls Head Road. Turn left onto NY-82 N. When the road ends, turn left onto NY-199/NY-82 N/ W Church Street. Turn right onto Bowman Road and right onto Ryan Road. Driving time: 20 minutes.

DUTCH'S SPIRITS
Harvest Homestead Farm | 98 Ryan Road |Pine Plains, NY | 12567
518.398.1022 | http://www.dutchsspirits.com/

When you visit Dutch's Spirits you are not just visiting a distillery but a part of prohibition history. In 1932, prohibition agents raided this 400-acre farm that at the time housed liquor bootlegger Dutch Schultz's stills in a massive underground distilling operation where thousands of gallons of moonshine were produced illegally. A few years after the raid it was purchased by a German group, then Janet and Charles Adams. Charles worked at the distillery thirty years earlier. The Adams family kept watch over the farm and its secrets. After the passing of the New York farm distillery law in the spring of 2008, Charles' grandson Alex Adams and close friend Ariel Schlein decided to move forward and bring the farm back to the distillery it once was. It is listed in the State and National Register of Historic Places as a "Bootleg Era Bunker Complex." Presently they produce Sugar Wash Moonshine, which is great mixed with lemonade. In the tasting room you will be able to taste a wide variety of New York craft spirits. Shop around in their New York designated farmer's market with a nice selection of products made in the Hudson Valley.

Head back towards Bowman Road and make a left. Turn left onto NY-199 E/W Church Street. Follow NY-199 E. Turn left onto NY-82 N. Slight left onto Pooles Hill Road. Driving time: 15 minutes.

HILLROCK DISTILLERY
408 Pooles Hill Road | Ancram, NY | 12502
518.329.1023 | http://www.hillrockdistillery.com/

Tucked away on a beautiful country road in Ancram, New York you will find Hillrock Farm, home to Hillrock Estate Distillery. Jeffrey Baker is producing whiskey under the direction of Master Distiller, Dave Pickerall who was the Master Distiller at Makers Mark. On this 100-acre estate there are 36 acres planted and rotational planting between barley and rye. Tour their facility and visit the first malt house built at a distillery in the United States since before prohibition. They bring the terroir to whiskey from field to glass. Tours and tastings must be pre-booked and are by appointment only.

South on Pooles Hill Road. Right onto NY-82. Turn right onto NY-199/ NY-82 and left onto S Main Street. It is right there at the intersection. Driving time: 10 minutes.

THE STISSING HOUSE
7801 S Main Street | Pine Plains, NY | 12567
518.398.8800 | http://www.stissinghouse.com/

A tavern and restaurant since the 1700's, the Stissing House features wide plank wood floors, revolutionary era beams, old local landscape paintings, and cozy rooms throughout for dining. Dine on French Italian fare by Chef Michael Jean who found his way from Provence to the Hudson Valley via New York City. The menu changes weekly and they source their food locally when possible. Bringing in your own wine, the corkage fee is $25.

Take NY-199 W and bear left onto NY-308 W. Turn left onto Mill Street. Beekman Arms will be on your right. Driving time: 30 minutes.

BEEKMAN ARMS
6387 Mill Street | Rhinebeck, NY | 12572
845.876.7077 | http://www.beekmandelamaterinn.com/
beekmanarms.htm

You'll find history at the Beekman Arms, America's oldest continuously operated hotel. Many famous people have slept here. President Franklin Delano Roosevelt concluded his campaign for governor and President, talking from the front porch. The main house might be old and historic, but all rooms have a private bath, TV, phone, and a decanter of sherry. The Guest House is a comfortable motel type accommodation located behind the main inn. These rooms have air conditioning and refrigerators and they are pet friendly. Other accommodations are also in "The Old Firehouse," which was the original firehouse to the village of Rhinebeck. If you have a group, The Townsend House will accommodate you in four large King size bedrooms with gas fireplaces.

Weekend Rendezvous

Dutchess Wine Trail & Hudson-Berkshire Beverage Trail

Three-Day Itinerary

Suggested Stops

Madava Farms|Crown Maple • Dover Stone Church • Millbrook Vineyards & Winery • Clinton Vineyards • Taconic Distillery • Dutch's Spirits • Hillrock Distillery • Tousey Winery • Clermont Vineyards • Olana State Historic Site • Hudson Chatham Winery • Chatham Brewery • Buttercup Farm Audubon Sanctuary

Suggested dining

Monte's Local Kitchen & Tap Room • McKinney & Doyle Millbrook Café • Red Devon • Otto's Market • Yainnis @ Chatham House

Suggested lodging

Old Drovers Inn • Wing Castle Bed & Breakfast • Inn at Silver Maple Farm

Friday

Traveling north on the Taconic State Parkway take Exit US-44 towards Poughkeepsie /Millbrook. Turn right onto US-44 E. Turn left on US-44 E. Continue straight onto E Main Street. Monte's will be on your right. Driving time: 15 minutes.

MONTE'S LOCAL KITCHEN & TAP ROOM

3330 Route 343 | Amenia, NY | 12501
845.789.1818 | http://www.monteskitchen.com/

You might have seen Dafna Mizrahi on the TV program Chopped but now is the chance to taste her food personally. Dafna, a graduate of the Culinary Institute of America, partnered with the Monte Family and features a menu of farm fresh products. Dafna highlights the local ingredients along with the farms where they are sourced. You will experience her creative talents in her locally inspired dishes. Corkage fee is $20

Head west on E Mains Street RT 343 turns into NY-22 S. Driving time: 30 minutes.

DARYL'S HOUSE
130 Route 22 | Pawling, NY | 12564
845.289.0185 | http://www.darylshouseclub.com/

This is the place to listen (and see) some great music and relax with your friends. It is owned by Daryl Hall of Hall & Oats. What you watched on Daryl's House on the internet now has a home for you to visit. This is his way of inviting you over for some wine. Housed in the building that was formerly the Towne Crier, Daryl renovated the building in an eighteenth century style. Make sure you check the website for the lineup of who is playing and purchase your tickets.

Take NY-22 N and turn right onto E Duncan Hill Road. The inn will be on your right. Driving time: 15 minutes.

OLD DROVERS INN
196 E Duncan Hill Road | Dover Plains, NY | 12522
845.832.9311 | http://www.olddroversinn.com/

The Old Drovers Inn dates back to 1750 when it opened as the Clear Water Tavern. In 2013, the Inn went through a huge renovation to bring it back to its original state. The Inn boasts six private rooms with en-suite bathrooms, cable TV, and high speed broadband ports. You'll enjoy afternoon tea, sherry, homemade sandwiches, breads, and desserts at 4.p.m, and a complimentary full breakfast in the morning with local farm to table ingredients fresh from the

Inn's gardens and local purveyors.

Saturday

Head west on E Duncan Hill Road and turn left onto NY-22 S. Turn right onto Old Route 22 and continue on Corbin Road. Turn left onto Charles Colman Blvd. Driving time: 15 minutes

MCKINNEY & DOYLE
10 Charles Colman Boulevard | Pawling, NY | 12564
845.855.3707 | http://www.mckinneyanddoyle.com/

Tucked in the little hamlet of Pawling, New York, what began as a bakery later expanded to a restaurant and today they have added a soda fountain. The décor is exposed brick, wooden booths and pictures of funky food quotes hanging on the walls. They open for brunch at 9 a.m. on Saturday and Sundays. Begin your day with Strawberry Cream Cheese Pancakes, Huevos Vertiz or Genoa Salami and Date Hash. Don't forget to check out the bakery.

Turn left onto Coulter Avenue to NY-22 N. Turn left onto Dover Furnace Road. Turn left onto Ridge Road. Turn left onto McCourt Road. Driving time: 25 minutes.

MADAVA FARMS|CROWN MAPLE
47 McCourt Road | Dover Plains, NY | 12522
845.877.0640 | https://www.crownmaple.com/visit-madava-farms

This is the place to see and learn about the process of making maple syrup. Set on 800 acres, Madava Farms is full of maple and red maple trees. Crown Maple is one of the best maple syrups around. In fact, it's the only one I purchase. Take the 60-minute tour of the sugarhouse where you'll see the journey of the maple sap as it travels from the trees to the barrel in their state-of-the-art facility. The tour concludes with a Crown Maple Syrup tasting. After the tour feel free to hike the property in the designated areas and take in the views.

Head north on McCourt Road and turn left onto Corbin Road. Turn right onto Chestnut Ridge Road. Turn right and stay on Chestnut Ridge Road (RT 24). Chestnut Ridge Road turns slightly left and become Halls Corners Road. Slight right onto Cart Road. Driving time: 10 minutes.

DOVER STONE CHURCH

Cart Road | Dover Plains, NY | 12522
http://townofdoverny.us/Stone_Church.cfm

If you think you are going to visit a historic church and admire the stained-glass windows, think again. The Dover Stone Church is an ancient cavern on the Stone Church Brook. It has been said that it served as a Native American hideout in the seventeenth century. The waterfall cascades at the cavern's entrance. If the water is low enough you can go right into the center of the cavern. There is no parking at the entrance, so I suggest parking at Dover Elementary School just south of the entrance on Route 22. The preserve entrance is accessed by walking down a gravel driveway between two homes. Look for the blue and yellow state historic marker. Make sure you wear the proper shoes for this hike and check yourself for ticks afterwards.

Head northwest on Cart Road and turn right onto Halls Corners Road. Turn left onto NY-343 W. Turn right onto Church Street and right onto Franklin Avenue. Driving time: 10 minutes.

MILLBROOK CAFÉ

3290 Franklin Avenue | Millbrook, NY | 12545
845.677.6956 | http://www.themillbrookcafe.com/

Eat where the locals eat. This nice cozy atmosphere will make you feel right at home. Meals are made fresh in their wood fired brick oven and generous portions are served on cast iron plates. If you are a burger person, try their burger from Walbridge Farm (which is local). Corkage fee is $15.

Continue on Franklin Avenue turn left onto Sharon Turnpike and right onto Valley Farm Road. Turn right onto Shunpike and next left onto Wing Road. Winery is on the right. Driving time: 10 minutes.

MILLBROOK VINEYARDS & WINERY
26 Wing Road | Millbrook, NY | 12545
845.677.8383 | http://www.millbrookwine.com/

Known as the "Flagship Winery of the Hudson Valley" John Dyson purchased the 130-acre Wing Dairy Farm in 1982, his first vineyard and winemaking venture with his brother-in-law and General Manager David Bova. Winemaker John Graziano has been with them since the beginning crafting amazing award-winning wines. Try their Proprietor's Special Reserve Cabernet Franc, Block Five East Pinot Noir, and their Tocai Friulano. Grab a bite to eat at their Vineyard Café and enjoy a bottle on the grounds or in the new Four Season room overlooking the vineyard. The views are spectacular! The Millbrook portfolio goes beyond the Hudson Valley as they own Williams Selyem in Sonoma, CA, Villa Pillo, Tuscany, Italy, and Pebble Ridge Vineyards in the North Central Coast in CA. Some of these wines are available for purchase in the tasting room.

Take a right out of the winery onto Wing Road. Turn left onto Ernest Road and a left onto N Anson Road. Right onto Sister's Hill Road. Right onto NY-82. Left onto Bulls Head Road and right onto Bowen Road. Driving time 10 minutes.

TACONIC DISTILLERY
179 Bowen Road | Stanfordville, NY | 12581
845.393.4583 | http://www.taconicdistillery.com/

In 2010, the Coughlin family purchased 113 acres of an old beef farm called Laufred Farms and renamed it Rolling Hills Farm. When you pull up to the distillery you will be in awe of its beauty with the rolling hills. Paul is an avid outdoorsman and bourbon aficionado. Grab a taste of their Dutchess Private Reserve, Barrel Strength, Founder's Rye Whiskey or Rolling Hills Rum. Take time to stroll through the grounds and enjoy the view.

Head north on Bowen Road and turn left onto Hicks Lane. Turn left onto Market Lane that then merges onto Salt Point Turnpike (NY-115). Turn right onto Corners Schultzville Road. Winery will be on your left. Driving time: 10 minutes.

CLINTON VINEYARDS
450 Clinton Corners Schultzville Road | Clinton Corners, NY | 12514
845.266.5372 | http://clintonvineyards.com/

Clinton Vineyards was established in 1976 when Ben Feder, a Bronx born book designer and artist purchased the property and turned the dairy farm into a beautiful vineyard and winery. He was inspired by the vineyards and wineries he loved in the French countryside. Celebrate with their estate bottled sparkling wines or their estate bottle Seyval. Make sure you try their famous Cassis too. You will find Clinton Vineyards to be small and intimate and most likely have a tasting with Ben's wife Phyllis who runs the vineyard/winery today.

Leaving winery turn right onto Clinton Corners Schultzville Road and turn right onto Salt Point Turnpike (NY-115). Bear left onto Clinton Corners Road. At end of road take a right onto NY-82 S. Turn right onto US-44 W and the restaurant will be on your left. Driving time: 10 minutes.

LA PUERTA AZUL
2510 US-44 | Salt Point, NY | 12578
845-677-2985 | http://www.lapuertaazul.com/

After a day of wine tasting, some high end Mexican food and a margarita is just what you need. Take one step into La Puerta Azul and you will feel like you are in Mexico complete with an indoor waterfall. The Guacamole is prepared at your table and it is delicious. They usually have live music on the weekends, so sit back, relax, and enjoy. Bringing in your own bottle is not permitted.

Turn right out of restaurant onto US-44 E and take a left onto NY-

82 N. Turn right onto Shunpike and left onto Bengall Road. Driving time: 10 minutes.

WING CASTLE BED & BREAKFAST
717 Bangall Road | Millbrook, NY | 12545
845.677.9085 | http://www.wingscastle.com/

With views overlooking Millbrook Winery (no relation to the winery), Storm King and the Catskill Mountain ranges, Wing's Castle is a fifteen-century country castle designed using 80 percent of recycled materials salvaged from antique buildings. This is the dream of Peter Wing and his wife, Toni Ann. If you ever had a dream about sleeping in the dungeon or tower room, this is the B&B for you to spend the night. Each of the rooms features a private bath and Wi-Fi.

Sunday

Head northeast on Bangall Road. It turns into Duell Road. Continue onto Bangall Amenia Road. Sharp left onto Stage Stop Way. Driving time: 5 minutes.

RED DEVON RESTAURANT
108 Hunns Lake Road | Bangall, NY | 12506
845.868.3175 | http://www.reddevonrestaurant.com/

When you step inside the Red Devon you are stepping inside history. Once known as James Cagney's Stage Stop Steakhouse, the actor owned a farm just down the road and frequented the restaurant. Now owned by the Widdowson's who owned a local farm and raised Devon beef, they are all about sustainability and supporting local products. Everything is homemade daily from their own scones, croissants, bread, pastries, donuts, and more.

Head north on Stage Stop Way towards Bengall Amenia Road. Turn left onto Hunns Lake Road and a right onto Millis Lane. Slight right onto NY-82 N. Driving time: 5 minutes.

BUTTERCUP FARM AUDUBON SANCTUARY
6862 State Route 82 | Stanfordville, NY | 12581
518.325.5203 | http://ny.audubon.org/buttercup

You can take a nice hike and partake in some great birdwatching on these 641 acres with six miles of trails. It is possible to see over eighty species of birds that live there – species such as Great Blue Herons, Wood Ducks, Bobolinks, and more. Stroll the open grasslands, mature woods, and former orchard. Make sure you wear the proper shoes.

Head north on NY-82, turn left onto NY-199 /W Church Street then right onto Bowman Road. Turn right onto Ryan Road. Driving time: 10 minutes.

DUTCH'S SPIRITS
Harvest Homestead Farm | 98 Ryan Road |Pine Plains, NY | 12567
518.398.1022 | http://www.dutchsspirits.com/

When you visit Dutch's Spirits you are not just visiting a distillery but a part of prohibition history. In 1932, prohibition agents raided this 400-acre farm that at the time housed liquor bootlegger Dutch Schultz's stills in a massive underground distilling operation where thousands of gallons of moonshine were produced illegally. A few years after the raid it was purchased by a German group, then Janet and Charles Adams. Charles worked at the distillery thirty years earlier. The Adams family kept watch over the farm and its secrets. After the passing of the New York farm distillery law in the spring of 2008, Charles' grandson Alex Adams and close friend Ariel Schlein decided to move forward and bring the farm back to the distillery it once was. It is listed in the State and National Register of Historic Places as a "Bootleg Era Bunker Complex." Presently they produce Sugar Wash Moonshine, which is great mixed with lemonade. In the tasting room you will be able to taste a wide variety of New York craft spirits. Shop around in their New York designated farmer's market with a nice selection of products made in the Hudson Valley.

Head back towards Bowman Road and make a left. Turn left onto NY-199 E/W Church Street. Follow NY-199 E. Turn left onto NY-82 N. Slight left onto Pooles Hill Road. Driving time: 10 minutes.

HILLROCK DISTILLERY
408 Pooles Hill Road | Ancram, NY | 12502
518.329.1023 | http://www.hillrockdistillery.com/

Tucked away on a beautiful country road in Ancram, New York you will find Hillrock Farm, home to Hillrock Estate Distillery. Jeffrey Baker is producing whiskey under the direction of Master Distiller, Dave Pickerall who was the Master Distiller at Makers Mark. On this 100-acre estate there are 36 acres planted and rotational planting between barley and rye. Tour their facility and visit the first malt house built at a distillery in the United States since before prohibition. They bring the terroir to whiskey from field to glass. Tours and tastings must be pre-booked and are by appointment only.

Head north on Poole Hill road and turn right onto Pats Road. Turn left onto NY-82. Turn left onto County Road 11. Make a slight right onto County Route 8. Turn left onto County Route 19. Brewery will be on your left. Driving time: 20 minutes

SLOOP BREWING
1065 Co. Rte. 19 | Elizaville, NY | 12523
518.751.9134 | http://www.sloopbrewing.com/

If you think you are pulling up to someone's home or farm, you are. Just follow the sign to the brewery and go through the last barn/garage door and then you will be transformed from quiet farm life to lively brewery with lots of conversation and great energy. The tap room opened in August 2015 and they specialize in sour and farmhouse ales. All of the beers are unfiltered and un-pasteurized. Black Raz, dark in color is aged in oak and it's one of their most popular sours. If you like grapefruit try The Confliction, a hoppy beer and grapefuit bomb in the mouth. This brew stop is great for the person who might not like beer to be swayed into a taste and become a beer lover. 2015 Thrillist rated Sloop the most underrated brewery in New York State.

Turn right from brewery onto Country Route 19. Turn left onto County Route 8. Turn left onto Buckwheat Road and left onto US-9 S. Winery will be on your left. Driving time: 5 minutes.

TOUSEY WINERY
1774 US 9 | Germantown, NY | 12526
518.567.5462 | http://www.touseywinery.com/

When Kimberly and Ben Peacock moved back to the states from Europe they joined forces with Kimberly's Dad, Ray Tousey, to realize Ray's dream of turning their grounds into a vineyard and winery. Ben was a former assistant at the Houses of Parliament in London who embraced this life changing position with open arms. They are a diamond in the ruff. Try their Riesling, Pinot Noir, and Queen of Clermont. New is their Blanc de Blanc sparkling wine. Check out the Scarlet Tiger label, a series of wines which tells a story about a missing tiger. As you walk into the tasting room you will see the empty cage. The Queen of Clermont is the only one who knows where the tiger is and each of the other varietals are supporting characters in this epic story. Each vintage is a different part of the story, so start collecting the bottles.

Take a right out of the parking lot and go straight onto County Route 6. Winery will be on your left. Driving time: 5 minutes.

CLERMONT VINEYARDS
241 County Route 6 | Clermont, NY | 12526
845.663.6611 | http://clermontvineyards.com/

More than a decade ago Tony transformed a former dairy farm into a vineyard and winery. Wine is produced in the traditional Portuguese fashion from grapes grown on their seven acres of land. The renovated barn that houses the winery and tasting room has floor to ceiling windows with spectacular views of the Catskills. Grab a bottle and sit on the deck and watch the sunset. They are open Friday and Saturday until sunset and Sunday until 5 p.m. April through December.

Head west on County Route 6 and turn right onto NY-9G N. Turn right onto Roundtop Road and left at the first cross street onto Church Avenue and left onto Main Street. Driving time: 7 minutes.

OTTO'S MARKET
215 Main Street | Germantown, NY | 12526
518.537.7200 | http://ottosmarket.com/

This will take you back to your old town grocery store days. Otto's has had a few owners in the past since opening in 1927 as Central Market owned by Tracy Osborn Rockefeller. Today it is owned by Otto Leuschel who was the Vice President for the Northeast Region of Whole Foods and is bringing the Whole Foods experience to a Main Street grocer. Stop in here for a sandwich. Eat it in or take out and picnic at Olana.

Take Main Street and turn right onto NY 9G-N. Turn right onto Olana State Historic Site. Driving time: 10 minutes.

OLANA STATE HISTORIC SITE
5720 Route 9G | Hudson NY | 12534
518.828.0135 | http://www.olana.org/

This is the home and estate of Hudson River School painter Frederic Church. This 250-acre estate is open year round. You'll find hiking, picnicking, and there is also a pond for kayaking and fishing. Tour the main house and see the mixture of Victorian architecture and Middle Eastern motifs.

Exit Olana and head north on NY-9G N and take NY-23 slight left onto NY-9H N turn right onto NY-66N. Winery should be on your left. Driving time: 25 minutes.

HUDSON-CHATHAM WINERY
1900 NY-66 | Ghent, NY | 12075
518.392.9463 | http://www.hudsonchathamwinery.com/

Authors and book publishers turned winery owners, Carlo and Dominique DeVito, purchased their farm in 2006. Their winemaker Steve Casscles strives for great quality and known for his Baco Noir. Taste and compare their Casscles Vineyard Block 3 North Creek Vineyard, Fieldstone and Old Vines Mason Place Vineyards Pultney Farms Baco Noir. Under the Paperbirch label is their small production of artisanal ports, sherries, and other dessert wines. New products include an entire line of balsamic-styled vinegars and a cognac-style brandy to be released in the not too distant future. Grab a bottle, have a picnic, and enjoy the views.

Take a left out of the winery onto NY-66 N. That turns into Hudson Avenue and Main Street. Driving time: 8 minutes.

CHATHAM BREWERY
59 Main Street | Chatham, NY | 12037
518.697.0202 | http://www.chathambrewing.com/

When I first visited Chatham Brewery we tasted beers in an alley from a tapped keg. They have come a long way from that back alley, the tasting room now located on Main Street with fourteen ales and lagers on tap along with seasonal offerings and a menu to pair it all with. Large picture windows offer views of Main Street and the small-town action. One of their most popular beers is the Farmer's Daughter Rye IPA made with rye malt from neighboring distillery Hillrock in Ancram, New York. Order that beer with your grass-fed burger. Their buns and greens are sourced from local farmers, plus anything else available locally.

Yainnis is right down the street, a 5-minute walk. If you must drive, head south on NY-66 ¼ mile.

YAINNIS AT CHATHAM HOUSE
29 Hudson Avenue | Chatham, NY | 12037
518.392.7700 | http://yiannisatchathamhouse.com/

Before you hit the road to go home, stop in at Yiannis at Chatham House for dinner. You will find nice country charm in the historic renovated 1859 hotel. The dining room has brick walls and beautiful chandeliers surrounded by cozy tavern tables and an open floor plan that looks up to the second floor. You will find a diverse menu that ranges from burgers to duck to pasta and everything in between. If you have a chance, taste their goat and feta cheeses. The corkage fee is $15 if you bring your own wine.

Head northeast on Hudson Avenue, and take a slight right onto Railroad Avenue. Continue onto NY-295/Spring Street. Turn left onto Bristol Road. Driving time: 10 minutes.

INN AT SILVER MAPLE FARM
1871 State Route 295 | East Chatham, NY | 12060
518.781.3600 | http://www.silvermaplefarm.com/

Where the Hudson Valley meets the Berkshires. It's truly a country inn complete with post and beam architecture. There are eleven nicely appointed guest rooms each with their own private ensuite bathroom, Wi-Fi, cable TV, and air-conditioning. Enjoy a full country breakfast each morning, and afternoon cookies and tea.

Hudson Valley

Breweries

Day Tripping

Lower Hudson Valley

One-Day Itinerary

Suggested Stops
Yonkers Brewing Company • Hudson River Museum • Broken Bow Brewery • Captain Lawrence Brewing Co. • TeaTown Lake Reservation • Peekskill Brewery •

Suggested Dining
The Hudson Room

Suggested Lodging
Holiday Inn Express

From New York City via I87 take exit 5 from the Saw Mill River Parkway. Continue on Nepperhan Avenue to Main Street. Driving time: 5 minutes. Also accessible via Metro North from Grand Central Station to Yonkers.

YONKERS BREWING COMPANY
92 Main Street | Yonkers, NY | 10701
914.226.8327 | http://www.yonkersbrewing.com/

Located approximately thirty minutes north of New York City, this is a great place to begin your day or take Metro North for some brews and food. Located in the historic Yonkers Trolley Barn, which is listed on the National Register of Historic Places, it is the last remaining trolley barn in Westchester County and the only remains of the Yonkers trolley system. You know the old saying, "It takes a lot of beer to make a good wine," well that's how the idea began to start Yonkers Brewing Company. John Rubbo and Nick Califano always helped their grandfathers make homemade wine, and as friends do, they chatted about their experiences over a cold beer. It was these discussions that led to them realizing they wanted to open a brewery. Beers range from the classics IPA, Stout, and Saison, and testing the limits of brewing like their Smoked Marzen and Farmhouse Ales. Food is also served so check out their gastropub menu and brunch on the weekends.

Head west on Main Street. Turn right onto Van Der Donck Street that turns into Alexander Street, that turns into Polychrome Place, that turns into Babcock Place. Turn left onto Warburton Avenue. Driving time: 5 minutes.

HUDSON RIVER MUSEUM
511 Warburton Avenue | Yonkers, NY | 10701
914.963.4550 | http://www.hrm.org/

The galleries at this museum showcase American art, history, and science along with exhibitions by regional artists and Hudson River painters. Connected to the museum is Glenview, home of the Trevor family. You'll find this restored home that was built in 1876 with rooms featuring stenciling, carved woodwork, ceramic tiles, period settings, paintings, and sculptures. You get a little bit of everything here as it is also the site for the Andrus Planetarium.

Head North on Warburton Avenue and take a right onto Arthur Street, turn right onto Gilbert Place, left onto Morsemere Place, left onto Park Avenue, right onto Roberts Avenue, left onto Old Nepperhan Avenue, left onto Saw Mill River Road, continue straight onto Tuckahoe Road that will turn right and become Garrett Avenue, turn left onto Armourvilla, slight left onto Lake Avenue, right onto Main Street, left onto Marbledale Road. Driving time: 20 minutes.

BROKEN BOW BREWERY
173 Marbledale Road | Tuckahoe, NY | 10707
914.268.0900 | http://www.brokenbowbrewery.com

It all began when Mike LaMothe ordered an online beer making kit and made beer in his apartment breaking his stove in the process.

However, he found his calling. The name Broken Bow is the town in Nebraska where Mike's mother grew up. Truly a family operation in the hamlet of Tuckahoe, New York, you will feel right at home in the tasting room. Their commitment is to offer quality beer that reflects their respect for sustainability and community. They have ten beers on tap in the tasting room with their Broken Auger Lager being their signature brew. Their American Pale Ale (APA), Lager, and Stout are their bestsellers. If you come up by train, it is walking distance from the Crestwood Metro North station.

Turn left onto Winter Hill Road and right onto Midland Avenue to Bronx River Parkway North ramp to the Sprain Brook Parkway North to I-287 West take Exit 2 for NY 9A towards Elmsford. Use the right two lanes and turn right onto NY-9A N/Saw Mill River Road. Driving time: 20 minutes.

CAPTAIN LAWRENCE BREWING CO.
444 Saw Mill River Road | Elmsford, NY | 10523
914.741.2337 | http://www.captainlawrencebrewing.com/

Scott Vaccaro began home brewing at the age of seventeen. It's only natural that the name of the brewing company is the name of the street he originally brewed it on. They celebrated their tenth year in 2016. In the tasting room you can belly up to the 30ft long oak bar where you'll find two twelve-tap towers to sample from. And don't think you have to stay inside. Outside you will find a nice patio area complete with a bocce ball court and cornhole set ups. Make sure you taste the brews created by their brew team's own recipes. These will only be available in the tasting room. If available, try the Cuvee de Castleton; their first Gold Medal beer won at the American Beer Festival. Don't be shy about getting your picture taken while visiting as you might end up on their blog.

Take the Taconic Parkway North to NY-134 toward Ossining. Turn left onto NY-134. Turn left onto Grants Lane, and right onto Spring Valley Road. Driving time: 15 minutes.

TEATOWN LAKE RESERVATION
1600 Spring Valley Road | Ossining, NY | 10562
914.762.2912 | http://www.teatown.org/

For a little break and some fresh air, this 194-acre gift from the Gerard Swope Sr. family, and has grown to a 1000-acre preserve. There are three lakes, streams, waterfalls, swamps, forests, meadows, hemlock forests, laurel groves, and fifteen miles of hiking trails. Stop in at the nature center, visit the two-acre Wildflower Island with more than 230 species of wildflowers, the bee and butterfly garden, or simply take a hike.

Take Spring Valley Road to US 9N. Take the South St/Hudson Avenue exit. Turn left onto Hudson Avenue, and turn right onto S Water Street. Driving time: 15 minutes

PEEKSKILL BREWERY
47-53 S Water Street | Peekskill, NY | 10566
914.734.2337 | http://www.peekskillbrewery.com/

End your day of touring at Peekskill Brewery for some brews and dinner if you wish. When you first walk in you will find yourself in the large bar area that exposes you to the brewery complete with an industrial look and concrete floors. Look up and the ceiling opens up to the dining room on the second floor. They have sixteen beers on tap in the tasting room that change depending on the season along with the special brews they've been brewing.

Head north on S Water Street to Central Avenue. Right onto Central Avenue, right onto Union Avenue. Turn left at the first cross street onto South Street, and turn right onto S Division Street. Driving time: 5 minutes.

THE HUDSON ROOM
23 S Division Street | Peekskill NY | 10566
914.788.3663 | https://www.hudsonroom.com/

Hudson Room is a fusion restaurant using locally sourced ingredients. Their tag line is "globally inspired, locally sourced." You'll find a mouthwatering menu with just about anything you're craving from Sushi to Penne and Sausage, Veal Milanese, to a Burger. Located in a former five-and-dime store, they have a full bar and a large stage that comes alive at 10 p.m. on Friday and Saturdays. If you bring in your own bottle of wine the corkage fee is $25.

Head north on S Division Street and turn left onto South Street. Turn right onto Hudson Avenue. Turn left at the first cross street onto Lower S St/Requa Street. Continue on Lower S Street and turn right onto Louisa Street and left onto John Walsh Blvd. Driving time: 5 minutes.

HOLIDAY INN EXPRESS
2 John Walsh Blvd | Peekskill, NY | 10566
914.743.5700 | http://snip.ly/dqqsm

With scenic views of the Hudson River and the Bear Mountain Bridge enjoy Hudson Valley hospitality complete with complimentary continental buffet breakfast in the morning. The hotel's triple sheeted beds are soft with firm pillows for a great comfy night's sleep. Hotel offers free Wi-Fi, an indoor heated pool, and a 24-hour fitness center.

Day Tripping

Southern Orange County Breweries

One-Day Itinerary

Suggested stops

Rushing Duck Brewing Company • Sugar Loaf Art & Craft Village • Orange County Distillery • Cocktail Room at Brown Barn Farms • Orchard Hill Cider Mill at Soons Orchard • Equilibrium Brewery • Westtown Brew Works • Warwick Valley Winery & Black Dirt Distillery

Suggested dining

19 Main St. Luncheonette • Scotchtown Craft Bar & Kitchen • Landmark Inn

Suggested lodging

Comfort Inn & Suites

Traveling on the New York State Thruway entering the region at the Harriman Interchange, Woodbury Toll Go west on NY-17/ US-6 W and take exit 127 towards Sugarloaf/Warwick. Turn right onto Lehigh Avenue. Left onto Greycourt Avenue. Greycourt becomes Howland Street. Turn left onto Main Street. Driving time: 10 minutes.

19 MAIN ST. LUNCHEONETTE
19 Main Street | Chester, NY | 10918
845.469.7499

Stop in for a quick breakfast or lunch and get some nice home-style cooking. An old-style luncheonette in a small town. Try their buttermilk pancakes for breakfast. Check their daily specials.

You can walk to Rushing Duck from the Luncheonette. Just go down

Main Street, turn right onto Howland, and it's your second right. Remember, it's the back of the building. If you must drive, make sure you follow the signs for parking. You will be towed if you don't park in designated areas.

RUSHING DUCK BREWING COMPANY
1 Battiato Lane | Chester, NY | 10918
845.610.5440 | http://www.rushingduck.com/

As you drive down Main Street in Chester, don't look for the brewery; it's actually around the back, on a side street that runs parallel to Main Street. Make sure you obey the parking signs. Dan Hitchcock entered college as a political science major then made a left turn after graduation to the American Brewer's Guild for a degree in Intensive Brewing Science and Engineering. In 2012, he opened Rushing Duck. Their brewing style is that they brew the beers they like to drink. You will find a lot of IPA's and Belgium style ales here. The tasting room is small and quaint with limited seating.

Follow Main Street and turn right onto NY-94 / Academy Avenue. Turn left onto Glenmere Road, left onto Pine Hill Road. Driving time: 10 minutes

SUGAR LOAF ART & CRAFT VILLAGE
1371 Kings Hwy | Chester, NY | 10918
http://www.sugarloafnewyork.com/fun/

As I traveled the Shawangunk Wine Trail I always ended up driving through Sugar Loaf and stopped each time, especially during the holidays. This is a small community of independent artists. They have beautiful art galleries, craft and jewelry shops, and more. You might even check the schedule at the Sugar Loaf Performing Arts Center and catch a show or play while in town. Since the stores are all independent the hours vary, but they are all open on the weekends. You must stop as you're driving through!

Pine Hill Road turns into Galet Road to left onto NY 94W/Randall

Street. Continue straight as it turns into Meadow Road, and then turn into Pumpkin Swamp Road. Turn right onto Pulaski Highway, left onto Maloney Lane. Driving time: 12 minutes.

ORANGE COUNTY DISTILLERY
19 Maloney Lane | Goshen, NY | 10924
845.651.2929 | http://orangecountydistillery.com/

(Note: Their second location at The Cocktail Room at Brown Barn Farms is closed Monday through Wednesday. Directions to the Brown Barn from the Distillery will be below.)

Orange County Distillery is a farm to bottle craft distillery. They grow it and they distill it. What began in 2014 with six thousand sugar beets sitting in John Glebocki's warehouse (he's a fifth generation-farmer) has turned out to be a business for friends John Glebocki and Bryan Ensall. Those sugar beets became vodka and the rest is history. They produce gin, whiskey, and vodka. If you have never visited the distillery before I suggest you do so to see how they make the spirits, and then you can see the farm where everything is grown. Afterwards, visit the Cocktail Room at Brown Barn Farms, sit down, relax, listen to music, and enjoy a cocktail made with their spirits.

Three miles from the distillery. Turn left onto Pulaski Hwy, left onto Cross Rd and left onto Maple Avenue. It will be on your right. Driving time: 5 minutes

COCKTAIL ROOM AT BROWN BARN FARMS
286 Maple Avenue | New Hampton, NY | 10958
845.347.2077 | http://orangecountydistillery.com/

This is the tasting room for Orange County Distillery. Here you can bring a picnic lunch and eat in the tasting room. They feature all their spirits and cocktails along with New York produced beer, cider, wine, and other spirits.

From the Distillery turn left onto Pulaski Highway, left onto Cross

Rd, left onto Maple Avenue. When road ends, turn right onto Lower Road. Right onto Soons Circle. Driving time: 10 minutes.

ORCHARD HILL CIDER MILL AT SOONS ORCHARD
29 Soons Circle | New Hampton, NY | 10958
845.374.2468 | http://www.orchardhillnyc.com

You will find the Orchard Hill Cider Mill tasting room right next door to the Farm Market. This nice cozy barn has a tasting bar, cider vats, and it also offers tastings of local spirits. They produce mainly dry style ciders from the fifty-six varieties of apples grown on Soons' family run farm. Try their Ten66 inspired by Pommeau de Normandie. The Red Label is brandy distilled and aged in French oak wine barrels then blended with fresh non-alcoholic sweet cider, and returned to the barrel for extra aging. Check the labels and learn what apples each cider was made from.

Turn right onto Lower Road and left at the first cross street onto Country Road 56. Take a slight left onto US-6 W and merge onto I84 E. Take exit 4E and turn left onto Crystal Run Road. Turn left onto Goshen Turnpike/Scotchtown Road. Turn left onto NY-211 W. Driving time: 15 minutes.

SCOTCHTOWN CRAFT BAR & KITCHEN
741 Route 211 East, Ste 6 | Middletown, NY | 10941
845.692.7360 | http://www.scotchtowncraft.com/home.html

This little bar is packed with awesome food and a wide selection of local beers. The ever-changing selection of beers are local and regional. Their menu is reasonably priced from $6 to $16. Wide variety of selections from mac & cheese, burgers, rack of lamb to crab cakes.

Head east on NY-211 W, take a slight right onto Highland Avenue, and turn left onto W Main Street and left onto Henry Street. Driving time: 10 minutes

EQUILIBRIUM BREWERY
22 Henry Street | Middletown, NY | 10940
http://www.eqbrew.com/

This is what happens when two environmental engineers apply scientific principles to their passion for craft brewing. They brew what they like to drink and share with you. They work with local farmers to bring the true craft from farm to glass. They are known for their IPA's Stouts and Farmhouse Ales.

Mill Street to left on Fulton Street. Turn right at the second cross street onto Wawayanda Avenue, slight left onto County Road 49. Turn left onto Mt. Orange Road, left onto US-6 E. Turn right onto NY-284 S. Turn left onto Jacobs Road, left onto County Rd 1, slight right onto Grusz Road, right onto Lower Road, and right onto Scheffiers Road. Driving time: 20 minutes

WESTTOWN BREW WORKS
236 Scheflers Road | Westtown, NY | 10998
845.381.3496 | http://westtownbrewworks.com/

A true farm brewery, they grow it, and what they don't grow they source within a five-mile radius and then they drink it. When you visit you will be on a full working farm. Relax with a brew in the tasting room and look at the valley views and the hop yard.

Turn left onto Lower Road, right onto County Route 1. Turn left onto Pine Island Turnpike, turn left onto Little Brooklyn Road, and left onto Little York Road. Driving time: 15 minutes.

WARWICK VALLEY WINERY & BLACK DIRT DISTILLERY
114 Little York Road | Warwick, New York | 10990
845.258.4858 | http://wvwinery.com/
http://blackdirtdistillery.com/

Set on an apple orchard purchased in 1989, Warwick Valley Winery

& Distillery has created wine and other fruit based alcoholic beverages since 1994. Their Doc's Hard Apple Ciders won many awards. In 2001, they were awarded a New York State grant to create a fruit distillery and became New York's first fruit micro distillery. Black Dirt Distilling LLC was formed in 2012 to meet the demand of their renowned Black Dirt Bourbon and Black Dirt Apple Jack. Don't forget to try Warwick Gin. During the Fall you can go apple picking. They also offer dining at their Pané Cafe/ Black Dirt Grill. Tours of the distillery are by appointment only.

Left onto Little York Road and take a left onto Pine Island Turnpike. Continue onto Grand Street and take a left onto Maple Avenue (NY 17-A w/NY-94 E). Inn will be on the right. Driving time: 18 minutes.

LANDMARK INN
526 Route 94 | Warwick, NY | 10990
845.986.5444 | http://www.landmarkinnwarwick.com/

End the day in the country with dinner at a charming country inn. The hardwood floors and bar give it nice cozy country charm. Chef owned and operated by Culinary Institute of America graduate Michael DiMartino, he offers a creative and well executed menu for all palates. Dine on fresh seafood, steaks, pasta, and Lobster Egg Rolls. If you bring a bottle of wine the corkage fee is $12.

Head north on NY-17A W/NY-94 E. turn left onto Hatfield Lane. Driving time: 15 minutes.

COMFORT INN & SUITES
20 Hatfield Lane | Goshen, NY | 10924
845.637.2476 | http://www.choicehotels.com

This Comfort Inn is centrally located, close to I84 and Rt 17, restaurants and shopping, and it is smoke free. It has a fitness center so you can work out in the morning before heading out to taste for the day, or you can take a swim in their outdoor pool. There is free high-speed internet access throughout the hotel. They also offer a complimentary hot breakfast in the morning. Rooms come with coffee maker, refrigerator, TV, hair dryer, and iron.

Weekend Rendezvous

Orange County & Dutchess County Breweries

Three-day Itinerary

Suggested stops

Pine Island Brewery • Rushing Duck Brewing Company • Orange County Distillery • Cocktail Room at Brown Barn Farms • Orchard Hill Cider Mill at Soons Orchard • Clemson Brothers Brewery • Newburgh Brewing Company • 2 Way Brewing Company • Denning's Point Distillery • North River Hops and Brewing • Mill House Brewing Company • Locust Grove Franklin D. Roosevelt Home National Historic Site • Hyde Park Brewery • Blue Collar Brewery • Sprout Creek Farm • Dutchess Hops at Eastern View Farm • Peekskill Brewery

Suggested dining

Craft 47 • Elsie's • Newburgh Waterfront • Mill House Brewing Company • Julie's Restaurant • Hyde Park Brewery • Peekskill Brewery

Suggested lodging

Comfort Inn & Suites • Hampton Inn & Suites • Holiday Inn Express

Friday

Traveling on the New York State Thruway entering the region at the Harriman Interchange, Woodbury Toll. Take Y-17 W / US-6 W to exit 126 NY-94 towards Florida/Chester. Take NY-94 to Pulaski Highway to Pine Island Turnpike. Driving time: 30 minutes.

PINE ISLAND BREWERY

682 County Route 1 Suite B | Pine Island, NY | 10969
http://pineislandbeer.com/

If you think you are pulling up to a firehouse, you are correct. Pine Island Brewery is set in the old firehouse; the new one is across the street. It has a nice cozy tasting room with a barn wood bar, mason jar lights, and a friendly staff. Mike Kraai began brewing beer in college and after years of being a CPA left the corporate world and opened Pine Island Brewery at the age of 29. The most popular beers are their American IPA and Scottish Ale. They rotate out other brews constantly with seasonal or occasional brews.

Pulaski Highway and turn right onto Pumpkin Swap Road to NY 94 E. Turn right onto Main Street, and right onto Howland Avenue. It's the second road on the right. Driving time: 20 minutes.

RUSHING DUCK BREWING COMPANY
1 Battiato Lane | Chester, NY | 10918
845.610.5440 | http://www.rushingduck.com/

As you drive down Main Street in Chester, don't look for the brewery; it's actually around the back, on a side street that runs parallel to Main Street. Make sure you obey the parking signs. Dan Hitchcock entered college as a political science major, he made a left turn after graduation to the American Brewer's Guild for a degree in Intensive Brewing Science and Engineering. In 2012, he opened Rushing Duck. Their brewing style is that they brew the beers they like to drink. You will find a lot of IPA's and Belgium style ales here. The tasting room is small and quaint with limited seating.

Take Main Street turn right at Bank Street turn right onto Hambletonian Avenue. Turn right onto NY 17M W, turn right onto Old Chester Road. Turn left onto West Main Street. Driving time: 10 minutes

CRAFT 47
47 West Main Street | Goshen, NY | 10924
845.360.5253 | http://craft47.com/

You might think you are in Soho but you are really in Goshen. Craft 47 is an upbeat Tapas bar with a great selection of craft brews on tap and a nice wine list. Sit back, relax, order, and experiment with different small plates. Try the Slow Roasted Wild Boar or Chipotle and Craft Beer Braised Short Rib Tacos or the Scallops with Apple and Serrano Ham Skewers. You will enjoy a fun, one-of-a-kind dining experience with a small town atmosphere.

Main Street and take a left onto New Street and right onto Greenwich Avenue. Turn right onto Hatfield Lane. Driving time: 5 minutes

COMFORT INN & SUITES
20 Hatfield Lane | Goshen, NY | 10924
845.637.2476 | http://www.choicehotels.com

This Comfort Inn is centrally located, close to I84 and Rt. 17, restaurants and shopping, and it is smoke free. It has a fitness center so you can work out in the morning before heading out to taste for the day, or you can take a swim in their outdoor pool. There is free high-speed internet access throughout the hotel. They also offer a complimentary hot breakfast in the morning. Rooms come with coffee maker, refrigerator, TV, hair dryer, and iron.

Hatfield Lane to US 6 E/ RT 17 E to Exit 126. Take a left onto Rt 94 E Turn right onto Brookside Avenue and right onto Kings Highway. Driving time: 15 minutes.

SUGAR LOAF PERFORMING ARTS CENTER
1351 Kings Highway | Sugar Loaf NY | 10981
http://www.sugarloafpac.org/

When planning your weekend, make sure you check out the Sugar Loaf Performing Arts Center schedule. They have concerts, plays, and readings both on indoor and outdoor stages. If something interests you, make sure you purchase your tickets. They might not be available the day of the show.

<u>Saturday</u>

Head southeast on Hatfield Lane and turn left onto Greenwich Avenue, and right onto W Main Street. Driving time: 5 minutes.

ELSIE'S
128 W. Main Street | Goshen, NY | 10924
845.294.5765

Elsie's is a small luncheonette located on Main Street. It's typical small town charm. Open from 6 a.m. to 2 p.m. it's a great place for breakfast or lunch. All food is cooked to order. They have fabulous pancakes, so try their blueberry or pumpkin cinnamon when in season.

To Distillery: Main Street to NY 17A E. Turn right on Pulaski Highway, left on Maloney Road. Driving time: 10 minutes.

ORANGE COUNTY DISTILLERY
19 Maloney Lane | Goshen, NY | 10924
845.651.2929 | http://orangecountydistillery.com/

(Note: Their second location at The Cocktail Room at Brown Barn Farms is closed Monday through Wednesday. Directions to the Brown Barn from the Distillery will be below.)

Orange County Distillery is a farm to bottle craft distillery. They grow it and they distill it. What began in 2014 with six thousand sugar beets sitting in John Glebocki's warehouse (he's a fifth generation farmer) has turned out to be a business for friends John Glebocki and Bryan Ensall. Those sugar beets became vodka and the rest is history. They produce gin, whiskey, and vodka. If you have never visited the distillery before I suggest you do so to see how they make the spirits, and then you can see the farm where everything is grown. Afterwards, visit the Cocktail Room at Brown Barn Farms, sit down, relax, listen to music, and enjoy a cocktail made with their spirits.

Three miles from the distillery. Turn left onto Pulaski Hwy, left onto Cross Rd and left onto Maple Avenue. It will be on your right. Driving time: 5 minutes

COCKTAIL ROOM AT BROWN BARN FARMS
286 Maple Avenue | New Hampton, NY | 10958
845.347.2077 | http://orangecountydistillery.com/

This is the tasting room for Orange County Distillery. Here you can bring a picnic lunch and eat in the tasting room. They feature all their spirits and cocktails along with New York produced beer, cider, wine, and other spirits.

From the Distillery: Maloney Lane to Pulaski Highway, left onto Cross Road, left onto Maple Avenue, left onto Lower Road, right onto Soons Circle. Driving time: 10 minutes

ORCHARD HILL CIDER MILL AT SOONS ORCHARD
29 Soons Circle | New Hampton, NY | 10958
845.374.2468 | http://www.orchardhillnyc.com

You will find the Orchard Hill Cider Mill tasting room right next door to the Farm Market. This nice cozy barn has a tasting bar, cider vats, and it also offers tastings of local spirits. They produce mainly dry style ciders from the fifty-six varieties of apples grown on Soons' family run farm. Try their Ten66 inspired by Pommeau de Normandie. The Red Label is brandy distilled and aged in French oak wine barrels then blended with fresh non-alcoholic sweet cider, and returned to the barrel for extra aging. Check the labels and learn what apples each cider was made from.

Take right onto Lower Road and left at the first cross street County Rd 56 to US-6 W, straight onto NY-17M W. Turn left onto E Main Street, right onto Roberts Street and right onto Cottage Street. Driving time: 10 minutes.

CLEMSON BROS. BREWERY
22 Cottage Street | Middletown, NY | 10940
845.775.4638 | http://www.clemsonbrewing.com

If you think it's an old warehouse, you guessed right. Back in the 1800's, the building was home to Clemson Bros., a manufacturing plant making hacksaw blades and precision lawn mowers. Today it has been restored and is home to Clemson Bros. Brewery. Get a tasting sample and watch the brewing process from the tasting room. If you are hungry try their tacos or a burger.

Right onto 211 W to Rt NY-17E to I84 East. Take exit 10 and turn right onto Rt 9W. Take your first left onto Plank Road that turns into Water Street. Turn right onto Colden Street. Driving time: 30 minutes

NEWBURGH BREWING COMPANY
88 Colden Street | Newburgh, NY | 12550
845.569.2337 | http://www.newburghbrewing.com/

Located in the heart of Newburgh, Paul Halayko, a CPA by trade who got his appetite for beers on a business trip to Germany, partnered with his high school buddy Christopher Basso who previously worked as Brewer at Brooklyn Brewery in 2012. The tap room replicates an indoor German beer hall with long tables and benches with spectacular views of the Hudson River. Their beer focus is lower alcohol beers (but there are a few that are high octane) and have a great flavor profile.

Colden Street to Washington Street. Right onto Washington and a left onto Front Street. Driving time: 8 minutes.

NEWBURGH WATERFRONT
Front Street | Newburgh, NY | 12550
http://www.ribworks.com/ http://www.blu-pointe.com/
http://cena2000.com/ http://www.therivergrill.com/

Choose from a variety of restaurants and sit on the banks of the Hudson River enjoying the view of Mt. Beacon and watch the boats on the river. Restaurants vary from Billy Joe's Ribworks, Blu-Pointe, The River Grill, Cena 2000, and many more. Take a walk along the water, look at the menus, take in the vibe, and enjoy.

Water Street to Plank Road. Make a right onto Rt 9W S and take I-84 E. Cross bridge and get off at the first exit (go to the toll booth on the right) Beacon NY 9D. Take right onto NY 9D S. Turn right onto Beekman Street, turn right onto Main Street. Driving time: 10 minutes.

2 WAY BREWING COMPANY
18 W Main Street | Beacon, NY | 12508
845.202.7334 | http://www.2waybrewingcompany.com/

Located overlooking the Hudson River this micro craft brewery opened its doors in September 2014 when 30-year-old Michael O'Herron came home from Colorado to follow his passion. 2 Way is named after the Hudson River, as it is a two-way river, a river that flows both ways. Their specialty beer is Confusion, made from proprietary blend of yeast Michael cultivated from his parents' farm. The tasting room is rustic and you are encouraged to sign the bar… just ask for a sharpie.

Head east on Main Street toward Beekman Street. Left onto Beekman Street, right onto North Avenue, left onto Main Street, left onto Chestnut Street. Use the public parking across the street from the distillery. Driving time: 5 minutes

DENNING'S POINT DISTILLERY
10 N. Chestnut Street | Beacon, NY | 12508
845.230.7905 | http://www.denningspointdistillery.com/

With the gentrification of Beacon, New York, what was once my car mechanic's garage is now Denning's Point Distillery. There are no remnants of the once garage except for the large garage door which now houses the only urban distillery in the Hudson Valley. Taste through their selection of gin, vodka, and whiskey, and on the weekend there is live music in front of the still.

Go down Chestnut Street and take a left onto Verplank Avenue. At the light take a right onto NY 9D. Turn right onto E. Main Street. You can turn in by Walgreens. Driving time: 20 minutes.

NORTH RIVER HOPS AND BREWING
1571 US Rt 9 | Wappingers Falls, NY | 12590
845.297.2190 | http://www.northriverbrews.com/

Don't let the strip mall fool you. Once inside it will remind you of an old time general store and instead of a soda fountain, you have a tasting bar with taps. The tasting menu you are handed will remind you of an old newspaper from back in the early 1900's. At the tasting bar you have a complete view of the brewing area. Their three flagship brews are always on tap, the Tarwe (Hefeweizen), BLM (Session AmberAle), and Paddle Steamer (IPA) there are an additional three to seven brews to choose from. Come prepared to bring home a growler!

They have plans to move into the Village of Wappingers in 2017 off Market Street. Please call ahead to get their location.

Take Route 9 North to Poughkeepsie and exit left on Rt 44/55 E Church Street. Turn left onto Academy Street, turn left onto Rt 44/55 W. Mill House will be on your right. Driving time: 20 minutes.

MILL HOUSE BREWING COMPANY
289 Mill Street | Poughkeepsie, NY | 12601
845.485.2739 | http://www.millhousebrewing.com/

In the heart of "The Queen City on the Hudson" (Poughkeepsie) you will receive the full Hudson Valley experience from the brews to the food. Executive Chef Daniel Crocco prepares a creative menu that features locally sourced ingredients, daily specials, and hand crafted sausages that you must try. Brewmasters Jamie Bishop and Larry Stock brew great beers for pairing with the meal. Try their Kölsch, Amber Ale or their Russian Imperial Stout. If you bring a bottle of wine the corkage fee is $15.

Head west on Rt 44/55. When you get behind the Civic Center stay in the right lane and get off onto US 9 N just before the bridge. Loop around to the Rt 9 South side. Take Route 9 south about 4 miles.

Driving time: 10 minutes.

HAMPTON INN & SUITES
2361 South Road | Poughkeepsie, NY | 12601
845.463.7500 | http://snip.ly/yrymj

Located close to the mall, restaurants, golf, and historic sites this hotel is easy to get to. The hotel offers 129 rooms and it is pet friendly. It has free Wi-Fi, workout center, indoor pool, and complimentary breakfast. The suites are spacious and named after Hudson Valley historic places and people. A true Hudson Valley experience, the hotel is decorated with pictures of the region's historic attractions and sights.

Sunday

Turn right and go south on US-9 and make a U turn at the next light. Go north on US-9 and take Spackenkill Road- NY-113 exit. Take a left hand turn onto Wilbur Avenue just past Oakwood School. At the end of Wilbur turn right onto Hooker Avenue. At the next light turn left onto Raymond Avenue. Julie's will be on the left after the third traffic circle. Driving time: 10 minutes.

JULIE'S RESTAURANT
49 Raymond Avenue | Poughkeepsie, NY | 12603
845.452.6078

A cozy family restaurant located by Vassar College. For a great home cooked breakfast this is the place to be and great value too. They offer a diverse menu of pancakes, omelets, breakfast wraps, and homemade muffins to get your day started before hitting the beverage trail.

At the traffic circle take the first exit onto College Avenue. Turn left onto Park Avenue, turn right onto Hooker Avenue. Turn left onto Ferris Lane at third traffic light. Ferris Lane turns into Beechwood Avenue. At intersection at Rt 9 go straight as that is the entrance to Locust Grove. Driving time: 10 minutes

LOCUST GROVE
2683 South Road (Rt 9) | Poughkeepsie, NY | 12601
845.454.4500 | http://www.lgny.org/

Take in some history and Morse code at the home of Samuel Morse. In 1895, William and Martha Young purchased the mansion, redecorated it, and added gardens. Today the grounds are beautiful, with gardens and hiking trails that will bring you down to the river. Take a tour of the mansion and see the Young's family collection of Hudson River School paintings and early nineteenth century American furniture. Tour the Museum Pavilion where you will see the exhibit that explores Samuel Morse's two careers, an artist first and inventor of the telegraph and Morse Code.

Take Route 9 north to Franklin D. Roosevelt's Home. Driving time: 15 minutes.

FRANKLIN D. ROOSEVELT HOME NATIONAL HISTORIC SITE
4097 Albany Post Road | Hyde Park, NY | 12538
845.229.9115 | http://snip.ly/czcui

Home to his Springwood Estate, President Franklin D. Roosevelt lived here from his birth in 1882 to 1945. Tour the property that includes grave sites, rose gardens, hiking trails, and the many places from which the President addressed the nation during his four terms as President. Roosevelt's life from the early years through his presidency, from the Great Depression to the New Deal era and World War II, are all presented here. It is also home to the first US Presidential Library.

After reliving all that history, across the street is the Hyde Park Brewery. Head south on Route 9.

HYDE PARK BREWERY
4076 Albany Post Road | Hyde Park, NY | 12538
845.229.8277 | http://hydeparkbrewing.com/

Probably the oldest craft brewery in the area, Hyde Park Brewery has been around since 1995. Brewmaster John Eccles, a former hospital administrator and grandson of a prohibition era brewmaster, brews all German style beers. Try their Big Easy Blonde, a light lager that's crisp and refreshing, or a Winkle Lager for something more hoppy. Their menu features local ingredients along with the best 'Beef on Weck' east of Western New York. Not sure what beer to pair with your meal? The menu offers pairing suggestions to steer you in the right direction.

Head south on Route 9 and take a left on Fulton Street (just opposite Marist College) turn right onto Fairview Avenue. Continue onto North Hamilton Street and turn left onto Cottage Street. Driving time: 10 minutes.

BLUE COLLAR BREWERY
40 Cottage Street | Poughkeepsie NY | 12603
845.454.2739 | http://www.thebluecollarbrewery.com/

When you step into the Blue Collar Brewery you step into a little history of Poughkeepsie. Brewmaster Randall Marquis studied at UC Davis and brought his love of craft brewing to his home town. Once the Morris and Co. meat packing, and several other blue collar businesses, the building has now been renovated but it still has the feel of the old businesses the building once housed. As you walk in, the open plan has you walking the length of the building looking down on the brewery and past the open kitchen to the tasting room. Try a sampling of five beers or have a pint of their light bodied Cream Ale or their Irish Stout with chocolate, coffee, and licorice flavors.

Take North Clinton Street to 44/55 East (Church Street) When 44/55 splits take Rt 55 E to Noxon Road (just past Page Lumber.) Take a right onto Noxon Road and a left onto Lauer Road. It's right there on the right. Driving time: 15 minutes

SPROUT CREEK FARM
34 Lauer Road | Poughkeepsie, NY | 12603
845.485.8438 | https://sproutcreekfarm.org/

Sprout Creek Farm is a working farm and educational center on 200 acres of land surrounding Sprout Creek. Visit and tour the farm. You'll see their free-range cows, sheep, goats, turkeys, chickens, and pigs. Stop into the creamery where the magic happens and view the cheese making. Their cheeses are made from their herd of grass-fed cows and goats, made in the old tradition of European farmstead cheese. Take home a container of their goat cheese (that freezes really well) or their Bogart, Toussaint, Margie to name a few. I haven't met a cheese from Sprout Creek that I didn't like.

Take a left back onto Noxon Road. Follow it as you have to make a left hand turn towards the on ramp to the Taconic North. It will be just under the overpass of the parkway. Driving time: 5 minutes.

DUTCHESS HOPS AT EASTERN VIEW FARM
1167 Noxon Road | Lagrangeville, NY | 12540
845.456.1227 | http://dutchesshops.com/

In the mid-1800s the Hudson Valley region was responsible for 85 percent of the hops grown in the country. Dutchess Hops is the first commercial hops farm in the Hudson Valley since blight ended that production. They have planted four thousand hop plants on four acres of land. To see the hops during their peak, visit during July and August. Stop in anytime and Ken will go through the process of growing hops and how they are used. Group tours need to be arranged in advance. Since it's also a nursery, you might bring home a plant or two.

Take the Taconic Parkway south to NY 301 Cold Spring. Turn right onto NY 301 W to US 9. Turn left onto US 9 South. At traffic circle take the third exit US 202 E/US-6/US 9 S. Take the exit towards Hudson Avenue. Turn right onto Hudson Avenue, and right onto S Water Street. Driving time: 40 minutes.

PEEKSKILL BREWERY
47-53 S Water Street | Peekskill, NY | 10566
914.734.2337 | http://www.peekskillbrewery.com/

End your day of touring at Peekskill Brewery for some brews and dinner. When you first walk in you will find yourself in the large bar area that exposes you to the brewery complete with an industrial look and concrete floors. Look up and the ceiling opens up to the dining room on the second floor. They have sixteen beers on tap in the tasting room that change depending on the season along with the special brews they've been brewing.

Head south on S Water Street and take a left onto Hudson Avenue. Turn right at the first cross street onto Lower S St/Requa Street. Continue on Lower S Street. Turn right onto Louisa Street and left onto John Walsh Blvd. Driving time: 5 minutes.

HOLIDAY INN EXPRESS
2 John Walsh Blvd | Peekskill, NY | 10566
914.743.5700 | http://snip.ly/dqqsm

With scenic views of the Hudson River and the Bear Mountain Bridge enjoy Hudson Valley hospitality complete with complimentary continental buffet breakfast in the morning. The hotel's triple sheeted beds are soft with firm pillows for a great comfy night's sleep. Hotel offers free Wi-Fi, an indoor heated pool, and a 24-hour fitness center.

Day Tripping

The Capital District Breweries

One-Day Itinerary

Suggested Stops

Nine Pins Cider Works • C.H. Evans Brewing Company at the
Albany Pump Station • Albany Distillery • Brown's Brewing
Company Troy Taproom / Malt Room • Rare Form Brewing
S & S Farm Brewery • Chatham Brewery

Suggested Dining

C.H. Evans Brewing Company at the Albany Pump Station •
Blue Plate

Suggested Lodging

Inn at Silver Maple Farm

*From the I-90 coming from the West or East Take I-787 to exit 4
towards US-9/US-20 W. Merge onto Quay Street. Quay Street to
Colonie Street, right onto Erie Blvd. Left onto N Ferry Street, and
right onto Broadway. Driving time: 15 minutes.*

NINE PIN CIDER WORKS

929 Broadway | Albany, NY | 12207
518.449.9999 | http://www.ninepincider.com

All it took was a sample of local hard cider and Alejandro was
hooked. Nine Pin Cider was New York's first farm cidery, and
in 2013 Alejandro's cider won a gold medal at the Great Lakes
International Cider Competition. The tasting room is located in
downtown Albany, in an old warehouse. Alejandro makes cider
from apples sourced from the Capital Region, Hudson Valley, and
his family farm. Signature is their flagship cider using apples from

Samascott Orchards. You will find a selection of seven ciders to taste and they rotate depending on production.

Head southwest on Broadway. Turn left onto Spencer and right onto Montgomery Street. It's on the right. Driving time: less than 5 minutes.

C.H. EVANS BREWING COMPANY AT THE ALBANY PUMP STATION
19 Quackenbush Square | Albany, NY | 12207
518.447.9000 | http://www.evansale.com/

The Evan's family has been in the commercial brewing business for three generations. The original brewery in Hudson, New York produced until prohibition. In keeping with the family tradition, Neil Evans relocated the brewery to the historic building of the Albany Pump Station in 1999. In its day the pump station drew water from the Hudson River to the Bleecker Reservoir until it ceased operation in 1932. When you walk in look up to the mezzanine floor that highlights multiple levels of brewing tanks. The brewery décor highlights the industrial feel of the pump station with high energy of the craft brewery scene. Their menu features a wide variety of dishes from burgers, specialty sandwiches, and entrees. Make sure you try their Albany Ale if they have it on tap. It's a recipe dating back to 1830 that Head Brewer Ryan Demler made a few tweaks to and uses New York grown malted barley ingredients.

Right next door to the Pump Station.

ALBANY DISTILLERY
78 Montgomery Street | Albany, NY | 12207
518.621.7191 | http://www.albanydistilling.com/

You don't have far to walk after visiting the Pump Station as the distillery is right next door. The building has 1800 charm while filled with modern day stills. This is Albany's first distillery since Prohibition. The distillery is currently open Thursday's from 5 p.m. to 8 p.m and Saturday from 2 p.m. to 7 p.m. To see how they make their whiskey and rum you can book your tour right from their website. Tours are given on Thursday at 6 p.m. and Saturday at 2 p.m., 4 p.m., and 6 p.m.

Hop on I-787 N from Broadway and follow I-787 N and get off at exit 8 for 23rd Street toward Watervliet/Green Island. Turn right onto Hudson Avenue and continue onto Lower Hudson Avenue. Turn right onto Albany Avenue/Green Island Bridge. Turn left onto King Street. Turn left onto Jacob Street. Turn left at the first cross street onto River Street. Driving time: 12 minutes.

BROWN'S BREWING COMPANY TROY TAPROOM / MALT ROOM
417 River Street \ Troy, NY | 12180
518.273.2337 | http://brownsbrewing.com/

This buzzing brewpub transformed an abandoned 150 year old warehouse into the Capital Region's first brewery restaurant, brewing over twenty-five different styles of ales and lagers with at least ten on tap. Pair the beers with some of the food on their extensive menu. If you visit after 5 p.m. check out the Malt Room, which is in the basement of Revolution Hall. Relax in large leather couches and listen to the smooth jazz playing in the background. Choose fancy cocktails or ask for a recommendation from their selection of forty scotches.

South on River Street, sharp left onto King Street, and continue onto Jacob Street. Turn right onto 6th avenue and right onto Congress Street. Driving time: 5 minutes.

RARE FORM BREWING
90 Congress Street | Troy, NY 12180
518.326.4303 | http://www.rareformbrewing.com/

A small locally owned brewery in downtown Troy owned by husband and wife team Kevin Mullen and Jenny Kemp. Their five-barrel brewing system is the main focal point of the taproom with the bar seats around it. The beer speaks about them, the places they've been, and the places they want to go. You will find their four mainstay beers on tap at all times; Sabbatical Session Ale, Cascadia Double IPA, Wee Plaid Scottish Ale, and Satan's Gut Imperial Stout. Other beers rotate in and out.

Get on I-787 and follow it to I-90 E. Take I-90 E to Exit 11E US-20. Take US-20 and make a right onto Jefferson Hill Road – take it to Middle Road. Driving time: 30 minutes.

S & S FARM BREWERY
173 Middle Road | Nassau, NY | 12123
518.336.0766 | http://sandsbrewery.com/

Formerly a dairy farm, The Sanford Farm has been in the family since the 1800's. Today they have re-purposed the family farm to a farm brewery. The fields are back planted with barley and hops. The old cow milking barn has turned into the brewery and the milking equipment replaced with brewery equipment. They are only open Friday from 6 p.m. to 8 p.m. Plan accordingly to have a pint or fill the growler.

Take Jefferson Hill Road and take a left onto Malden Bridge Road and continue onto Albany Turnpike. Take a sharp right onto NY-66 S. At traffic circle take second exit onto Main Street. Driving time: 15 minutes.

CHATHAM BREWERY
59 Main Street | Chatham, NY | 12037
518.697.0202 | http://www.chathambrewing.com/

When I first visited Chatham Brewery we tasted beers in an alley from a tapped keg. They have come a long way from that back alley, the tasting room now located on Main Street with fourteen ales and lagers on tap along with seasonal offerings and a menu to pair it all with. Large picture windows offer views of Main Street and the small-town action. One of their most popular beers is the Farmer's Daughter Rye IPA made with rye malt from neighboring distillery Hillrock in Ancram, New York.

You can walk to the Blue Plate from the Brewery. Go down Main Street and turn left toward Kinderhook and left onto Kinderhook. To drive go up Main Street to the traffic circle. Take the third exit onto Kinderhook Street. Restaurant is on right. Driving or walking will take less than 5 minutes.

BLUE PLATE
1 Kinderhook Street | Chatham, NY | 12037
518.392.7711 | http://chathamblueplate.net/

If it's good enough for Bill and Hilary Clinton, you will enjoy it too. This cozy restaurant has wooden floors, and a menu that features traditional American meals with a flare. The locals love the Bacon Topped Meatloaf with whipped potatoes and brown gravy and a piece of Chocolate Bourbon Espresso Cake for dessert. If you haven't had enough beer, their craft beer menu features local and regional beer and a New York Cider list. Bringing your own wine, corkage fee is $15.

Head east on Kinderhook Street to traffic circle. Continue straight onto River Street. Keep right to continue onto Austerlitz Street. Turn left onto NY-295 and left onto Bristol Road. Driving time: 15 minutes.

INN AT SILVER MAPLE FARM
1871 State Route 295 | East Chatham, NY | 12060
518.781.3600 | http://www.silvermaplefarm.com/

Where the Hudson Valley meets the Berkshires. It's truly a country inn complete with post and beam architecture. There are eleven nicely appointed guest rooms each with their own private en-suite bathroom, Wi-Fi, cable TV, and air-conditioning. Enjoy a full country breakfast each morning, and afternoon cookies and tea.

Weekend Rendezvous

Breweries Albany and South

Three-Day Itinerary

Suggested Stops

Nine Pin Cider Works • Druthers Brewing Company • Harvest Spirits • Chatham Brewery • The Hudson Brewing Co. • Old Klaverack Brewery • Tousey Winery • Sloop Brewing • Grand Cru Beer & Cheese Market • Kingston Farmers Market • Hudson River Maritime Museum • Keegan Ales • Thomas Cole National Historic Site

Suggested Dining

Druthers Brewing Company • Café Madison • Baba Louie's Pizza • Licks Ice Cream • Terrapin Restaurant • Dolce • Dutch Ale House • Crossroads Brewing Co

Suggested Lodging

Hilton Garden Inn • Beekman Arms • The Country Squire Bed & Breakfast

Friday

I-787 to exit 4 towards US-9/US-20 W. Merge onto Quay Street. Quay Street to Colonie Street to right onto Erie Blvd. Left onto N Ferry Street and right onto Broadway. Driving time: 15 minutes.

NINE PIN CIDER WORKS
929 Broadway | Albany, NY | 12207
518.449.9999 | http://www.ninepincider.com

All it took was a sample of local hard cider and Alejandro was hooked. Nine Pin Cider was New York's first farm cidery, and in 2013 Alejandro's cider won a gold medal at the Great Lakes International Cider Competition. The tasting room is located in downtown Albany, in an old warehouse. Alejandro makes cider from apples sourced from the Capital Region, Hudson Valley, and his family farm. Signature is their flagship cider using apples from Samascott Orchards. You will find a selection of seven ciders to taste and they rotate depending on production.

Head northeast on Broadway. Druthers will be on the right. Driving time: 1 minute. Walking will take you 5 minutes.

DRUTHERS BREWING COMPANY
1053 Broadway | Albany, NY | 12204
518.650.7996 | http://www.druthersbrewing.com/

This Albany brewpub is housed in a converted warehouse with 11,000 sq. ft of brewery space. The brick, tables and exposed piping maintain the industrial look of the once warehouse. The brewery operation is visible through the glass windows and from the main dining room you can view the open kitchen. Their five signature beers, Golden Rule Blonde, Fist of Karma Brown, All-In IPA, The Dare, and Against the Grain Hefeweizen are usually on tap along with seasonal and guest brews. Their food is for comfort and they use local ingredients. Try the Loaded Monkey Bread or Wood Fired Mussels with Smoked Hefeweizen, Roasted Garlic Miso Butter, Bacon, Tarragon and Scallions. Then move on to a wood fired pizza, burgers, and six choices for Mac N Cheese.

Take Broadway and turn right onto Loudonville Road. Continue onto Shaker Road. It turns into Albany Shaker Road. At traffic circle continue on Albany Shaker Road. It turns into NY-155 W / Albany Shaker Road. Follow it to hotel. Driving time: 15 minutes.

HILTON GARDEN INN - ALBANY AIRPORT
800 Albany Shaker Road | Albany, NY | 12211
518.464.6666 | http://snip.ly/mt1pc

The Hilton Garden Inn is convenient to all sites in the Albany area.

The hotel features complimentary Wi-Fi, fitness center, indoor pool, and 24-hour business center. All rooms come equipped with microwaves, refrigerators, and coffee makers. There is a nice lounge area and an outdoor fire pit to relax and have a night cap with friends.

Saturday

Head southeast on Albany Shaker Road to NY-155 E and merge onto I-87 S. Exit 1E and follow signs for I-90E/Albany/Boston. Merge onto I-90 E and take exit 3 towards the State Offices. Merge onto Campus Access Road and continue onto Soc Ring Road. Turn right and stay on Campus Access Road. Turn left onto Western Avenue and the road turns into Madison Avenue. Driving time: 15 minutes.

CAFÉ MADISON
1108 Madison Avenue | Albany, NY | 12208
518.935.1094 | http://www.cafemadisonalbany.com

Located in the heart of Albany, the décor has a nice upbeat jazzy feeling. Get there early as it is small but they do offer outdoor seating, weather permitting. Taking breakfast to the next level, Café Madison is known for its oatmeal raspberry pancakes and specially prepared weekend menu that changes weekly. Check their Facebook page for the current specials.

Head northwest on Madison Avenue. Turn left onto Ormond Street. Turn right and merge onto NY-85E. Get on I-90 E to exit 12 for US-9 toward Hudson. Turn right onto US 9 S. Harvest Spirits will be on your left. Driving time: 25 minutes.

HARVEST SPIRITS
3074 US Route 9 | Valatie, NY | 12184
518.758.1776 | http://www.harvestspirits.com/

Harvest Spirits is located at Golden Harvest Farms, where fifteen varieties of apples are grown on two 100 acre orchards. Derek Grout is a third-generation apple farmer turned distiller. Known for their Core Vodka, made from their apples, it's a must-try and as smooth as can be. All you need is to shake it up on some ice and serve. Their range of spirits include vodka, applejack, brandy, and whiskey.

Head south on US 9. At traffic circle take third exit and stay on US 9 S. Turn right onto Albany Avenue and continue onto Main Street. Turn right onto NY-203 S / Chatham Street. Turn left onto Hudson Avenue and continue to Main Street. Driving time: 15 minutes.

CHATHAM BREWERY
59 Main Street | Chatham, NY | 12037
518.697.0202 | http://www.chathambrewing.com/

When I first visited Chatham Brewery we tasted beers in an alley from a tapped keg. They have come a long way from that back alley, the tasting room now located on Main Street with fourteen ales and lagers on tap along with seasonal offerings and a menu to pair it all with. Large picture windows offer views of Main Street and the small town action. One of their most popular beers is the Farmer's Daughter Rye IPA made with rye malt from neighboring distillery Hillrock in Ancram, New York. Order that beer with your grass-fed burger. Their buns and greens are sourced from local farmers, plus anything else available locally.

Take NY-66 S. Continue straight onto Columbia Street. Turn left to stay on Columbia Street. Turn left onto Park Place and right onto Warren Street. Driving time: 20 minutes.

BABA LOUIE'S PIZZA
517 Warren Street | Hudson, NY | 12534
518.751.2155 | http://babalouiespizza.com/

People come from all over to go to Baba Louie's and they rave about their wood-fired pizzas. The sourdough pizza crusts combined with fresh ingredients are to die for. But don't worry, it's not all about pizza; they also offer sandwiches and paninis, fresh salads, and gluten-free pizza.

If you are an ice cream lover, take a short walk to Licks Ice Cream.

LICKS – ICE CREAM
253 Warren Street | Hudson NY | 12534
518.828.7254 | http://www.lickhudson.com/

While walking down Hudson Street stop in at Licks for some delicious ice cream. They source their ice cream locally from Jane's (http://janesicecream.com/), which makes their ice cream in small batches from a recipe that has been handed down through the generations. A must-stop if you're an ice cream lover!

Continue walking down Warren Street towards the river and turn left onto S Front Street. Walking time: 10 minutes. Enjoy the antique window shopping along the way. (you can also drive and the same directions apply).

THE HUDSON BREWING CO.
Tasting Room | 60 S Front Street | Hudson, NY 12534
518.828.0438 | http://www.hudsonbrew.com/

Sharing the same building as Cafe Relish, you will find a large outdoor space, lawn games, and a beer garden. Come and share in the stories from the past at the same time as creating new ones. The Hudson Brewing Co. is bringing back brewery life to Hudson New York, which was once filled with whalers, and sailors telling stories over pints of beers. Prohibition put an end to all that and now it's alive again. Their hops and grains come from the local farmers. The names of their beers are a reflection from an era past. Create your stories and memories here.

S Front Street turn right onto Warren. Street and left onto Park Place. Park Place turns right and becomes Columbia Street. Take a slight right onto Columbia Turnpike. Turn right onto NY-23B E/Columbia Turnpike. Continue onto NY-23. Slight left onto NY-217 E. Turn right onto Roxbury Road. Turn right onto Thielman Road. The brewery will be on your right. Driving time: 15 minutes.

OLD KLAVERACK BREWERY
150 Thielman Road | Hudson, NY | 12534
518.965.1437 | http://www.oldklaverackbrewery.com/

Erik Bell opened the Town of Claverack's first brewery to showcase his beer crafted from locally sourced ingredients. In an effort to help his son, Erik's dad planted hops and started Old Klaverack Hop Farm. It is his hope to not only supply his son the hops he needs but also other local breweries. Stop in for a pint or fill a growler. Mainstays are his Red Mills Amber Ale, Uncle Fud, and a seasonal beer or two.

Thielman Road to NY 217 W. Continue onto NY 23 W. Bear left onto NY 23 and merge onto US 9 S. Driving time: 25 minutes.

TOUSEY WINERY
1774 US 9 | Germantown, NY | 12526
518.567.5462 | http://www.touseywinery.com/

When Kimberly and Ben Peacock moved back to the states from Europe they joined forces with Kimberly's Dad, Ray Tousey, to realize Ray's dream of turning their grounds into a vineyard and winery. Ben was a former assistant at the Houses of Parliament in London who embraced this life changing position with open arms. They are a diamond in the ruff. Try their Riesling, Pinot Noir, and Queen of Clermont. New is their Blanc de Blanc sparkling wine. Check out the Scarlet Tiger label, a series of wines which tells a story about a missing tiger. As you walk into the tasting room you will see the empty cage. The Queen of Clermont is the only one who knows where the tiger is and each of the other varietals are supporting characters in this epic story. Each vintage is a different part of the story, so start collecting the bottles.

Turn left onto US 9 North and right onto Buckwheat Road. Turn right onto County Route 8. Turn right onto County Route 19. Brewery will be on your left. Driving time: 5 minutes.

SLOOP BREWING
1065 Co. Rte. 19 | Elizaville, NY | 12523
518.751.9134 | http://www.sloopbrewing.com/

If you think you are pulling up to someone's home or farm, you are. Just follow the sign to the brewery and go through the last barn/garage door and then you will be transformed from quiet farm life to lively brewery with lots of conversation and great energy. The tap room opened in August 2015 and they specialize in sour and farmhouse ales. All of the beers are unfiltered and unpasteurized. Black Raz, dark in color is aged in oak and it's one of their most popular sours. If you like grapefruit try The Confliction, a hoppy beer and grapefuit bomb in the mouth. This brew stop is great for the person who might not like beer to be swayed into a taste and become a beer lover. 2015 Thrillist rated Sloop the most underrated brewery in New York State.

Turn left onto County Route 19. Turn right onto Hapeman Road, turn right onto Pleasantville Road. Turn left onto US 9 S. Terrapin will be on your left. A block down the road is Beekman Arms. You might want to check in and walk to the restaurant. Driving time: 25 minutes.

TERRAPIN RESTAURANT
6426 Montgomery Street | Rhinebeck, NY | 12572
845.876.3330 | http://www.terrapinrestaurant.com/

Housed in a former church Chef Josh Kroner combines global flavors and cultural influences to create mouthwatering dishes using farm fresh local ingredients. Whether you are looking for an elegant diner in the dining room or a casual dinner in the Red Bistro bar, you will be sure to have an outstanding meal. If you choose to bring your own bottle of wine the corkage fee is $20.

Walking distance from the Beekman Arms. Just one block away.

BEEKMAN ARMS
6387 Mill Street | Rhinebeck, NY | 12572
845.876.7077 | http://www.beekmandelamaterinn.com/
beekmanarms.htm

You'll find history at the Beekman Arms, America's oldest continuously operated hotel. Many famous people have slept here. President Franklin Delano Roosevelt concluded his campaign for governor and President, talking from the front porch. The main house might be old and historic, but all rooms have a private bath, TV, phone, and a decanter of sherry. The Guest House is a comfortable motel type accommodation located behind the main inn. These rooms have air conditioning and refrigerators and they are pet friendly. Other accommodations are also in "The Old Firehouse," which was the original firehouse to the village of Rhinebeck. If you have a group, The Townsend House will accommodate you in four large king size bedrooms with gas fireplaces.

Across the street from the Beekman Arms.

GRAND CRU BEER & CHEESE MARKET
6384 Mill Street | Rhinebeck, NY | 12572
845.876.6992 | http://grandcrurhinebeck.com/

Mingle with the locals at Grand Cru, located just across the street from the Beekman Arms. This hidden gem has the largest collection of craft beer anywhere. Grand Cru is not only a bar but also a bottle shop, so you can mix and match your six-pack to go. With sixteen beers on tap curated personally by Rod the owner, you'll find a mix of local and not so local craft beers. They also have a liquor license and serve wine by the glass. Although they don't have a kitchen, they have a great selection of local artisan cheeses and charcuterie plates to start or end your evening. Don't forget to take in the local artwork that decorates the tasting room. Artwork changes monthly. Here you'll find great conversation, and tips on what to do next.

Sunday

Take Montgomery Street – US-9 N and turn left to stay on Montgomery Street in front of the Hospital. Continue on Old Post Road. Continue straight onto Mt Rutsen Road to River Road. Take a left onto NY-199. Once over the bridge it becomes NY-209. Get off onto NY-28 E. At the traffic circle take the second exit onto I587 E. At the end of I587 E take a left onto Maiden Lane and a right onto Wall Street. Driving time: 15 minutes

KINGSTON FARMERS MARKET
278 Wall Street | Kingston, NY | 12401
347.721.7386 | http://kingstonfarmersmarket.org/

Begin your day shopping among the producers and growers of our region. Shop for farm products, wine, spirits, grass fed beef, cheese, baked goods, and more. Their market runs May through November.

From Wall Street, turn right onto John Street. Turn right turn onto Clinton Avenue, left turn onto Albany Avenue, and take a slight right onto Broadway. Follow Broadway down towards the Rondout Creek. Driving time: 10 minutes.

DOLCE
27 Broadway | Kingston, NY | 12401
845.339.9021

Start your day in this quaint little restaurant walking distance to the Rondout. Known for their crepes, try the Organic Buckwheat and Organic Spelt crepes. Also good is the French toast style Challah Roll stuffed with ham, Swiss cheese, and egg with local maple syrup. Breakfast specials change daily.

You can leave your car parked on Broadway and walk 328 feet to Rondout Landing. Take a right and the museum will be on your right. Walking time: 3 minutes and half a mile.

HUDSON RIVER MARITIME MUSEUM
50 Rondout Landing | Kingston, NY | 12401
845.338.0071 | http://www.hrmm.org/

Learn about the history of the Hudson River, its tributaries, and the commercial industries that lined and developed the river. Formed in 1980 by steamboat and tugboat enthusiasts to preserve the shipping history of the river, the museum features two galleries that display artifacts, ship models, and exhibits on ferries and tugboats.

Head up Broadway and turn left onto Liberty Street. Turn right at the first cross street onto Prospect Street, and left onto St. James Street. Driving time: 10 minutes.

KEEGAN ALES
20 Saint James Street | Kingston, NY | 12401
845.331.2739 | http://www.keeganales.com/

Founded in 2003 by Tommy Keegan and housed in the building that formerly housed the Woodstock Brewery, the building dates back to the early 1800's and still has the brick walls exposed in the interior. The most popular and famous selections that are a must-try are Mother's Milk, which is a dark and creamy milk stout; Hurricane Kitty an India Pale Ale; and Old Capital named after Kingston, New York which was New York State's first Capital. Tours are given on Friday, Saturday, and Sunday from 1 p.m. to 5 p.m.

Head southwest on St. James Street and take a right onto Clinton Avenue and a right onto Maiden Lane. Turn right onto Albany Avenue and a left onto I-587 to I-87 North. Take I-87 North to exit 20 – Saugerties. Turn right onto NY-32 S. Turn left onto Main Street. Brewery will be on the right. Driving time: 15 minutes.

BREWERY @THE DUTCH ALE HOUSE
255 Main Street | Saugerties, NY | 12477
845-247-2337 | http://www.dutchalehouse.com/

Following their passion for beer, Johnny and Karyn Pavich opened The Dutch Ale House with a three-barrel brew system and gastropub menu. Sit at the antique bar and taste Johnny's craft brews on tap, such as Ale-X and Karyn's Pale Ale and other craft brews from regional breweries. If you're hungry, their Culinary Institute of America trained Chef prepares menu delights with fresh local ingredients.

Head back to NY-32 N toward I-87. Take I-87 N to exit 21. Turn left onto Main Street. Turn left and merge onto NY*23 E towards the Rip Van Winkle Bridge. Take a slight right towards Spring Street. Driving time: 20 minutes.

THOMAS COLE NATIONAL HISTORIC SITE
218 Spring Street | Catskill, NY | 12414
518.943.7465 | http://thomascole.org/

Get into the heart of the founder of the first American Art movement of landscape artists. Cedar Grove, as it's called, is the former home of the Hudson River School of Art where Thomas Cole lived. You can take the 50-minute tour of the house, studio, and grounds. Watch a short film about his life and view the special exhibition of the Hudson River School paintings.

Take Spring Street back toward NY-23. Spring Street turns into N-385. Take NY-385 4.1 miles and turn left onto 2nd Street. Driving time: 5 minutes.

CROSSROAD BREWING CO
21 2nd St | Athens, NY | 12015
518.945.2337 | http://crossroadsbrewingco.com/

Located in the former Brooks Opera House, Ken Landin and Janine Bennett opened their seven-barrel brew house, tasting room, and pub, and realized their dream. Brewmaster Adam Krawczak brews something for every palate. Executive Chef Paul Parillo sources the meats, produce, and cheese locally. The menu has nice comfort food to mouthwatering salads and great appetizers. They have ten brews on taps and they rotate weekly, and there is a New York State wine list for the non-beer drinker.

Head southeast on 2nd Street and turn right onto NY-385 S. Turn left onto NY-23 and cross the Rip Van Winkle Bridge. Slightly turn left onto NY 23B/NY-9GN. Turn left onto Allen Street. Driving time:15 minutes.

THE COUNTRY SQUIRE BED & BREAKFAST

251 Allen Street | Hudson NY | 12534
518.822.9229 | http://www.countrysquireny.com/

Built in 1900 as a rectory and later turned into a convent for the sisters of St. Mary's Academy, this B&B is Queen Ann style, restored with its original stained glass, woodwork, and mantels. Its warm intimate atmosphere features a grand mahogany staircase and five cozy rooms all filled with antiques and pillow top mattresses. They have free Wi-Fi, flat screen TV, and private bathrooms. Continental breakfast featuring local products, baked goods, organic yogurt, cereals, and quiche served in the morning.

Day Tripping

Orange and Dutchess County Breweries
One-Day Itinerary

Suggested Stops
Angry Orchard Cider • Newburgh Brewing Company • 2 Way
Brewing Company • North River Hops and Brewery • Dutchess
Hops at Eastern View Farm • Sprout Creek Farm • Blue Collar
Brewery • Mill House Brewing Company

Suggested Dining
Mrs Fairfax • Mill House Brewing Company

Suggested Lodging
Hampton Inn & Suites

*Traveling on the New York State Thruway, enter the region at the
Harriman Interchange, Woodbury Toll. Follow I87 north Exit 17,
Newburgh – I84. Take I84 east to Exit 6 and turn right onto NY-17K
W. Take a right onto Coldenham Road. Take a right onto Orange
Avenue (NY-208). Merge onto Main Street. Turn left and stay on
Main Street NY-52. Turn right onto Albany Post Road. Driving time:
15 minutes.*

ANGRY ORCHARD CIDER
2241 Albany Post Road | Walden, NY | 12586
http://angryorchard.com/

Look for the red barn on the corner. This facility was opened up
by Angry Orchard Cider to be used for research and development.
It is a state-of-the-art facility on a 60-acre farm. You will learn
everything about apples – how apples are grown and how cider is
made. The farm itself dates back to the 1700's with it becoming

a full-time orchard around the 1950's. You will be able to taste ciders created just for this local market that may eventually become available across the country, as well as new and old ciders in the tasting room. The interactive Visitor's Center will give you a lesson on the history and heritage of cider making.

Take a right onto Albany Post Road towards NY-52E. Take a left onto NY-52 E continue onto Orange Avenue and take a left onto Coldenham Road, turn left onto NY-17K E. Turn left onto I-84 E and take exit 10 (last exit before bridge and toll). Take a right onto 9W and get into one of the two left lanes. You will make a left at the light onto Plank Road. Turn right onto Washington Street and left onto Colden Street. Driving time: 25 minutes.

NEWBURGH BREWING COMPANY
88 Colden Street | Newburgh, NY | 12550
845.569.2337 | http://www.newburghbrewing.com/

Located in the heart of Newburgh, Paul Halayko, a CPA by trade who got his appetite for beers on a business trip to Germany, partnered with his high school buddy Christopher Basso who previously worked as Brewer at Brooklyn Brewery in 2012. The tap room replicates an indoor German beer hall with long tables and benches with spectacular views of the Hudson River. Their beer focus is lower alcohol beers (but there are a few that are high octane) and have a great flavor profile.

Head north on Colden Street and turn left onto Washington Street and right onto Liberty Street. You can walk it. It's .2 miles and will take 5 minutes.

MRS FAIRFAX
105 Liberty Street | Newburgh, NY | 12550
845.565.0169

Mrs. Fairfax was named after George Washington's true love. It's a very quaint place and it has a casual atmosphere. It's like eating at Mom's house. The menu leans towards Mediterranean and brunch is offered on the weekends. You have to try their crepes or their grilled cheese sandwich. They have local beers on tap and a full bar.

Liberty Street turn left onto Water Street to Plank Road. Right onto 9W-S and right onto I-84 E to Beacon. Stay to the right and take the toll booth on the right because you will be getting off at this exit – NY-9D. Take a right onto NY-9D, turn right onto Beekman Street, and right onto West Main Street. The brewery will be on your right. Diving time: 15 minutes.

2 WAY BREWING COMPANY
18 W Main Street | Beacon, NY | 12508
845.202.7334 | http://www.2waybrewingcompany.com/

Located overlooking the Hudson River this micro craft brewery opened its doors in September 2014 when 30-year-old Michael O'Herron came home from Colorado to follow his passion. 2 Way is named after the Hudson River, as it is a two-way river, a river that flows both ways. Their specialty beer is Confusion, made from proprietary blend of yeast Michael cultivated from his parents' farm. The tasting room is rustic and you are encouraged to sign the bar... just ask for a sharpie.

Turn left out of the parking lot onto W Main Street, left onto Beekman Street, and left onto NY-9D. Follow NY-9D to Wappingers. Turn right onto E. Main Street. You can turn in by Walgreens. Driving time: 15 minutes.

NORTH RIVER HOPS AND BREWING
1571 US Rt 9 | Wappingers Falls, NY | 12590
845.297.2190 | http://www.northriverbrews.com/

Don't let the strip mall fool you. Once inside it will remind you of an old time general store and instead of a soda fountain, you have a tasting bar with taps. The tasting menu you are handed will remind you of an old newspaper from back in the early 1900's. At the tasting bar you have a complete view of the brewing area. Their three flagship brews are always on tap, the Tarwe (Hefeweizen), BLM (Session AmberAle), and Paddle Steamer (IPA) there are an additional three to seven brews to choose from. Come prepared to bring home a growler!

They have plans to move into the Village of Wappingers in 2017 off Market Street. Please call ahead to get their location.

Exit the parking lot by McDonalds and go south on US 9. Get in the left lane. At the next intersection you will take a left onto Myers Corners Road. Then take a right onto NY-376 S and continue onto Hillside Lake Road. Keep left and then turn left onto Arthursburgh Road and turn right onto Noxon Road. Farm will be on your left. Driving time: 15 minutes.

DUTCHESS HOPS AT EASTERN VIEW FARM
1167 Noxon Road | Lagrangeville, NY | 12540
845.456.1227 | http://dutchesshops.com/

In the mid 1800s the Hudson Valley region was responsible for 85 percent of the hops grown in the country. Dutchess Hops is the first commercial hops farm in the Hudson Valley since blight ended that production. They have planted 4000 hop plants on four acres of land. To see the hops during their peak, visit during July and August. Stop in anytime and Ken will go through the process of growing hops and how they are used. Group tours need to be arranged in advance. Since it's also a nursery, you might bring home a plant or two.

West on Noxon then turn right onto Noxon. Right onto Lauer. Driving time: 5 minutes.

SPROUT CREEK FARM
34 Lauer Road | Poughkeepsie, NY | 12603
845.485.8438 | https://sproutcreekfarm.org/

Sprout Creek Farm is a working farm and educational center on 200 acres of land surrounding Sprout Creek. Visit and tour the farm. You'll see their free-range cows, sheep, goats, turkeys, chickens, and pigs. Stop into the creamery where the magic happens and view the cheese making. Their cheeses are made from their herd of grass-fed cows and goats, made in the old tradition of European farmstead cheese. Take home a container of their goat cheese (that freezes really well) or their Bogart, Toussaint, Margie to name a few. I haven't met a cheese from Sprout Creek that I didn't like.

Take Lauer Road and turn left onto Bushwick Road. You will come to a funky intersection. Turn right onto Titusville Rd and left at the light onto NY-55 W. Turn right onto N Clinton Street and right onto Cottage Street. Brewery will be on the left. Driving time: 15 minutes.

BLUE COLLAR BREWERY
40 Cottage Street | Poughkeepsie NY | 12603
845.454.2739 | http://www.thebluecollarbrewery.com/

When you step into the Blue Collar Brewery you step into a little history of Poughkeepsie. Brewmaster Randall Marquis studied at UC Davis and brought his love of craft brewing to his home town. Once the Morris and Co. meat packing, and several other blue collar businesses, the building has now been renovated but it still has the feel of the old businesses the building once housed. As you walk in, the open plan has you walking the length of the building looking down on the brewery and past the open kitchen to the tasting room. Try a sampling of five beers or have a pint of their light bodied Cream Ale or their Irish Stout with chocolate, coffee, and licorice flavors.

Head west on Cottage Street which becomes Cottage as it bends left. Take Catherine Street to Mill Street NY 44/55 W. Mill House Brewing Company will be on the right. Driving time: 5 minutes.

MILL HOUSE BREWING COMPANY
289 Mill Street | Poughkeepsie, NY | 12601
845.485.2739 | http://www.millhousebrewing.com/

In the heart of "The Queen City on the Hudson" (Poughkeepsie) you will receive the full Hudson Valley experience from the brews to the food. Executive Chef Daniel Crocco prepares a creative menu that features locally sourced ingredients, daily specials, and hand crafted sausages that you must try. Brewmasters Jamie Bishop and Larry Stock brew great beers for pairing with the meal. Try their Kölsch, Amber Ale or their Russian Imperial Stout. If you bring a bottle of wine the corkage fee is $15.

Take NY 44/55 E towards the bridge. You will be bearing right and stay in the right lane. Get off onto US 9 South. The exit is just before you go onto the bridge. Take US 9 south to the Hampton Inn. It's just past IBM on the right. Driving time: 10 minutes.

HAMPTON INN & SUITES
2361 South Road | Poughkeepsie, NY | 12601
845.463.7500 | http://snip.ly/yrymj

Located close to the mall, restaurants, golf, and historic sites this hotel is easy to get to. The hotel offers 129 rooms and it is pet friendly. It has free Wi-Fi, workout center, indoor pool, and complimentary breakfast. The suites are spacious and named after Hudson Valley historic places and people. A true Hudson Valley experience, the hotel is decorated with pictures of the region's historic attractions and sights.

Weekend Rendezvous

A Taste of the Region

Three-Day Itinerary

Suggested Stops

Angry Orchard Cider • Newburgh Brewing Company • Heart of the Hudson Valley Farmers Market • Bad Seed Cider • Hudson Ale Works • Blue Collar Brewery • Mill House Brewing Company • Dutchess Hops at Eastern View Farm • Sprout Creek Farm • North River Hops and Brewing • Piano Piano Wine Bar • Beacon Farmers Market • 2 Way Brewing Company • Dennings Point Distillery • Hudson Beach Glass • Peekskill Brewery

Suggested Dining

El Solar Café • Frida's Bakery, • Mill House Brewing Company • Aroma Osteria • Red Line Diner • Home Spun Foods • Peekskill Brewery

Suggest Lodging

4 Points by Sheraton • Courtyard by Marriott • Holiday Inn Express

Friday

Traveling on the New York State Thruway entering the region at the Harriman Interchange, Woodbury Toll. Follow I87 north Exit 17, Newburgh – I84. Take I84 east to Exit 6 off I 84 turn right onto NY-17K W. Take a right onto Coldenham Road. Take a right onto Orange Avenue (NY-208). Merge onto Main Street. Turn left and stay on Main Street NY-52. Turn right onto Albany Post Road. Driving time: 15 minutes.

ANGRY ORCHARD CIDER
2241 Albany Post Road | Walden, NY | 12586
http://angryorchard.com/

Look for the red barn on the corner. This facility was opened up by Angry Orchard Cider to be used for research and development. It is a state-of-the-art facility on a 60-acre farm. You will learn everything about apples – how apples are grown and how cider is made. The farm itself dates back to the 1700's with it becoming a full-time orchard around the 1950's. You will be able to taste ciders created just for this local market that may eventually become available across the country, as well as new and old ciders in the tasting room. The interactive Visitor's Center will give you a lesson on the history and heritage of cider making.

Take a right onto Albany Post Road towards NY-52E. Take a left onto NY-52 E continue onto Orange Avenue and take a left onto Coldenham Road, to left onto NY-17K E. Turn left onto I-84 E and take exit 10 (last exit before bridge and toll). Take a right onto 9W and get into one of the two left lanes. You will make a left at the light onto Plank Road. Turn right onto Washington Street and left onto Colden Street. Driving time: 25 minutes.

NEWBURGH BREWING COMPANY
88 Colden Street | Newburgh, NY | 12550
845.569.2337 | http://www.newburghbrewing.com/

Located in the heart of Newburgh, Paul Halayko, a CPA by trade who got his appetite for beers on a business trip to Germany, partnered with his high school buddy Christopher Basso who previously worked as Brewer at Brooklyn Brewery in 2012. The tap room replicates an indoor German beer hall with long tables and benches with spectacular views of the Hudson River. Their beer focus is lower alcohol beers (but there are a few that are high octane) and have a great flavor profile.

Head north on Colden and take a left onto Broadway. Restaurant will be on your right. Driving time: 5 minutes.

EL SOLAR CAFE
346 Broadway | Newburgh, NY | 12550
845.561-3498

Located on Broadway in Newburgh this restaurant is a little gem. You will feel like you are in the Mediterranean with a combination of eclectic Latin and Mediterranean dishes. Jose Hernandez and his wife Gisela Pacheco are passionate about their restaurant and are there to answer all your questions. The food is fresh and delicious and their Sangria will not disappoint. If you bring your own bottle of wine the corkage fee is $10.

Continue straight on Broadway and it turns into NY-17K. Just past the I-84 interchange take a right and hotel will be on your left. Driving time: 15 minutes.

4 POINTS BY SHERATON AT STEWART AIRPORT
5 Lakeside Road | Newburgh, NY | 12550
845.567.0567 | http://www.starwoodhotels.com/

This property is fairly new and centrally located right off I-84. Rooms are nicely appointed in a contemporary style. There is free wireless internet and each room has a mini refrigerator and a 50-inch flat screen TV. There is a restaurant and bar just off the lobby, and the hotel has a small workout room.

Saturday

Left onto NY17-K and left onto I-84 E. Get off at exit 10 (last exit before toll) and take a left onto US-9W N. Turn right onto James Road and right onto S Road. Turn left to stay on S road and turn left onto Main Street. Parking is in back.

FRIDA'S BAKERY
26 Main Street | Milton, NY | 12547
845.795.5550 | http://www.fridasbakeryny.com/

Located in the sleepy town of Milton, a town time forgot. Park in the back of the building and take the elevator to the second floor (which is on street level). The menus are on the counter to the left. Make sure you look at the specials, and if they have the Funky

Grilled Cheese for breakfast get it, it's awesome! You can also build your own breakfast sandwich or burrito. If you have a sweet tooth, it is a bakery so enjoy. (Look for the free samples by the cashier.)

Take S Road Southwest and turn right onto Willow Tree Road. Be careful crossing Rt 9W as the market is on the other side.

HEART OF THE HUDSON VALLEY FARMER'S MARKET
Cluett Schantz Park | 1801-1805 Route 9W | Milton, NY | 12547
http://www.hhvfarmersmarket.com/

This farmers market opens at the end of June and runs through mid-October from 9 a.m. to 2 p.m. Make sure you check the website for dates. You will find a large selection of Hudson Valley items from baked goods, pickles, jams, maple syrup to farm fresh veggies and fruits.

Head north on US 9W and turn left onto New Road. Left onto Mahoney Road, bear right to stay on Mahoney Road. Turn right onto Milton Crossroads and left onto Baileys Gap Road. Driving time: 5 minutes.

BAD SEED CIDER
43 Baileys Gap Road | Highland, NY | 12528
845.236.0956 | http://www.badseedhardcider.com/

There are two orchards I go apple picking at in the Hudson Valley and Wilklow Orchards is one of them. I've followed sixth generation apple farmer Albert through all the family newsletters from when he was a little kid. Albert and his friend Devin grew up together and in 2011 they put together their savings and turned their hobby into a reality for the love of cider. It's their pastime, their passion, their life, and it shows through the quality of their cider. The base of their cider comes from three apples, Winesap, Ida Red, and Empire. Then they mix in some Northern Spy, Braeburn, Pink Lady, and others. Their main ciders are a dry cider based on a French cider almost like a cider champagne, very crisp. Belgian

Abby Cider has sour apple tones and yeasty characters. For people who like Belgian sours, Bourbon Barrel Cider is a dry cider aged in bourbon barrel for eight weeks and it picks up some oak and smoke and rounds out some of the acidity in the apples. It's more of a still cider. If you visit in the fall, try their Apple Pie Dry, it's the best apple pie you'll drink.

Head southeast on Baileys Gap Road and take a left onto Orchard Road and right onto US-44 E. Turn right onto Milton Avenue. Driving time: 7 minutes.

HUDSON ALE WORKS
17 Milton Avenue | Highland, NY | 12528
845.384.2531 | http://www.hudsonaleworks.com/

A fairly new addition to the brew scene, this is a small craft brewery that has up to seven beers on tap. Stop in for a taste.

Milton Avenue to a slight right onto US 44 E/ US -9W S. Get in the right lane and take the exit for the Mid-Hudson Bridge NY 44/55 E. Cross bridge and stay in the left lane and take a left onto Hamilton Street. Turn right onto Cottage Street. The brewery will be on your left. Driving time: 10 minutes.

BLUE COLLAR BREWERY
40 Cottage Street | Poughkeepsie NY | 12603
845.454.2739 | http://www.thebluecollarbrewery.com/

When you step into the Blue Collar Brewery you step into a little history of Poughkeepsie. Brewmaster Randall Marquis studied at UC Davis and brought his love of craft brewing to his home town. Once the Morris and Co. meat packing, and several other blue collar businesses, the building has now been renovated but it still has the feel of the old businesses the building once housed. As you walk in, the open plan has you walking the length of the building looking down on the brewery and past the open kitchen to the tasting room. Try a sampling of five beers or have a pint of their light bodied Cream Ale or their Irish Stout with chocolate, coffee, and licorice flavors.

Head west on Cottage Street and it becomes Cottage as it bends left. Take Catherine Street to Mill Street NY 44/55 W. Mill House Brewing Company will be on the right. Driving time: 5 minutes.

MILL HOUSE BREWING COMPANY
289 Mill Street | Poughkeepsie, NY | 12601
845.485.2739 | http://www.millhousebrewing.com/

In the heart of "The Queen City on the Hudson" (Poughkeepsie) you will receive the full Hudson Valley experience from the brews to the food. Executive Chef Daniel Crocco prepares a creative menu that features locally sourced ingredients, daily specials, and hand crafted sausages that you must try. Brewmasters Jamie Bishop and Larry Stock brew great beers for pairing with the meal. Try their Kölsch, Amber Ale or their Russian Imperial Stout. If you bring a bottle of wine the corkage fee is $15.

Take a right onto NY 44/55 W and loop around the Civic Center onto NY 44/55 E. When 44/55 split stay to the right onto NY 55 E. Turn right onto Noxon Road just after Page Lumber. Turn left and stay on Noxon Road. Farm will be on the left. Driving time: 15 minutes.

DUTCHESS HOPS AT EASTERN VIEW FARM
1167 Noxon Road | Lagrangeville, NY | 12540
845.456.1227 | http://dutchesshops.com/

In the mid-1800s the Hudson Valley region was responsible for 85 percent of the hops grown in the country. Dutchess Hops is the first commercial hops farm in the Hudson Valley since blight ended that production. They have planted four thousand hop plants on four acres of land. To see the hops during their peak, visit during July and August. Stop in anytime and Ken will go through the process of growing hops and how they are used. Group tours need to be arranged in advance. Since it's also a nursery, you might bring home a plant or two.

Take a right onto Noxon Road and turn right to stay on Noxon Road. Turn right onto Lauer and Sprout Creek is right there on the right.

Driving time: 5 minutes.

SPROUT CREEK FARM
34 Lauer Road | Poughkeepsie, NY | 12603
845.485.8438 | https://sproutcreekfarm.org/

Sprout Creek Farm is a working farm and educational center on 200 acres of land surrounding Sprout Creek. Visit and tour the farm. You'll see their free-range cows, sheep, goats, turkeys, chickens, and pigs. Stop into the creamery where the magic happens and view the cheese making. Their cheeses are made from their herd of grass-fed cows and goats, made in the old tradition of European farmstead cheese. Take home a container of their goat cheese (that freezes really well) or their Bogart, Toussaint, Margie to name a few. I haven't met a cheese from Sprout Creek that I didn't like.

Turn right onto Noxon Road, left onto Robinson Lane and right onto Diddell Road. Turn right onto NY 376 N. Just past airport stay to the right and turn left onto New Hackensack Road. At end of road turn right onto NY 9 S. Right at the next light onto Main Street and left into parking lot at Walgreens. Driving time: 15 minutes.

NORTH RIVER HOPS AND BREWING
1571 US Rt 9 | Wappingers Falls, NY | 12590
845.297.2190 | http://www.northriverbrews.com/

Don't let the strip mall fool you. Once inside it will remind you of an old time general store and instead of a soda fountain, you have a tasting bar with taps. The tasting menu you are handed will remind you of an old newspaper from back in the early 1900's. At the tasting bar, you have a complete view of the brewing area. Their three flagship brews are always on tap, the Tarwe (Hefeweizen), BLM (Session AmberAle), and Paddle Steamer (IPA) there are an additional three to seven brews to choose from. Come prepared to bring home a growler!

They have plans to move into the Village of Wappingers in 2017 off Market Street. Please call ahead to get their location.

Exit parking lot at McDonalds and turn right onto NY 9 S. At light at Adams turn left onto Old Post Road. Aroma will be on your right. Driving time: 5 minutes.

AROMA OSTERIA
114 Old Post Road | Wappingers Falls, NY | 12590
845.298.6790 | http://aromaosteriarestaurant.com/

You are in wine country, so think of yourself on the rolling hills of Tuscany in this authentic Italian restaurant. It's the perfect place for a romantic dinner for two, a celebration, or simply to eat a great meal. They offer impressive appetizers, main dishes that never fail to satisfy, and an exceptional wine list. Don't forget to leave room for the desserts... the tiramisu is a standout. They do have a private room for small groups. If you bring your own bottle of wine, the corkage fee is $30.

Go back to NY 9 S and take a left. The Marriott will be on your right just before the I-84 interchange. Driving time: 5 minutes.

COURTYARD BY MARRIOTT
17 Westage Drive (Rt 9 & I84) | Fishkill, NY | 12524
845.897.2400 http://snip.ly/o1k06

Located at the crossroad of the East – the intersection of Interstate 84 and Route 9 – this hotel is close to it all. You'll be greeted by a nice friendly staff and you will enjoy free Wi-Fi, fitness center, and indoor pool. They offer standard guest rooms with King, two Queens or two Doubles, and one-bedroom suites with a King and sofa bed or two Doubles and a sofa bed. Rooms are equipped with hair dryers, iron, and complementary coffee/tea.

Go north on NY 9 to Main Street. Take a left onto Main Street. Piano Piano will be on the left. Driving time: 5 minutes.

PIANO PIANO WINE BAR
1064 Main Street | Fishkill, NY | 12524
845.896.8466 | http://www.pianopianowinebar.com/

Stop in here for a nightcap. Create your own wine flights and experiment with wines from around the world or have one of their many micro brews. The décor provides a relaxing atmosphere where you'll find it friendly, cozy, and relaxing at the end of your day.

Sunday

Right across the street from the Courtyard is the Red Line Diner. Head north on US-9.

RED LINE DINER
588 U.S. 9 | Fishkill, NY | 12524
845.765.8401 | http://dineatredline.com/

Red Line Diner is your typical but not so typical diner. You'll find your usual breakfast entreés and then some. If you like Portobello mushrooms, try their Portobello Powerhouse, mushroom cap stuffed with fresh spinach, egg whites, mozzarella cheese, and a touch of house made tomato sauce, or dine on one of their breakfast wraps or quesadillas. Don't forget to have a cup of coffee, as it's the best cup you'll have for the entire stay of your trip.

Head south on US 9 to I-84 E. Get on I-84 E to exit 11. Take a left off exit onto NY-9D. Turn right at Beekman Street and continue to Long Dock Road. Take a slight right onto Red Flynn Drive. Driving time: 10 minutes.

BEACON FARMERS MARKET
Red Flynn Drive | Beacon, NY | 12580
http://www.beaconfarmersmarket.org/

Stop here to get some local produce and other items to bring home. You'll find farm fresh veggies, grass-fed beef, local cheeses, flowers, soap, wine tasting, and other culinary specialties. The market is open every Sunday from 10 a.m. to 3 p.m. from May 15 into late fall.

South on Red Flynn Drive to Long Dock Road to Beekman Street N.

Turn right onto Beekman Street. It's a two-minute car drive and a five-minute walk.

DIA: BEACON
3 Beekman Street | Beacon, NY 12508
845.440-0100 | http://www.diaart.org/sites/main/beacon

This museum opened in the renovated Nabisco box factory on the banks of the Hudson River. Spend some time viewing contemporary art collections from the 1960's to the present. You'll see some amazing and quirky art. See works by such artists as Joseph Beuys, John Chamberlain, and Robert Irwin. The Warhol exhibit is worth the trip in itself.

Head north on Beekman Street and turn left onto W Main Street. The brewery will be on your right. It's half a mile, and less than a five-minute drive.

2 WAY BREWING COMPANY
18 W Main Street | Beacon, NY | 12508
845.202.7334 | http://www.2waybrewingcompany.com/

Located overlooking the Hudson River this micro craft brewery opened its doors in September 2014 when 30-year-old Michael O'Herron came home from Colorado to follow his passion. 2 Way is named after the Hudson River, as it is a two-way river, a river that flows both ways. Their specialty beer is Confusion, made from proprietary blend of yeast Michael cultivated from his parents' farm. The tasting room is rustic and you are encouraged to sign the bar... just ask for a sharpie.

Up W Main Street and turn left onto Beekman Street and right onto NY-9D (North Avenue). At light take a left onto Main Street. Restaurant will be on your left. Driving time: 2 minutes.

HOMESPUN FOODS
232 Main Street | Beacon, NY | 12508
845.831.5096 | http://www.homespunfoods.com/

Sit down for some fresh homemade food. Choose from unique sandwiches and salads, such as Cheddar and Chutney, Goat Gouda Pecan, or from their daily specials. For breakfast, order the deep dish baked French Toast, which is only available on the weekends. Local beers and wine are available and don't forget to save room for some homemade dessert.

Walk up four blocks to left on N. Chestnut to the distillery. If you drive there is a parking lot across from the distillery.

DENNING'S POINT DISTILLERY

10 N. Chestnut Street | Beacon, NY | 12508
845.230.7905 | http://www.denningspointdistillery.com/

With the gentrification of Beacon, New York, what was once my car mechanic's garage is now Denning's Point Distillery. There are no remnants of the once garage except for the large garage door which now houses the only urban distillery in the Hudson Valley. Taste through their selection of gin, vodka, and whiskey, and on the weekend there is live music in front of the still.

Take a right onto Main Street. Driving time is three minutes, walking time is eight minutes.

HUDSON BEACH GLASS

162 Main Street | Beacon, NY 12508
845.440.0068 | http://www.hudsonbeachglass.com/

Located in a restored firehouse on the west end of Main Street enjoy a gallery of beautiful crafted hand blown glass pieces. If you are lucky and you are there on the day they are blowing glass you can watch them create their pieces. There is also a small art gallery upstairs with locally inspired works of art.

Main Street to left onto NY 9D (Wolcott Avenue) to left onto NY 403 S that runs into US 9 S. US 9. Turn left onto US 9 South. At traffic circle take third exit US 202 E/US-6/US 9 S. Take the US 202/Main Street exit. Turn right onto Main Street. Main Street turns left and becomes Water Street. Driving time: 30 minutes

PEEKSKILL BREWERY
47-53 S Water Street | Peekskill, NY | 10566
914.734.2337 | http://www.peekskillbrewery.com/

End your day of touring at Peekskill Brewery for some brews and dinner. When you first walk in you will find yourself in the large bar area that exposes you to the brewery complete with an industrial look and concrete floors. Look up and the ceiling opens up to the dining room on the second floor. They have sixteen beers on tap in the tasting room that change depending on the season along with the special brews they've been brewing.

Head south on S Water Street and take a left onto Hudson Avenue. Turn right at the first cross street onto Lower S St/Requa Street. Continue on Lower S Street. Turn right onto Louisa Street and left onto John Walsh Blvd. Driving time: 5 minutes.

HOLIDAY INN EXPRESS
2 John Walsh Blvd | Peekskill, NY | 10566
914.743.5700 | http://snip.ly/dqqsm

With scenic views of the Hudson River and the Bear Mountain Bridge enjoy Hudson Valley hospitality complete with complimentary continental buffet breakfast in the morning. The hotel's triple sheeted beds are soft with firm pillows for a great comfy night's sleep. Hotel offers free Wi-Fi, an indoor heated pool, and a 24-hour fitness center.

Day Tripping

A Taste of Dutchess County Breweries

One-Day Itinerary

Suggested Stops

Dutchess Hops at Eastern View Farm • Sprout Creek Farm •
Blue Collar Brewery • Mill House Brewing Company • Franklin
D. Roosevelt Home National Historic Site • Mill House Brewing
Company • Walkway Over the Hudson • Hyde Park Brewery

Suggested Dining

Mill House Brewing Company • Ice House

Suggested Lodging

Hampton Inn & Suites

*Driving north on the Taconic Parkway exit at Arthursburg Road
and take the exit toward Noxon Road. Turn right onto Noxon Road.
Driving time from highway is two minutes.*

DUTCHESS HOPS AT EASTERN VIEW FARM

1167 Noxon Road | Lagrangeville, NY | 12540
845.456.1227 | http://dutchesshops.com/

In the mid-1800s the Hudson Valley region was responsible for
85 percent of the hops grown in the country. Dutchess Hops is the
first commercial hops farm in the Hudson Valley since blight ended
that production. They have planted four thousand hop plants on
four acres of land. To see the hops during their peak, visit during
July and August. Stop in anytime and Ken will go through the
process of growing hops and how they are used. Group tours need
to be arranged in advance. Since it's also a nursery, you might
bring home a plant or two.

Take a right onto Noxon Road and turn right to stay on Noxon Road. Turn right onto Laur and Sprout Creek is right there on the right. Driving time: 5 minutes.

SPROUT CREEK FARM
34 Lauer Road | Poughkeepsie, NY | 12603
845.485.8438 | https://sproutcreekfarm.org/

Sprout Creek Farm is a working farm and educational center on 200 acres of land surrounding Sprout Creek. Visit and tour the farm. You'll see their free-range cows, sheep, goats, turkeys, chickens, and pigs. Stop into the creamery where the magic happens and view the cheese making. Their cheeses are made from their herd of grass-fed cows and goats, made in the old tradition of European farmstead cheese. Take home a container of their goat cheese (that freezes really well) or their Bogart, Toussaint, Margie to name a few. I haven't met a cheese from Sprout Creek that I didn't like.

Take Lauer Road and turn left onto Bushwick Road. You will come to a funky intersection. Turn right onto Titusville Rd and left at the light onto NY-54 W. Turn right onto N Clinton Street and right onto Cottage Street. Brewery will be on the left. Driving time: 15 minutes.

BLUE COLLAR BREWERY
40 Cottage Street | Poughkeepsie NY | 12603
845.454.2739 | http://www.thebluecollarbrewery.com/

When you step into the Blue Collar Brewery you step into a little history of Poughkeepsie. Brewmaster Randall Marquis studied at UC Davis and brought his love of craft brewing to his hometown. Once the Morris and Co. meat packing, and several other blue collar businesses, the building has now been renovated but it still has the feel of the old businesses the building once housed. As you walk in, the open plan has you walking the length of the building looking down on the brewery and past the open kitchen to the tasting room. Try a sampling of five beers or have a pint of their light bodied Cream Ale or their Irish Stout with chocolate, coffee, and licorice flavors.

Head west on Cottage Street and becomes cottage as it bends left. Take Catherine Street to Mill Street NY 44/55 W. Mill House Brewing Company will be on the right. Driving time: 5 minutes.

MILL HOUSE BREWING COMPANY
289 Mill Street | Poughkeepsie, NY | 12601
845.485.2739 | http://www.millhousebrewing.com/

In the heart of "The Queen City on the Hudson" (Poughkeepsie) you will receive the full Hudson Valley experience from the brews to the food. Executive Chef Daniel Crocco prepares a creative menu that features locally sourced ingredients, daily specials, and hand crafted sausages that you must try. Brewmasters Jamie Bishop and Larry Stock brew great beers for pairing with the meal. Try their Kölsch, Amber Ale or their Russian Imperial Stout. If you bring a bottle of wine the corkage fee is $15.

Take a right onto NY 44/55 – Mill Street. At light in front of the Poughkeepie Grand take a right then a left. At the light at the Mobil Station take a right onto Washington Avenue. Take this to US 9 N. Bear right onto US 9 N to FDR Site. Driving time: 10 minutes.

FRANKLIN D. ROOSEVELT HOME NATIONAL HISTORIC SITE
4097 Albany Post Road | Hyde Park, NY | 12538
845.229.9115 | http://snip.ly/czcui

Home to his Springwood Estate, President Franklin D. Roosevelt lived here from his birth in 1882 to 1945. Tour the property that includes grave sites, rose gardens, hiking trails, and the many places from which the President addressed the nation during his four terms as President. Roosevelt's life from the early years through his presidency, from the Great Depression to the New Deal era and World War II, are all presented here. It is also home to the first US Presidential Library.

Just across the street from FDR's Home. Head south on US 9.

HYDE PARK BREWERY
4076 Albany Post Road | Hyde Park, NY | 12538
845.229.8277 | http://hydeparkbrewing.com/

Probably the oldest craft brewery in the area, Hyde Park Brewery has been around since 1995. Brewmaster John Eccles, a former hospital administrator and grandson of a prohibition era brewmaster, brews all German style beers. Try their Big Easy Blonde, a light lager that's crisp and refreshing, or a Winkle Lager for something more hoppy. Their menu features local ingredients along with the best 'Beef on Weck' east of Western New York. Not sure what beer to pair with your meal? The menu offers pairing suggestions to steer you in the right direction.

Head south on US 9. Turn left onto NY 9G N by Mid-Hudson Regional Hospital. Turn left onto Parker Avenue. Driving time: 10 minutes.

WALKWAY OVER THE HUDSON
61 Parker Avenue | Poughkeepsie, NY | 12601
https://walkway.org/

Before heading to the Ice House for dinner stop for a stroll across the Walkway. Once a railroad bridge at 212 ft. above the Hudson River and 1.25 miles across, it is now the longest pedestrian bridge in the world. It crosses the Hudson River from Poughkeepsie to Highland with rail trails going as far east as East Fishkill and west to New Paltz. Signage gives a brief history of the bridge, and the views are magnificent so don't forget your camera.

Head back towards 9G and take a left onto Washington Street. Just after the traffic light take a right onto Verazzano Blvd. At light go straight onto Mill Street and take a left onto Davies Place. Turn right onto Main Street. You can park in the circle or take a right onto N. Water Street as you come down Main. Just past the train station, take a left and the Ice House is on the left. There is parking just past the boat ramp as well as back up on the hill. Driving time: 5 minutes.

ICE HOUSE
1 Main Street | Poughkeepsie, NY | 12601
845.232.5783 | http://poughkeepsieicehouse.com/

Back in the day ice was harvested from the Hudson River and stored in icehouses such as the Poughkeepsie Ice House, which today is a restaurant. The exposed bricks and stamped concrete floors are reminiscent of the era before. Dine inside or out on the banks of the Hudson River and watch the sunset. Start your meal with "Le Cast" Mac n Cheese made with local cheese, or their Seafood Mac & Cheese. Choose your entreé from options such as Sesame Crusted Ahi Tuna or choose from their daily specials and sip on local brews and wine. If you bring your own bottle of wine the corkage fee is $15.

Go up to Main Street and get on US-9 S. Driving time: 5 minutes

HAMPTON INN & SUITES
2361 South Road | Poughkeepsie, NY | 12601
845.463.7500 | http://snip.ly/yrymj

Located close to the mall, restaurants, golf, and historic sites this hotel is easy to get to. The hotel offers 129 rooms and it is pet friendly. It has free Wi-Fi, workout center, indoor pool, and complimentary breakfast. The suites are spacious and named after Hudson Valley historic places and people. A true Hudson Valley experience, the hotel is decorated with pictures of the region's historic attractions and sights.

Weekend Rendezvous

The Breweries of Dutchess and Westchester Counties

Three-Day Itinerary

Suggested Stops

Dutchess Hops at Eastern View Farm • Sprout Creek Farm • Blue Collar Brewery • Mill House Brewing Company Franklin D. Roosevelt Home National Historic Site • Frances Lehman Loeb Arts Center • Hyde Park Brewery • North River Hops and Brewing • 2 Way Brewing Company • Denning's Point Distillery • Beacon Farmers Market • Dia: Beacon • Peekskill Brewery • Captain Lawrence Brewing Co. • Broken Bow Brewery • Yonkers Brewing Company

Suggested Dining

• Mill House Brewing Company • BC Kitchen • The Vault • Beacon Bread Company • X20: Xaviars on the Hudson

Suggested Lodging

Hampton Inn & Suites • Hyatt House • Hyatt Place

Friday

Taconic Parkway North and exit at Arthursburg Road and take the exit toward Noxon Road. Turn right onto Noxon Road. Driving time from highway: 2 minutes.

DUTCHESS HOPS AT EASTERN VIEW FARM

1167 Noxon Road | Lagrangeville, NY | 12540
845.456.1227 | http://dutchesshops.com/

In the mid-1800s the Hudson Valley region was responsible for

85 percent of the hops grown in the country. Dutchess Hops is the first commercial hops farm in the Hudson Valley since blight ended that production. They have planted four thousand hop plants on four acres of land. To see the hops during their peak, visit during July and August. Stop in anytime and Ken will go through the process of growing hops and how they are used. Group tours need to be arranged in advance. Since it's also a nursery, you might bring home a plant or two.

Take a right onto Noxon Road and turn right to stay on Noxon Road. Turn right onto Laur and Sprout Creek is right there on the right. Driving time: 5 minutes.

SPROUT CREEK FARM
34 Lauer Road | Poughkeepsie, NY | 12603
845.485.8438 | https://sproutcreekfarm.org/

Sprout Creek Farm is a working farm and educational center on 200 acres of land surrounding Sprout Creek. Visit and tour the farm. You'll see their free-range cows, sheep, goats, turkeys, chickens, and pigs. Stop into the creamery where the magic happens and view the cheese making. Their cheeses are made from their herd of grass-fed cows and goats, made in the old tradition of European farmstead cheese. Take home a container of their goat cheese (that freezes really well) or their Bogart, Toussaint, Margie to name a few. I haven't met a cheese from Sprout Creek that I didn't like.

Take Lauer Road and turn left onto Bushwick Road. You will come to a funky intersection. Turn right onto Titusville Rd, and left at the light onto NY-55 W. NY 55 merges with NY 44. Stay in the right two lanes. Follow NY 44/55 to Mill House Brewing Company. It will be on your right. Driving time: 15 minutes.

MILL HOUSE BREWING COMPANY
289 Mill Street | Poughkeepsie, NY | 12601
845.485.2739 | http://www.millhousebrewing.com/

In the heart of "The Queen City on the Hudson" (Poughkeepsie) you will receive the full Hudson Valley experience from the brews to the food. Executive Chef Daniel Crocco prepares a creative menu that features locally sourced ingredients, daily specials, and hand crafted sausages that you must try. Brewmasters Jamie Bishop and Larry Stock brew great beers for pairing with the meal. Try their Kölsch, Amber Ale or their Russian Imperial Stout. If you bring a bottle of wine the corkage fee is $15.

Take NY 44/55 E towards the bridge. You will be bearing right and stay in the right lane. Get off onto US 9 South. The exit is just before you go onto the bridge. Take US 9 south to the Hampton Inn. It's just past IBM on the right. Driving time: 10 minutes.

HAMPTON INN & SUITES
2361 South Road | Poughkeepsie, NY | 12601
845.463.7500 | http://snip.ly/yrymj

Located close to the mall, restaurants, golf, and historic sites this hotel is easy to get to. The hotel offers 129 rooms and it is pet friendly. It has free Wi-Fi, workout center, indoor pool, and complimentary breakfast. The suites are spacious and named after Hudson Valley historic places and people. A true Hudson Valley experience, the hotel is decorated with pictures of the region's historic attractions and sights.

Saturday

Turn right and go south on US-9 and make a U turn at the next light. Go north on US-9 and take Spackenkill Road- NY-113 exit. Make a left hand turn onto Wilbur Avenue just past Oakwood School. At the end of Wilbur turn right onto Hooker Avenue. At the next light turn left onto Raymond Avenue. At the third traffic circle take the first exit and the restaurant will be on your left. Driving time: 10 minutes.

BC KITCHEN
(formerly BabyCakes)
1 Collegeview Avenue #3 | Poughkeepsie, NY | 12603
845.485-8411 | http://bckitchenbar.com/

BC Kitchen began as a small place to enjoy a coffee and homemade baked goods, known as BabyCakes. Now expanded and called BC Kitchen, the space is fresh and hip. You will find at least something to order from the delectable menu. Breakfast options include dishes such as Stuffed French Toast, or Brioche French Toast, homemade granola, Tofu Tex-Mex for vegans, and also gluten free bread. Don't be surprised if you are dining with the students from Vassar College. They love BC Kitchen too and the campus is right across the street. Lunch and dinner are served as well.

Leave your car and walk across the street and up Raymond Avenue to Vassar College. You can also walk through the college. The Arts Center is on the grounds just south of the main entrance.

FRANCES LEHMAN LOEB ARTS CENTER
124 Raymond Avenue | Poughkeepsie, NY | 12603
845.437.5237 | http://fllac.vassar.edu/

After breakfast take a walk across the street to Vassar College. There is a beautiful lake toward the back, and then head over to the Frances Lehman Loeb Arts Center. This art gallery was founded in 1864 and was the first college-university in the country to include an art museum in their original plan. There are over nineteen thousand works to catch a glimpse of in six galleries. You will see impressive paintings, sculptures, drawings, prints, photographs, textiles, glass, and ceramic wares. Memorable items to view are the Warburg Collection of Old Master prints, a group of Hudson River School paintings given by Matthew Vassar at the college's inception. There are many other works of art by major European and American twentieth century painters to view.

Take Raymond Avenue north and turn left onto NY 44/55. Turn right onto N Clinton Street and then right onto Cottage Street. Brewery is on the left. Driving time: 10 minutes.

BLUE COLLAR BREWERY
40 Cottage Street | Poughkeepsie NY | 12603
845.454.2739 | http://www.thebluecollarbrewery.com/

When you step into the Blue Collar Brewery you step into a little history of Poughkeepsie. Brewmaster Randall Marquis studied at UC Davis and brought his love of craft brewing to his home town. Once the Morris and Co. meat packing, and several other blue collar businesses, the building has now been renovated but it still has the feel of the old businesses the building once housed. As you walk in, the open plan has you walking the length of the building looking down on the brewery and past the open kitchen to the tasting room. Try a sampling of five beers or have a pint of their light bodied Cream Ale or their Irish Stout with chocolate, coffee, and licorice flavors.

Take right onto N Clinton Street from Cottage. Turn right onto Parker Avenue, which is also NY 9G. Follow that and take a left onto St. Andrews Road. At the end take a right onto US 9 N (Albany Post Road) FDR's Home will be on your left. Driving time: 12 minutes.

FRANKLIN D. ROOSEVELT HOME NATIONAL HISTORIC SITE
4097 Albany Post Road | Hyde Park, NY | 12538
845.229.9115 | http://snip.ly/czcui

Home to his Springwood Estate, President Franklin D. Roosevelt lived here from his birth in 1882 to 1945. Tour the property that includes grave sites, rose gardens, hiking trails, and the many places from which the President addressed the nation during his four terms as President. Roosevelt's life from the early years through his presidency, from the Great Depression to the New Deal era and World War II, are all presented here. It is also home to the first US Presidential Library.

Take a right out of FDR's Home to US 9 S and the Brewery is on the left. Driving time: less than a minute.

HYDE PARK BREWERY
4076 Albany Post Road | Hyde Park, NY | 12538
845.229.8277 | http://hydeparkbrewing.com/

Probably the oldest craft brewery in the area, Hyde Park Brewery has been around since 1995. Brewmaster John Eccles, a former hospital administrator and grandson of a prohibition era brewmaster, brews all German style beers. Try their Big Easy Blonde, a light lager that's crisp and refreshing, or a Winkle Lager for something more hoppy. Their menu features local ingredients along with the best 'Beef on Weck' east of Western New York. Not sure what beer to pair with your meal? The menu offers pairing suggestions to steer you in the right direction.

Head South on US 9. At the Dairy Queen in Wappingers take a right onto Main Street and left into the parking lot at Walgreens. Driving time: 25 minutes.

NORTH RIVER HOPS AND BREWING
1571 US Rt 9 | Wappingers Falls, NY | 12590
845.297.2190 | http://www.northriverbrews.com/

Don't let the strip mall fool you. Once inside it will remind you of an old time general store and instead of a soda fountain, you have a tasting bar with taps. The tasting menu you are handed will remind you of an old newspaper from back in the early 1900's. At the tasting bar you have a complete view of the brewing area. Their three flagship brews are always on tap, the Tarwe (Hefeweizen), BLM (Session AmberAle), and Paddle Steamer (IPA) there are an additional three to seven brews to choose from. Come prepared to bring home a growler!

They have plans to move into the Village of Wappingers in 2017 off Market Street. Please call ahead to get their location.

Exit the parking lot at Walgreens and take a left onto Main Street. At the light take a left onto NY 9D S. Turn right onto Beekman Street and then left onto W Main Street. Brewery will be on your right. Driving time: 15 minutes.

2 WAY BREWING COMPANY
18 W Main Street | Beacon, NY | 12508
845.202.7334 | http://www.2waybrewingcompany.com/

Located overlooking the Hudson River this micro craft brewery opened its doors in September 2014 when 30-year-old Michael O'Herron came home from Colorado to follow his passion. 2 Way is named after the Hudson River, as it is a two-way river, a river that flows both ways. Their specialty beer is Confusion, made from proprietary blend of yeast Michael cultivated from his parents' farm. The tasting room is rustic and you are encouraged to sign the bar... just ask for a sharpie.

Head east on Main Street toward Beekman Street. Left onto Beekman Street, right onto North Avenue, left onto Main Street, left onto Chestnut Street. Use the public parking across the street from the distillery. Driving time: 5 minutes

DENNING'S POINT DISTILLERY
10 N. Chestnut Street | Beacon, NY | 12508
845.230.7905 | http://www.denningspointdistillery.com/

With the gentrification of Beacon, New York, what was once my car mechanic's garage is now Denning's Point Distillery. There are no remnants of the once garage except for the large garage door which now houses the only urban distillery in the Hudson Valley. Taste through their selection of gin, vodka, and whiskey, and on the weekend there is live music in front of the still.

Take a left onto Main Street. Driving time: less than 5 minutes. Or you can walk from the distillery.

THE VAULT
446 Main Street | Beacon, NY | 12508
845.202.7735 | http://thevaultbeacon.com/

Housed in an old bank, look to the right as you walk in and see the open vault whose door weighs nearly four tons. You'll find a nice selection of tapas prepared with local ingredients from their culinary educated chefs. Try small plates and share. If you need to have a big meal their entrees are all under $30. Outdoor seating is available during the summer months.

Double back on Main Street and head west. Take a right onto NY-52 (Fishkill Avenue). Follow this through Fishkill (You can stop at Piano Piano Wine Bar on the way if you wish). At intersection at US 9 take a right turn and go south. Right turn onto Westage Business Center Drive at Walmart. At the traffic light Walmart will be on your right take a left and hotel is on your right. Driving time: 15 minutes.

HYATT HOUSE
100 Westage Business Center Drive | Fishkill, NY | 12524
845.897.5757 | http://snip.ly/o7cbq

Nestled in the crossroad of the Hudson Valley, don't be alarmed when you are turning into Walmart to find your hotel. This hotel is spaciously designed to make you feel like you are at home. They offer standard guestrooms, studios, one and two-bedrooms kitchen suites, free Wi-Fi, HDTV flat screen TV, indoor pool, and fitness center. The hotel is also dog friendly if your pup is traveling with you.

Sunday

Turn left onto US-9 S and get on I-84 W. Take exit 11 N-9D S. Left onto Main Street. Driving time: 10 minutes.

BEACON BREAD COMPANY
193 Main Street | Beacon, NY | 12508
845.838.2867 | http://www.beaconbread.com/

Get your bread on for breakfast! If you want lunch for breakfast you can get that too! From the time they open until they close, Beacon Bread Company serves breakfast and lunch. Prices are reasonable with nothing costing more than $12, and it's all homemade, including the jam. Try their In-house Beet Cured Salmon, French Toast, choice of omelets, or choose from a selection of sandwiches and grilled cheese. The place is small and it only seats twenty people, so keep that in mind when you arrive.

Head down Main Street and take a right onto NY 9D and a left onto Beekman Street. Turn right onto Beekman Street N and continue on Long Dock Road. Take a slight right onto Red Flyn Drive. Driving time: 5 minutes.

BEACON FARMERS MARKET
Red Flynn Drive | Beacon, NY | 12580
http://www.beaconfarmersmarket.org/

Stop here to get some local produce and other items to bring home. You'll find farm fresh veggies, grass-fed beef, local cheeses, flowers, soap, wine tasting, and other culinary specialties. The market is open every Sunday from 10 a.m. to 3 p.m. from May 15 into late fall.

South on Red Flynn Drive to Long Dock Road to Beekman Street N. Turn right onto Beekman Street. It's a 2-minute car drive and a 5-minute walk from the farmer's market.

DIA: BEACON
3 Beekman Street | Beacon, NY 12508
845.440-0100 | http://www.diaart.org/sites/main/beacon

This museum opened in the renovated Nabisco box factory on the banks of the Hudson River. Spend some time viewing contemporary art collections from the 1960's to the present. You'll see some amazing and quirky art. See works by such artists as Joseph Beuys, John Chamberlain, and Robert Irwin. The Warhol exhibit is worth the trip in itself.

Beekman Street and take a right onto NY 9D (Wolcott Avenue) to left onto NY 403 S that runs into US 9 S. US 9. Turn left onto US 9 South. At traffic circle take third exit US 202 E/US-6/US 9 S. Take the US

202/Main Street exit. Turn right onto Main Street. Main Street turns left and becomes Water Street. Driving time: 30 minutes.

PEEKSKILL BREWERY
47-53 S Water Street | Peekskill, NY | 10566
914.734.2337 | http://www.peekskillbrewery.com/

Stop in at Peekskill Brewery for some brews and lunch. When you first walk in you will find yourself in the large bar area that exposes you to the brewery complete with an industrial look and concrete floors. Look up and the ceiling opens up to the dining room on the second floor. They have sixteen beers on tap in the tasting room that change depending on the season along with the special brews they've been brewing.

Water Street to a left onto Hudson Avenue and right onto Lower S Street/Requa Street. Merge onto US 9 S. Exit on NY – 100/ NY 9A / Saw Mill River Road in Mount Pleasant. Follow NY 9A/ Saw Mill River Road. Driving time: 25 minutes.

CAPTAIN LAWRENCE BREWING CO.
444 Saw Mill River Road | Elmsford, NY | 10523
914.741.2337 | http://www.captainlawrencebrewing.com/

Scott Vaccaro began home brewing at the age of seventeen. It's only natural that the name of the brewing company is the name of the street he originally brewed it on. They celebrated their tenth year in 2016. In the tasting room you can belly up to the 30ft long oak bar where you'll find two twelve-tap towers to sample from. And don't think you have to stay inside. Outside you will find a nice patio area complete with a bocce ball court and cornhole set ups. Make sure you taste the brews created by their brew team's own recipes. These will only be available in the tasting room. If available, try the Cuvee de Castleton; their first Gold Medal beer won at the American Beer Festival. Don't be shy about getting your picture taken while visiting as you might end up on their blog.

Left turn onto NY 9A/Sawmill River Road. Take the ramp onto I 287

E. Take exit 3 towards New York City / Sprain Brook Parkway. Take the Tuckahoe Road exit. Take Tuckahoe Road E. Tuckahoe Road, which turns right and becomes Garrett Avenue. Turn left onto Armourvilla and a slight left onto Lake Avenue. Turn right onto Main Street, and left onto Marbledale Road. Driving time: 25 minutes.

BROKEN BOW BREWERY

173 Marbledale Road | Tuckahoe, NY | 10707
914.268.0900 | http://www.brokenbowbrewery.com

It all began when Mike LaMothe ordered an online beer making kit and made beer in his apartment breaking his stove in the process. However, he found his calling. The name Broken Bow is the town in Nebraska where Mike's mother grew up. Truly a family operation in the hamlet of Tuckahoe, New York, you will feel right at home in the tasting room. Their commitment is to offer quality beer that reflects their respect for sustainability and community. They have ten beers on tap in the tasting room with their Broken Auger Lager being their signature brew. Their American Pale Ale (APA), Lager, and Stout are their bestsellers. If you come up by train, it is walking distance from the Crestwood Metro North station.

Turn right onto Midland Avenue. Turn left onto the Cross County Parkway W ramp. Take exit 2 and merge onto Saw Mill River Parkway N (towards Albany) take exit 5 for Yonkers Avenue/ Dunwoodie GC. Turn right onto Yonkers Avenue. Slight left onto Neppperhan Avenue, turns into Prospect Street. Right onto Buena Vista Avenue. Left onto Main Street. Driving time: 20 minutes.

YONKERS BREWING COMPANY

92 Main Street | Yonkers, NY | 10701
914.226.8327 | http://www.yonkersbrewing.com/

Located approximately thirty minutes north of New York City, this is a great place to begin your day or take Metro North for some brews and food. Located in the historic Yonkers Trolley Barn, which is listed on the National Register of Historic Places, it is the last remaining trolley barn in Westchester County and the only remains of the Yonkers trolley system. You know the old saying, "It takes a lot of beer to make a good wine," well that's how the idea began to start Yonkers Brewing Company. John Rubbo and Nick Califano always helped their grandfathers make homemade wine, and as friends do, they chatted about their experiences over a cold beer. It was these discussions that led to them realizing they wanted to open a brewery. Beers range from the classics IPA, Stout, and Saison, and testing the limits of brewing like their Smoked Marzen and Farmhouse Ales. Food is also served so check out their gastropub menu and brunch on the weekends.

If you have good parking leave your car there and walk. Otherwise there is valet parking at X2O. Turn left on Main Street and it's right there. It's .2 miles.

X2O XAVIARS ON THE HUDSON
71 Water Grant Street | Yonkers, NY | 10701
914.965.1111 | http://www.xaviars.com/restaurants/xaviars-x2o-on-the-hudson/

Dine on the waterfront in Yonkers with amazing views of New York City and the Palisades, floor to ceiling windows that will make you feel like you are floating in the middle of the Hudson River. Executive Chef, Peter X. Kelly has set the stage for a wonderful dining experience. You might know of him from the Food Network Iron Chef as he beat Bobby Flay in the battle Cowboy Rib Eye. Between the food, the wine list, the desserts, and the view you can't go wrong. There's great attention to detail and farm to table focused, you will find many of the dishes made with local ingredients sourced throughout the Hudson Valley. This is a great way to end your holiday weekend. If you choose to bring in your own wine, the corkage fee is $25

Take Buena Vista Avenue to Nepperhane Avenue. Use the two right lanes and turn onto Yonkers Avenue. Take a sharp right and get onto the Cross County Parkway. Use the right lane and take exit 4 s-5-6-7 for Kimball Avenue / W Broad Street. Keep right and continue on Exit 4S. Follow signs for I-87 S/Central Avenue/Thruway and merge onto Central Avenue. Use the left lane to turn left at the first cross street onto Mile Square Road. Sharp left onto Central Park Avenue. Take a slight right onto South Drive. Then turn left. Driving time: 15 minutes.

HYATT PLACE NEW YORK/YONKERS
7000 Mall Walk | Yonkers, NY | 10704
914.377.1400
http://newyorkyonkers.place.hyatt.com/en/hotel/home.html

Located at the crossroads for New York City, Long Island, Connecticut, and New Jersey, all rooms are spacious and feature state-of-the-art media and work centers. Watch TV on a 42" HDTV and enjoy free Wi-Fi. In the morning experience their complimentary Kitchen Skillet breakfast and coffee made with Starbucks espresso roast.

Hudson Valley

Historic Sites and More

Day Tripping

Historic Orange County

One-Day Itinerary

Suggested Stops
Palaia Winery • West Point Military Academy • Washington Headquarters • Storm King Arts Center • Newburgh Brewing • Motorcyclepedia

Suggested dining
Thayer Hotel • Newburgh Waterfront

Suggested lodging
4 Points by Sheraton

Traveling on the New York State Thruway entering the region at the Harriman Interchange, Woodbury Toll. From the toll booth take the NY-17 ramp to NY-32 Suffern/Newburgh. Turn right onto NY-17 N/ Averill Avenue and keep left to NY-32 N. Driving time: 15 minutes.

PALAIA WINERY
10 Sweet Clover Road | Highland Mills, NY | 10930
845.928.5384 | http://www.palaiavineyards.com/

Take a trip back to the seventies where it was all about peace, love, and rock-n-roll. That is the vibe at Palaia Winery. In the year 2000, Jan and her husband Joe purchased a 200-year-old cow farm "The Seaman Homestead at Sweet Clover Farm" and planted 1500 vines. Built in the early 1800's the homestead now sits on thirty-two acres of what is left from the tract of land purchased from Aaron Burr in 1784. In 1888, the barn was added to the property and today it is home to the winery and tasting room. Their wines range from dry to sweet. They have music every weekend and a kickass outdoor stage venue that rocks in the summer months. *Take a left onto NY-32 turn right onto Quaker Avenue. Right merge onto US 9W south to West Point. Driving time: 20 minutes. (If NY-218 is open, take that as it is beautiful as you go through the mountain and view the valley and river. Unfortunately, it is closed more often than it's open)*

**Please note when entering West Point all passengers in the car must have photo identification. You will need to show it at the gate and your car is subject to a search. **

WEST POINT MILITARY ACADEMY
West Point, NY | 10996
http://www.westpoint.edu

The grounds are full of history and great views. Public and private tours are available. Take a short hike up to Ft. Putnam, or tour of Constitution Island, where there are many Revolutionary War fortifications. The West Point Museum contains the largest collection of military artifacts in the United States from ancient Egypt to today. Allow three hours to see it all.

THAYER HOTEL
674 Thayer Road | West Point, NY | 10996
845.446.4731 | http://www.thethayerhotel.com/

On the grounds of West Point, Thayer Hotel has a few restaurants to choose from and fantastic views. They are known for their Sunday Champagne Brunch from 10:30 a.m. to 2:30 p.m. MacArthur's Riverview Restaurant brunch features homemade waffles, Bananas Fosters, Smoked Salmon, carving stations, and more. And don't forget to take advantage of their unlimited champagne, Mimosa or Bloody Mary's. You won't leave hungry! If brunch is too much for you then you can always grab a burger, sandwich or salad at General Patton's Tavern.

US 9W north. Take the exit towards Cornwall. Left onto Quaker Avenue, right onto NY-32. Left onto Orrs Mills Road. Left onto Old Pleasant

Hill Road, left onto Museum Road. Driving time: 16 minutes.

STORM KING ARTS CENTER
1 Museum Road | New Windsor, NY | 12553
845.534.3115 | http://stormking.org/

This outdoor sculpture park and open air museum sits on 500 acres so make sure you wear shoes comfortable for walking. Explore the collection of more than one hundred modern sculptures created by some of the most acclaimed artists of our era. Tours are offered or you can stroll the grounds and look at the art on your own.

Directions: Turn right onto Old Pleasant Hill Road, right onto Orrs Mills Road. Take a left onto NY-32 N. Turn right onto Blooming Grove Turnpike. Continue on River Road and turn left onto Renwick Street, left onto Liberty Street. Driving time: 15 minutes.

WASHINGTON HEADQUARTERS
84 Liberty Street | Newburgh, NY | 12550
845.562.1195 | http://snip.ly/d1nyb

Tour the grounds that were General George Washington's Continental Army headquarters during the Revolutionary War. It is at these headquarters that General Washington rejected the idea that he should be king after the war and created the Badge of Military Merit that was the forerunner of the Purple Heart. This site was acquired by the New York State in 1850 and was the first publicly owned and operated historic site in the nation. The home is open for tours Wednesday through Saturday until 4:30 p.m. April through October. Check the website for the winter hours.

Take a right onto Renwick Street and a left onto Colden Street. Brewery will be on your right. Driving time: less than 1 minute.

NEWBURGH BREWING COMPANY
88 Colden Street | Newburgh, NY | 12550
845.569.2337 | http://www.newburghbrewing.com/

Located in the heart of Newburgh, Paul Halayko, a CPA by trade who got his appetite for beers on a business trip to Germany, partnered with his high school buddy Christopher Basso who previously worked as Brewer at Brooklyn Brewery in 2012. The tap room replicates an indoor German beer hall with long tables and benches with spectacular views of the Hudson River. Their beer focus is lower alcohol beers (but there are a few that are high octane) and have a great flavor profile.

Head south on Colden and take a right onto S William Street. Turn left onto Lake Street (NY-32). Motorcyclepedia will be on your right. Driving time: 5 minutes.

MOTORCYCLEPEDIA
250 Lake Street | Newburgh, NY | 12550
845.569.9065 | http://www.motorcyclepediamuseum.org/

Motorcyclepedia is a motorcycle enthusiast's paradise with over 450 American motorcycles mainly from the first half of the twentieth century. Gerald A. Doering a motorcycle enthusiast collected Indian motorcycles from 1901-1953. His son Ted also shared in his passion for motorcycles, and in 1971 they began a wholesale motorcycle parts business. With the success of the business they expanded their motorcycle collection. In 2011, they opened Motorcyclepedia "A Family's Attic Full of Motorcycles" featuring more than 400 motorcycles. Along with the motorcycles you will find photographs, posters, memorabilia, machinery, and other items related to bikes.

Head northeast on Lake Street and turn right onto Washington Street. Turn left onto Water Street. Turn right onto Carpenter Street and left onto Front Street. Driving time: 5 minutes.

NEWBURGH WATERFRONT
Front Street | Newburgh, NY | 12550
http://www.ribworks.com/ http://www.blu-pointe.com/
http://cena2000.com/ http://www.therivergrill.com/

Choose from a variety of restaurants and sit on the banks of the Hudson River enjoying the view of Mt. Beacon and watch the boats on the river. Restaurants vary from Billy Joe's Ribworks, Blu-Pointe, The River Grill, Cena 2000, and many more. Take a walk along the water, look at the menus, take in the vibe, and enjoy.

Get back to Water Street and take that to RT 9W. Turn right onto 9W and get in the left hand lane to get onto I84W. Get off at Exit 6 and take a ight. Lakeside Drive is on the right at the Diner. Driving time 10 minutes.

4 POINTS BY SHERATON AT STEWART AIRPORT
5 Lakeside Road | Newburgh, NY | 12550
845.567.0567 | http://www.starwoodhotels.com/

This property is fairly new and centrally located right off I-84. Rooms are nicely appointed in a contemporary style. There is free wireless internet and each room has a mini refrigerator and a 50-inch flat screen TV. There is a restaurant and bar just off the lobby, and the hotel has a small workout room.

Weekend Rendezvous

Historic Orange County

Three-Day Itinerary

Suggested Stops

Goshen Farmers Market • Harness Racing Museum • Museum Village • Palaia Winery • Storm King Arts Center • Newburgh Brewing Company • Karpeles Manuscript Library Museum • Motorcyclepedia • Benmarl Winery • Konx's Headquarters • West Point Military Academy

Suggested Dining

Delanceys • Howell's Deli & Café • Woody's Farm to Table • Il Cenacolo • Frida's • Jones Farm • Thayer Hall

Suggested Lodging

Comfort Inn & Suites • 4 Points by Sheraton • Thayer Hall

Friday

Traveling on the New York State Thruway entering the region at the Harriman Interchange, Woodbury Toll. Take US-6W/ NY-17 W to exit 125 for NY-17M E/South Street. Turn left onto NY-17M / Chester Avenue. Turn right onto South Street and left onto S Church Street. Driving time: 15 minutes.

GOSHEN FARMERS MARKET

Main Street & South Church Street | Goshen, NY | 10924
845.294.7741

Located at the Village Square the market is on Friday's from the end of May through October from 10 a.m.to 5 p.m. Their mission is to promote local and regional agriculture and to ensure a supply of fresh local produce for their community. It's a great place to begin your tour with local products. Try and get a good parking space and walk to dinner afterwards.

Head southeast on S Church Street and left onto Park Place. It's only .2 miles so if you have a good parking place I would suggest a nice walk.

DELANCEYS
40 Park Place | Goshen, NY | 10924
845-294.8254 | http://delanceysny.com/

Don't let the outside fool you! Step inside and choose between dining at the bar or in the intimate dining room overlooking the historic Goshen Race Track. Bring your appetite because the portions of American and Italian cuisine are generous. Start with their Thai Chili Wings or Grandma Annie's Meatballs. Then choose from a Sirloin Steak or Chicken Francese, a thick juicy burger or a big dish of pasta. There is a full wine, beer, and cocktail list available. You certainly won't leave hungry.

Head north on Park Place and turn left onto Main Street. Slight left onto Greenwich Avenue. Turn right onto Hatfield Lane. Driving time: 5 minutes.

COMFORT INN & SUITES
20 Hatfield Lane | Goshen, NY | 10924
845.637.2476 | http://www.choicehotels.com

This Comfort Inn is centrally located, close to I84 and Rt 17, restaurants and shopping, and it is smoke free. It has a fitness center so you can work out in the morning before heading out to taste for the day, or you can take a swim in their outdoor pool. There is free high-speed internet access throughout the hotel. They also offer a complimentary hot breakfast in the morning. Rooms come with coffee maker, refrigerator, TV, hair dryer, and iron.

Saturday

Head southeast on Hatfield Lane. Turn left onto Greenwich Avenue. Greenwich Avenue turns right and becomes Main Street. Driving time: 5 minutes.

HOWELL'S DELI & CAFE
27 Main Street | Goshen, NY | 10924
845.294.5561 | http://www.howellscafe.com/

Howell's Deli is a great small town café with a friendly atmosphere. Begin your day with a skillet dish, seven eggs scrambled on a bed of home fries, and choose from options such as the Bostonian with smoked salmon, sautéed onions, and warm cream cheese or the Hoboken with bacon, sausage, and cheddar cheese. If you don't want something that filling, choose from a three egg omelet or a specialty wrap (two eggs). The pastries are fresh and prepared daily, and don't forget to check out the specials.

Head east on Main Street. It's .2 miles. Driving time: less than a minute.

HARNESS RACING MUSEUM
240 Main Street | Goshen, NY | 10924
845.294.6330 | http://www.harnessmuseum.com/

If you're a harness racing fan this museum is for you. Harness Racing Museum is housed in the Good Time Stable formerly known as "The Trotting Horse Museum." In 1996 it changed its name to the Harness Racing Museum and Hall of Fame. The museum houses artifacts relating to the greatest steeds, such as Goldsmith's Maid who was the most winning horse in harness racing history. Visit the art gallery where you will view paintings of the famed horses and "The Story of Harness Racing" by Currier and Ives. View informative films and take part in the interactive exhibits. If you ever wanted to be a harness racing jockey, try their 3D simulated ride. The museum overlooks Goshen's Historic Track that was established in 1838 as the oldest working racetrack in the country. The best part is admission is free.

Main Street and left onto Park Place. Left onto South Church Street. Right onto South Street. Turn left onto NY-17M and merge onto NY-17 E/US-6 E. Take exit 129 for Museum Village Road. Turn left towards NY-17M E, then right towards NY-17M E, and left onto NY-17M E. Driving time: 15 minutes.

MUSEUM VILLAGE
1010 State Route 17M | Monroe, NY 10950
845.782.8248 | http://museumvillage.org/

If you are a history buff, you will enjoy the Museum Village. See, hear, touch, and understand life in nineteenth century America in this unique open-air historical museum. This village is the vision of Rosco William Smith who was the founder of Orange and Rockland Electric Company in 1905. He was an avid collector of items from textiles and porcelain to horse-drawn carriages. At times, he accepted farm tools as payment for electricity. He began to display these artifacts to educate people, and in 1950 he opened Museum Village to display it all. Visit the different buildings like the Blacksmith to learn about the importance of repairing the equipment and making necessary farming items for the community; the Wagon Shop; the Candle Shop where you can dip your own candle; the School House where you can see what it was like in rural school in the nineteenth century; the Livery area which shows the many different kinds of transportation vehicles that were used. There are many other buildings that house displays and exhibits dating back through American history.

Head back towards NY-17 – turn right onto Museum Village Road and left onto NY-208 N. Turn right onto Mountain Road, which turns into Seven Springs Mountain Road. Turn slightly to the left and stay on Seven Springs Mountain Road and then merge onto Seven Springs Road. Go left onto Ridge Road and left onto NY-32 N, then left onto Sweet Clover Road. Driving time: 15 minutes.

PALAIA WINERY

10 Sweet Clover Road | Highland Mills, NY | 10930
845.928.5384 | http://www.palaiavineyards.com/

Take a trip back to the seventies where it was all about peace, love, and rock- n -roll. That is the vibe at Palaia Winery. In the year 2000, Jan and her husband Joe purchased a 200-year-old cow farm "The Seaman Homestead at Sweet Clover Farm" and planted 1500 vines. Built in the early 1800's the homestead now sits on thirty-two acres of what is left from the tract of land purchased from Aaron Burr in 1784. In 1888, the barn was added to the property and today it is home to the winery and tasting room. Their wines range from dry to sweet. They have music every weekend and a kickass outdoor stage venue that rocks in the summer months.

Left onto NY-32. Turn right onto Quaker Avenue. Woody's will be in town on the right. Driving time: 8 minutes.

WOODY'S FARM TO TABLE

30 Quaker Avenue | Cornwall, NY | 12518
845.534.1111 | http://www.woodysfarmtotable.com/

Woody's Farm to Table is an old fashioned burger joint using fresh local farm to table ingredients, known for their 100 percent all natural grass-fed, grain finished beef burgers, onion hay, and hand cut fries. You must try a fountain soda or milkshake too. If you don't eat beef burgers, you can choose a Portobello Mushroom burger or a Beet Burger. They also serve wraps, soups, and salads.

Take Quaker Avenue and turn right onto NY-32 N. Left onto Orrs Mills Road and left onto Old Pleasant Hill Road. Turn left onto Museum Road. Driving time: 5 minutes.

STORM KING ARTS CENTER

1 Museum Road | New Windsor, NY | 12553
845.534.3115 | http://stormking.org/

This outdoor sculpture park and open air museum sits on 500 acres so make sure you wear shoes comfortable for walking. Explore the collection of more than one hundred modern sculptures created by some of the most acclaimed artists of our era. Tours are offered or you can stroll the grounds and look at the art on your own.

Directions: Turn right onto Old Pleasant Hill Road, right onto Orrs Mills Road to NY-32 S. Turn left onto Quaker Lane. Turn right onto ramp for US-9W N. Take US 9W north to right on River Road. River Road turns into Water Street. Turn left onto Washington Street and right onto Colden Street. Driving time: 15 minutes.

NEWBURGH BREWING COMPANY
88 Colden Street | Newburgh, NY | 12550
845.569.2337 | http://www.newburghbrewing.com/

Located in the heart of Newburgh, Paul Halayko, a CPA by trade who got his appetite for beers on a business trip to Germany, partnered with his high school buddy Christopher Basso who previously worked as Brewer at Brooklyn Brewery in 2012. The tap room replicates an indoor German beer hall with long tables and benches with spectacular views of the Hudson River. Their beer focus is lower alcohol beers (but there are a few that are high octane) and have a great flavor profile.

Colden Street to left onto Broadway. Driving time: less than 2 minutes.

KARPELES MANUSCRIPT LIBRARY MUSEUM
94 Broadway | Newburgh, NY | 12550
845.569.4997 | http://www.rain.org/~karpeles/

The library was founded in 1983 by David and Marsha Karpeles with the goal of stimulating interest in learning. It is the world's largest private collection of original manuscripts and documents. The documents rotate throughout the nine museums in the country. The Newburgh location also houses the Dona McPhillips Historical Painting Series. These series include many portraits of famous Americans grouped together. Check the website to see what documents are on display as they change often. Admission is free.

Head up Broadway and take a left onto Lake Street. Motorcyclepedia will be on your right. Driving time: 5 minutes.

MOTORCYCLEPEDIA
250 Lake Street | Newburgh, NY | 12550
845.569.9065 | http://www.motorcyclepediamuseum.org/

Motorcyclepedia is a motorcycle enthusiast's paradise with over 450 American motorcycles mainly from the first half of the twentieth century. Gerald A. Doering a motorcycle enthusiast collected Indian motorcycles from 1901-1953. His son Ted also shared in his passion for motorcycles, and in 1971 they began a wholesale motorcycle parts business. With the success of the business they expanded their motorcycle collection. In 2011, they opened Motorcyclepedia "A Family's Attic Full of Motorcycles" featuring more than 400 motorcycles. Along with the motorcycles you will find photographs, posters, memorabilia, machinery, and other items related to bikes.

Head northeast on Lake Street and turn left onto Lake Drive and left onto Cerone Place. Turn left onto Little Britain Road and left onto Wisner Avenue. Left onto Dupont Avenue. Left onto S Plank Road. Restaurant will be on your right. Driving time: 10 minutes.

IL CENACOLO
228 South Plank Road | Newburgh, NY | 12550
845.564.4494 | http://ilcenacolorestaurant.com/

If you like Northern Italian cuisine, you will be in Heaven here. Shades of Tuscany sets the tone for a delicious homemade Italian dinner. Scan the menu and make a choice, but be prepared to change your mind once you hear the list of specials. The wait staff will recite the specials in great detail and if you have any questions just ask. Everything is prepared by hand, with lots of love, herbs and fresh ingredients. Reservations are recommended. Corkage fee is $25 if you bring your own bottle.

Take a right onto S Plank Road. Turn left onto Lake Side Road. Hotel will be on your right. Driving time: 5 minutes.

4 POINTS BY SHERATON
AT STEWART AIRPORT
5 Lakeside Road | Newburgh, NY | 12550
845.567.0567 | http://www.starwoodhotels.com/

This property is fairly new and centrally located right off I-84. Rooms are nicely appointed in a contemporary style. There is free wireless internet and each room has a mini refrigerator and a 50-inch flat screen TV. There is a restaurant and bar just off the lobby, and the hotel has a small workout room.

Sunday

Left onto NY17-K and left onto I-84 E. Get off at exit 10 (last exit before toll) and take a left onto US-9W N. Turn right onto James Road and right onto S Road. Turn left to stay on S road and turn left onto Main Street. Parking is in back.

FRIDA'S BAKERY
26 Main Street | Milton, NY | 12547
845.795.5550 | http://www.fridasbakeryny.com/

Located in the sleepy town of Milton, a town time forgot. Park in the back of the building and take the elevator to the second floor (which is on street level). The menus are on the counter to the left. Make sure you look at the specials, and if they have the Funky Grilled Cheese for breakfast get it, it's awesome! You can also build your own breakfast sandwich or burrito. If you have a sweet tooth, it is a bakery so enjoy. (Look for the free samples by the cashier.)

Main Street turn right onto S Road and left onto St James Road. Turn left onto US-9W S. When you enter Marlboro, turn right onto Western Avenue, and left onto Highland Avenue. Driving time: 12 minutes.

BENMARL WINERY
156 Highland Avenue | Marlboro, NY | 12542
845.236.4265 | www.benmarl.com

Benmarl Winery sits on the oldest continuously planted vineyard in the United States, Slate Hill Vineyard, home to New York's Farm Winery License #1. Located on thirty-seven scenic acres overlooking the Hudson River and Berkshire Mountains with a kickass view for great picture taking. This historic winery was purchased by artist Mark Miller from Andrew J. Caywood, an early American viticulturist in 1957, and in 2006 it was purchased by Victor Spaccarelli who fulfilled his lifelong dream of owning a vineyard. Victor's son Matt is the General Manager and winemaker focusing on producing small batch wines that capture the unique terroir of the vineyard. In addition, Matt and his partner Casey have produced a line of wines, Fjord Vineyards from very small estate grown acre lots and small batches sourced regionally. At the time of writing this, Fjord tasting room was open on sporadic days and times. Ask for directions to their Ridge Road tasting room from the Benmarl staff, and if you visit, make sure to try their award winning Albariño.

Head north on Vineyard Avenue, turn left onto Highland Avenue, and turn right onto US-9W S. Turn left onto Albany Post Road and left onto Old Balmville Road. Go left onto Leroy Place and it turns into Water Street then River Road. Continue onto Blooming Grove Turnpike. (NY-94). Turn left onto Forge Hill Road. Driving time: 20 minutes.

KNOX'S HEADQUARTERS
289 Forge Hill Road | New Windsor, NY | 12553
845.561.5498 | http://snip.ly/8ijfu

This beautiful Georgian style house was built for John Ellison in 1754. General Henry Knox, Commander of the American artillery used the home as his headquarters from 1782 until 1783. Today it reflects the wealth of the Ellison family as well as its military heritage. Knox's Headquarters is open from Memorial Day weekend to Labor Day, Wednesday to Sunday from 1 p.m. to 4 p.m.

Head southeast on Forge Hill Road. Turn right onto US-9W S. Get off at the Angola Road exit and turn left onto Angola Road. Driving time: 8 minutes.

JONES FARM
190 Angola Road | Cornwall, NY | 12518
845.534.4445 | http://www.jonesfarminc.com/

Take a trip out to the farm. As you enter the farm, watch out for livestock wandering around. When entering the barn house - bakery & gift shop your mouth will begin to water simply as a result of the delicious smell of the baked goods. The country store is the place to shop for local produce, eggs, honey, gourmet foods, and more. They have daily specials for breakfast and lunch. Then wander over to the old dairy barn that has been converted to a large gift shop. It's a great place to look for a unique gift that you will not find anywhere else. Just when you thought you were done, stop at the Art Gallery where the walls are covered with original oils, pastels and watercolors, unique prints of the Hudson Valley and West Point, and local photography.

Get back onto US-9W S and follow it to the Stony Lonesome Gate.

Please note when entering West Point all passengers in the car must have photo identification. You will need to show it at the gate and your car is subject to a search.

WEST POINT MILITARY ACADEMY
West Point, NY | 10996
http://www.westpoint.edu

The grounds are full of history and great views. Public and private tours are available. Take a short hike up to Ft. Putnam, or tour of Constitution Island, where there are many Revolutionary War fortifications. The West Point Museum contains the largest collection of military artifacts in the United States from ancient Egypt to today. Allow three hours to see it all.

On the grounds of West Point.

THAYER HOTEL
674 Thayer Road | West Point, NY | 10996
845.446.4731 | http://www.thethayerhotel.com/

Since you are on the grounds of West Point, end your day at Thayer Hotel and one of their fantastic restaurants and stay for the evening. MacArthur's Riverview Restaurant has old world charm and beautiful views of the valley. A nice day, sit outside on the patio. If you aren't looking for a big meal visit General Patton's Tavern where you can grab a burger, sandwich or salad and have a view of the river. After dinner have a cocktail at Zulu Time Roof Top Bar and then retire to one of their guest rooms. You will have all the modern comforts like high speed internet, 32" flat screen TV with Direct TV.

Day Tripping

The Sites of the Capital Region

One-Day Itinerary

Suggested Stops
New York State Museum • Albany Distillery • Nine Pin Cider Works • Albany Institute of History and Art • USS Slater DE766 • Albany Pine Bush Preserve Commission

Suggested Dining
Café Madison • C.H. Evans Brewing at the Albany Pump Station • Barcelona Restaurant

Suggested Lodging
Albany Thruway Courtyard by Marriott

From I-90 E take exit 3 towards the State Offices. Merge onto Campus Access Road and continue onto Soc Ring Road. Turn right and stay on Campus Access Road. Turn left onto Western Avenue and the road turns into Madison Avenue. It should take approximately 15 minutes depending on where you are coming from.

CAFÉ MADISON
1108 Madison Avenue | Albany, NY | 12208
518.935.1094 | http://www.cafemadisonalbany.com

Located in the heart of Albany, the décor has a nice upbeat jazz feeling. Get there early as it is small but they do offer outdoor seating, weather permitting. Taking breakfast to the next level, Café Madison is known for its oatmeal raspberry pancakes and specially prepared weekend menu that changes weekly. Check their Facebook page for the current specials.

Head right down Madison Avenue. It should take you about 7 minutes depending on lights.

NEW YORK STATE MUSEUM
222 Madison Avenue | Albany, NY | 12230
518.474.5877 | http://www.nysm.nysed.gov/

Firstly, don't be intimidated by all those steps. The museum showcases the history of the Empire State from prehistoric times to the present. Learn about the Iroquois Indians, longhouse, and view many artifacts from 9-11. Learn about the World Trade Center Rescue, Recovery, and Response. The museum encompasses it all from the history of New York City to bones of a prehistoric mastodon (they were found in Hyde Park, NY), and the best part is, it's free, although they do ask for a donation.

Turn right onto South Swan Street. Keep left and stay on South Swan Street. Turn right onto S Mall Arterial. Take the I-787 N / US 9 N ramp towards Troy. Keep right at the fork and follow signs for US-9 N / Clinton Avenue. Continue on US 9 N. Keep left and stay on US 9 N. Turn right onto Broadway and left onto Spencer Street. Turn right onto Montgomery and the Restaurant/Brewery is on the right. Driving time: 7 minutes.

C.H. EVANS BRWING COMPANY AT THE ALBANY PUMP STATION
19 Quackenbush Square | Albany, NY | 12207
518.447.9000 | http://www.evansale.com/

The Evan's family has been in the commercial brewing business for three generations. The original brewery in Hudson, New York produced until prohibition. In keeping with the family tradition, Neil Evans relocated the brewery to the historic building of the Albany Pump Station in 1999. In its day the pump station drew water from the Hudson River to the Bleecker Reservoir until it ceased operation in 1932. When you walk in look up to the mezzanine floor that highlights multiple levels of brewing tanks. The brewery décor highlights the industrial feel of the pump station with high energy of the craft brewery scene. Their menu features a wide variety of dishes from burgers, specialty sandwiches, and entrees. Make sure you try their Albany Ale if they have it on tap. It's a recipe dating back to 1830 that Head Brewer Ryan Demler made a few tweaks to and he uses New York grown malted barley ingredients.

Right next door to the Pump Station.

ALBANY DISTILLERY
78 Montgomery Street | Albany, NY | 12207
518.621.7191 | http://www.albanydistilling.com/

You don't have far to walk after visiting the Pump Station as the distillery is right next door. The building has 1800 charm while filled with modern day stills. This is Albany's first distillery since Prohibition. The distillery is currently open Thursday's from 5 p.m. to 8 p.m. and Saturday from 2 p.m. to 7 p.m. To see how they make their whiskey and rum you can book your tour right from their website. Tours are given on Thursday at 6 p.m. and Saturday at 2 p.m., 4 p.m., and 6 p.m.

Montgomery Street turn left onto Spencer Street and right onto Broadway. Nine Pin is on the right. Driving time: 3 minutes.

NINE PIN CIDER WORKS
929 Broadway | Albany, NY | 12207
518.449.9999 | http://www.ninepincider.com

All it took was a sample of local hard cider and Alejandro was hooked. Nine Pin Cider was New York's first farm cidery, and in 2013 Alejandro's cider won a gold medal at the Great Lakes International Cider Competition. The tasting room is located in downtown Albany, in an old warehouse. Alejandro makes cider from apples sourced from the Capital Region, Hudson Valley, and his family farm. Signature is their flagship cider using apples from Samascott Orchards. You will find a selection of seven ciders to taste and they rotate depending on production.

Head southeast on Broadway. Turn right onto Clinton Avenue and left onto Chapel Street. Turn right onto Columbia Street and left onto Eagle Street. Bear straight onto Washington Avenue. The Institute will be on your right. Driving time: 5 minutes.

ALBANY INSTITUTE OF HISTORY AND ART
125 Washington Avenue | Albany, NY | 12210
518.463.4478 | http://www.albanyinstitute.org/

The Albany Institute of History and Art is dedicated to collecting, preserving, and promoting interest in the history art and culture of Albany and the Upper Hudson Valley region. Ongoing exhibits include works by the Hudson River School, and an Ancient Egypt exhibit about mummies. Learn about the people who shaped Albany.

Washington Avenue, turn left onto Eagle Street. Turn right onto Pine Street and right onto Broadway to Quay Street. Driving time: 6 minutes.

USS SLATER DE766
Broadway and Quay Streets | Albany, NY | 12202
518.431.1943 | http://www.ussslater.org/

Named after sailor Frank O. Slater who hailed from Alabama, the USS Slater is the only World War II destroyer escort in existence with its original battle armament. Destroyer escorts were a vital component of the Allied strategy for victory in the Atlantic. The USS Slater served in both the Atlantic and the Pacific in World War II. The ship was deactivated after the war until 1951 when it was transferred to the Hellenic Navy. It was renamed AETOS and stayed in the Greek service until 1991. Then it was transfered back to the United States under the care of the Destroyer Escort Historical Foundation. The restoration began in New York City, in 1993, and was moved to it's permanent home in 1997. Guided tours are available April through November, Wednesday through Sunday from 10 a.m. to 4 p.m.

I-787 N ramp towards Troy. Merge onto I-90 W towards Buffalo. Take exit 2 for Fuller Road toward University of Albany. At the traffic circle take the third exit onto Fuller Road. Use the right lane to take the Crossgate Road ramp. Merge onto Washington Avenue Ext. Turn right onto New Kramer Road. Preserve will be on your right. Driving time: 15 minutes.

ALBANY PINE BUSH PRESERVE COMMISSION

195 New Karner Road | Albany, NY | 12205
518.456.0655 | http://www.albanypinebush.org/

There are only twenty inland pine barrens left in the entire world, and this one is considered to be the best. The 3,200 acre preserve has gently rolling sand dunes supporting a fire dependent habitat that is home to more than 1,500 plant and animal species. There are eighteen miles of trails so pack comfortable shoes and stop into the Discover Center and learn about the geologic significance of the preserve.

Head north on New Karner Road (NY-155). Turn right onto Central Avenue (NY-5). Take a slight right onto the ramp for New York State Thruway I-87 S. Keep left and continue on Adirondack Northway. Stay in the left two lanes and turn left onto US-20 E – Western Avenue. Restaurant will be on the right. Driving time: 10 minutes.

BARCELONA RESTAURANT

1192 Western Avenue | Albany, NY | 12203
518.438.1144 http://www.barcelona-albany.com/

A little bit of Italian and a little bit of Spain is what you will find at Barcelona. The dining room is quaint and homey with large windows overlooking Western Avenue. Try the Veal Daniel, which is battered veal, mushrooms, and prosciutto in a Jack Daniel's cream sauce over linguini or the Paella. Save room for dessert and try the Tiramisu Cake or the Tres Leches Cake. If you bring your own wine, the corkage fee is $15.

Take a nice drive through SUNY Albany. Take Western Avenue and turn right onto SUNY at Albany. Turn left at the first cross street onto E University Drive, which turns into W University Drive. Turn left onto SUNY at Albany and turn left onto Washington Avenue. Driving time: 7 minutes.

ALBANY THRUWAY COURTYARD BY MARRIOTT

1455 Washington Avenue | Albany, NY | 12206
518.435-1600 | http://www.marriott.com/hotels/travel/albws-courtyard-albany-thruway/

Located close to the University of Albany and many sites in the Capital District, guest rooms are nicely appointed. There is a small gym to workout in before you begin the day, and free Wi-Fi.

Weekend Rendezvous

The Sites of the Capital Region and South

Three-Day Itinerary

Suggested Stops

Nine Pin Cider Works • USS Slater DE766 • Brookview Station Winery • Martin Van Buren National Historic Site • Hawthorne Valley Farm • Hudson-Chatham Winery • Omni International Arts Center • FASNY Museum of Firefighting • Olana State Historic Site • Kaaterskill Falls Pratt Rock • Bronck Museum

Suggested Dining

Angelo's 677 Prime • The French Press • Baba Louie's Pizza • Licks Ice Cream • Helsinki Hudson • Nolita's Bakery Café • 394 Main • Jack's Oyster House

Suggested Lodging

The Desmond Hotel • WM Farmer & Sons

Friday

I-787 to exit 4 towards US-9/US-20 W. Merge onto Quay Street. Quay Street to Colonie Street, right onto Erie Blvd. Left onto N Ferry Street and right onto Broadway. Driving time: 15 minutes.

NINE PIN CIDER WORKS

929 Broadway | Albany, NY | 12207
518.449.9999 | http://www.ninepincider.com

All it took was a sample of local hard cider and Alejandro was hooked. Nine Pin Cider was New York's first farm cidery, and in 2013 Alejandro's cider won a gold medal at the Great Lakes International Cider Competition. The tasting room is located in downtown Albany, in an old warehouse. Alejandro makes cider from apples sourced from the Capital Region, Hudson Valley, and his family farm. Signature is their flagship cider using apples from Samascott Orchards. You will find a selection of seven ciders to taste and they rotate depending on production.

Head southwest on Broadway.Driving time: 2 minutes.

ANGELO'S 677 PRIME
677 Broadway | Albany, NY | 12207
518.427.7463 | http://677prime.com/

This upscale steakhouse welcomes you with a gorgeous cherry wine cabinet where hardwood floors, leather chairs, and mahogany accents draw you into the dining room. You will find mouth watering steaks and fresh seafood to dine on, plus a wine list of more than four hundred international selections to pair with your meal. Valet parking is offered so you don't have to worry about the car. If you bring your own wine, the corkage fee is $25.

Head north on Broadway. Turn left onto Loundonville Road. It turns into Shaker Road and then turns into Albany Shaker Road. Driving time: 20 minutes.

THE DESMOND ALBANY HOTEL
660 Albany Shaker Road | Albany, NY | 12211
518.448.3500 | http://www.desmondhotelsalbany.com/

Family owned and operated, the Desmond has 322 rooms and suites. Sleep in a king-size four-poster beds, that is a reproduction of a model owned by George Washington. They also feature queen size beds, executive suites, and junior suites. Explore their two indoor courtyards that feature mock storefronts, a koi pond, and beautiful fountains. Enjoy complimentary high speed Wi-Fi, complimentary coffee outside Simpson's from 6:30 a.m. to 9 a.m., use of the indoor pool, hot tub, fitness center, and complimentary parking.

__Saturday__

Albany Shaker Road turns into Shaker Road turns into Loudonville Road. Turn right onto N. Pearl Street. Turn right onto Clinton Avenue. Turn left at the first cross street, which is Orange Street, and turn left onto Clinton Square. Driving time: 15 minutes.

THE FRENCH PRESS
5 Clinton Square | Albany, NY | 12207
518.275.0478 | http://frenchpresscafeandcrepes.com/

This quaint little spot is a great way to begin your day. Start with a delicious cup of coffee, espresso or tea and dine on awesome pastries, breakfast sandwiches, breakfast burritos, and of course crêpes. The crêpes are large thin and tasty! Be healthy and have the Holy Kale, which is baby kale sautéed in garlic with mushrooms and Swiss cheese, or if you have a sweet tooth, try The Nutoli, a Nutella crêpe rolled in a cone and stuffed with their homemade cannoli filling. If you think you will have more than one cup of coffee, order the personal coffee press.

Head southwest on Clinton Square and turn left onto Orange Street. Get in the right lane and take the ramp to US-9 S. Keep right at fork and follow signs for I-787 S / US 9 S / New York Thruway / Rensselaer. Use the middle land and continue on Frontage Road. Turn left onto NY-5 and left onto Quay. Driving time: 5 minutes.

USS SLATER DE766
Broadway and Quay Streets | Albany, NY | 12202
518.431.1943 | http://www.ussslater.org/

Named after sailor Frank O. Slater who hailed from Alabama, the USS Slater is the only World War II destroyer escort in existence with its original battle armament. Destroyer escorts were a vital component of the Allied strategy for victory in the Atlantic. The USS Slater served in both the Atlantic and the Pacific in World War II. The ship was deactivated after the war until 1951 when it was transferred to the Hellenic Navy. It was renamed AETOS and stayed in the Greek service until 1991. Then it was transfered back to the United States under the care of the Destroyer Escort Historical Foundation. The restoration began in New York City, in 1993, and was moved to it's permanent home in 1997. Guided tours are available April through November, Wednesday through Sunday from 10 a.m. to 4 p.m.

US-9 N to I 787 N to I90 E. Get off at exit 11E. Merge onto US-20 E. Turn right onto NY-150 S (S Old Post Road). Turn right onto Brookview Station Road. Driving time: 15 minutes.

BROOKVIEW STATION WINERY
1297 Brookview Station Road | Castleton, NY 12033
518.732.7317 | http://www.brookviewstationwinery.com/

Located at Goold Orchard, Brookview Station Winery opened in 2006 when third generation owner Sue Goold Miller and her husband Ed began making wine. Brookview Station is named after the small train station where Sue's grandparents arrived. Their wine names are train themed. Try their award-winning Whistle Stop White, a semi-dry apple wine. They also produce three hard apple ciders. Look around their store and pick up one of their fresh baked pies and cider donuts. In the Fall take an hour or two to go apple picking.

Brookview Station road to Simons Road. Left onto Maple Hill Road. Turn right onto S Schodack Road. Turn right onto Clove Road. Slight left onto Muitzeskill Road. Continue on County Road 21. Turn left onto Bishop Nelson Road to NY-9H S. Turn right onto Old Post Road. Driving time: 30 minutes.

MARTIN VAN BUREN
NATIONAL HISTORIC SITE
1013 Old Post Road | Kinderhook, NY | 12106
518.758.9689 | https://www.nps.gov/mava/index.htm

Home to Kinderhook native and the eighth President of the United

States (1837-1841) Martin Van Buren settled here following his defeat for a second term in 1862. This Georgian-style Lindenwald is where he entertained politicians and dignitaries. Van Buren farmed Lindenwald's grounds which have orchards, ponds, meadows, and formal gardens. Allow at least an hour or more to explore his home and grounds.

Directions: Take Old Post Road to NY-9H S. Turn right onto NY-66 S / Union Turnpike and go straight onto Columbia Street. Turn left and stay on Columbia Street. Turn left onto Park Place and right onto Warren Street. Driving time: 20 minutes.

BABA LOUIE'S PIZZA
517 Warren Street | Hudson, NY | 12534
518.751.2155 | http://babalouiespizza.com/

People come from all over to go to Baba Louie's and they rave about their wood fired pizzas. The sourdough pizza crusts combined with fresh ingredients are to die for. But don't worry, it's not all about pizza; they also offer sandwiches and paninis, fresh salads, and gluten-free pizza

Directions: Take a stroll up the street for some ice cream and look at the antique shops.

LICKS – ICE CREAM
253 Warren Street | Hudson NY | 12534
518.828.7254 | http://www.lickhudson.com/

While walking down Hudson Street stop in at Licks for some delicious ice cream. They source their ice cream locally from Jane's (http://janesicecream.com/), which makes their ice cream in small batches from a recipe that has been handed down through the generations. A must-stop if you're an ice cream lover!

Directions: Warren Street to left onto Park Place. Park Place turns right and becomes Columbia Street. Turn right onto NY-23B E to NY-23 E to Taconic State Parkway North. Take the NY-217 exit toward

Harlemville/Philmont. Turn right onto County Road 21C Farm will be on your left. Driving time: 20 minutes.

HAWTHORNE VALLEY FARM
327 County Route 21C | Ghent, NY | 12075
518.672.7500 | http://hawthornevalleyfarm.org/

This 500-acre Demeter certified 650A Biodynamic farm houses a herd of sixty dairy cows, ten acres of vegetables, twenty pigs, forty chickens, a creamery, organic bakery, sauerkraut cellar, and more. Stop into their farm store and pick up some organic, local meats, vegetables, and dairy products. Their cheese tastes really good! You can also take a self-guided tour around the farm. Visit the pigs, wander through the garden, visit the Creek, and hike Phudd Hill. Maps are available in the Farm Store.

Head northeast on County Road 21C and turn left onto Harlemville Road. Continue straight onto Tice Hill Road. Take a slight right onto Ghent Mellenville. Turn left onto NY-66 S. Driving time: 10 minutes.

HUDSON-CHATHAM WINERY
1900 NY-66 | Ghent, NY | 12075
518.392.9463 | http://www.hudsonchathamwinery.com/

Authors and book publishers turned winery owners, Carlo and Dominique DeVito, purchased their farm in 2006. Their winemaker Steve Casscles strives for great quality and known for his Baco Noir. Taste and compare their Casscles Vineyard Block 3 North Creek Vineyard, Fieldstone and Old Vines Mason Place Vineyards Pultney Farms Baco Noir. Under the Paperbirch label is their small production of artisanal ports, sherries, and other dessert wines. New products include an entire line of balsamic-styled vinegars and a cognac-style brandy to be released in the not too distant future. Grab a bottle, have a picnic, and enjoy the views.

Head southwest on NY-66 and turn right onto Waltermire Road. Turn left onto Snyder Road and take a slight left onto Habeck Road. Turn right and stay on Habeck Road. Turn left onto County Route 22. The

Omni Center will be on the right. Driving time: 10 minutes.

OMNI INTERNATIONAL ARTS CENTER
1405 County Route 22 | Ghent, NY | 12075
518.392.4747 | http://www.omiartscenter.org/

Omni International Arts Center is a nonprofit international arts center founded in 1992 by Francis Greenburger. The Fields Sculpture Park features beautiful rotating art exhibitions in an indoor setting and a 60-acre outdoor sculpture park with beautiful and inspiring works of art embedded in the breathtaking landscape of Columbia County. Wear good walking shoes and allow at least an hour to tour the park. Admission is free.

Head southwest on County Route 22 and turn left onto NY-9H S. Turn right onto NY-66 S / Union Turnpike. Straight onto Columbia Street. Turn left and stay on Columbia Street. Driving time: 20 minutes.

HELSINKI HUDSON
405 Columbia Street | Hudson, NY | 12534
518.828.4800 http://www.helsinkihudson.com/

Come for dinner and enjoy the nightlife afterwards in the club. The restored nineteenth century former industrial building is home to the restaurant, the club, and event space. Inside the restaurant, you'll find high ceilings with exposed brick and beams. Executive Chef Hugh Horner menu is inspired by the spirit of the Helsinki culture, his love of the Hudson Valley, and his southern roots. He sources from the local community of farmers and cheese-makers. The Rustic Cuisine will excite you. Feast on the Applewood Smoked Ribs 'Two Ways' or the 7 Hour Braised Short Rib Pot Pie. There is a nice list of local beer, cider, and spirits, but if you bring your own bottle the corkage fee is $25.

Continue down Columbia Street and turn left onto N Front Street. Driving time: 5 minutes.

WM FARMER AND SONS

20 S. Front Street | Hudson, NY | 12534
518.828.1635 | http://www.wmfarmerandsons.com/

You'll find comfortable and eclectic rooms in this historic boarding house in downtown Hudson. You'll be surrounded by great hospitality, history, and warmth from the moment you make the reservation. Each of ten rooms each with their own personality. Enjoy a night cap in the Barroom downstairs. It is in a very convenient location, walking distance to local shops, galleries, and antique stores.

Sunday

Head northeast on S Front Street and turn right onto Warren Street. Driving time: 5 minutes or a 15-minute walk.

NOLITA'S BAKERY CAFÉ

454 Warren Street | Hudson, NY | 12534
518.828.4905

This is a great place to begin your day. Chat with the locals while enjoying your cup of coffee and dine outside, eating your breakfast wrap. You'll get the best breakfast in town here!

Directions: Head northwest on Warren Street and turn right onto N 4th Street. Turn right onto State Street and left onto Carroll Street. Turn left onto Short Street and it turns into Harry Howard Avenue. Driving time: 5 minutes.

FASNY MUSEUM OF FIREFIGHTING

117 Harry Howard Avenue | Hudson, NY | 12534
518.822.1875 http://www.fasnyfiremuseum.com/

You will find the world's premier collection of American Firefighting artifacts at this museum. The museum began with four antique fire engines donated by the Exempt Firemen's Association of the City of New York. Included in this donation is the oldest documented fire engine in New York State, a Newsham Engine, from 1731, a gooseneck-style engine, a piano-style engine, and a double-decker-style engine. Today the collection includes over ninety pieces of fire apparatus. View rare Viking axes and telegraph alarm systems, to firefighter gear both past and present.

Directions: Take Harry Howard Avenue to Short Street. Turn right onto Carroll Street and then right onto State Street. Turn left onto N 3rd Street. Continue on NY-23B/NY-9G to Olana. Driving time: 15 minutes.

OLANA STATE HISTORIC SITE
5720 Route 9G | Hudson NY | 12534
518.828.0135 | http://www.olana.org/

This is the home and estate of Hudson River School painter Frederic Church. This 250-acre estate is open year round. You'll find hiking, picnicking, and there is also a pond for kayaking and fishing. Tour the main house and see the mixture of Victorian architecture and Middle Eastern motifs.

Directions: Take 9G N to NY-23 W and cross over the Rip Van Winkle Bridge. Turn left onto Colewood Avenue and turn right onto High Street. Turn left onto Spring Street and right onto Thompson Street then left onto Main Street. Driving time: 10 minutes.

394 MAIN
394 Main Street | Catskill, NY | 12414
518.947.4774

This charming café & wine bar serves innovative cuisine in a casual, sophisticated setting. It is nicely decorated with a warm feel, granite table tops, and a fireplace in the back corner adding to the ambiance. Try their home-made smoked meats, bread, pastries, and amazing coffee.

Directions: Head south on Main Street and turn right onto Bridge

Street. Turn left onto W Bridge Street and continue straight onto NY-23A to Kaaterskill Wild Forest. Driving time: 20 minutes.

KAATERSKILL FALLS
Rt 23A | Haines Falls, NY | 12436
518.357.2161

If you like to view beautiful waterfalls, this is a must-see. Kaaterskill Falls is a 260-foot two stage waterfalls. Take the yellow trail to the falls on this 1.6 mile round-trip hike. Keep in mind it is a hike and so it can be steep and rocky. Bring sneakers and leave your flip flops and heels in the car. The hike should take between one and one and a half hours.

Directions: Continue on NY-23 A and it meets up with NY-23. Driving time: 30 minutes.

PRATT ROCK
Rt 23 | Prattsville, NY | 12468
518.299.3125 | https://zadockprattmuseum.com/

Called "America's first Mt. Rushmore," view the carvings made for Zadock Pratt, a wealthy entrepreneur who ran the biggest shoe leather tannery in the world. The story told is that a stonecutter was looking for work and Zadock pointed to the cliff overlooking his farm and told him to begin to carve his life story. He carved for twenty-eight years until Zadock's death. The climb to view the carvings is steep but the path is clear. Wear comfortable shoes.

Directions: Head back on NY-23 E. Turn right onto County Road 85. Turn left onto County Road 41 A. Turn left onto Jerome Avenue. Continue on County Road 41/Lake Mills Road. Take a sharp right onto County Road 67. Turn left onto Gayhead-Earlton Road. Turn right and stay on Gayhead-Earlton Road. Continue onto County Road 45. Turn right onto NY-81 E and it turns into NY-385 E. Turn right onto Washington Avenue and left onto New Street. Driving time: 50 minutes.

BRONCK MUSEUM
90 County Highway 42 | Coxsackie, NY | 12051
518.731.6490 | http://www.gchistory.org/bronckmuseum.html

The oldest surviving house in Upstate New York was home to eight generations of Bronk's for 276 years. The estate consists of two homes built in 1663 and 1738, a kitchen dependency, a Northern European side-aisle barn, a thirteen-sided hay barn, and other Victorian agricultural buildings. Rooms are furnished with period furniture and many of the original Bronck family china, glass, and silverware...Guided tours are offered from Wednesday through Sunday.

Directions: New Street to right onto Washington Avenue. Right onto Mansion Street and left onto Elm Street. Left onto Prospect Street and left onto Lafayette Avenue. Right turn onto NY-385 N/Mansion Street to US 9W N to I87 N. Take exit 23 for I-787 N toward Troy. Take exit 4 US-9N/US-20W. Merge onto Quay Street. Turn left onto NY-5 to State Street. Driving time: 35 minutes.

JACK'S OYSTER HOUSE
42 State Street | Albany, NY | 122007
518.465.8854 | http://www.jacksoysterhouse.com/

This restaurant was opened in 1913 by Jack Rosenstein and today it's still in the family and run by his grandson Brad Rosenstein. This restaurant has exceptional service with waiters dressed in black jackets and bow ties. You will photographs throughout the restaurant depicting Albany's past. Executive Chef Larry Schepici has introduced creative international dishes blended in with the traditional 1913 menu items. You have to try Jack's Famous Oysters for six or the Crabcakes Jack's 1913 recipe. Beyond the appetizers choose from Steak Diane to Cowboy Steak, Chicken Lemonardo or a Two and a Half Pound Maine Lobster. Jack's has it all and service you will be talking about way after you get home. Corkage fee is $25 if you bring your own bottle.

Directions: State Street to right onto Broadway. Turn left onto NY-5/State Route 5. Turn left onto Quay Street and continue onto US-9 N. Get in the left lane and take I-787 N ramp to Troy. Use the right two lanes and take exit 5 and merge onto I-90 towards Buffalo. Keep left and stay on I-90W and use the two right lanes to merge onto I-87 N (Northway) to Saratoga. Take exit 4 to NY-155 W/Albany Shaker Road. Use the left two lanes and turn left onto Wolf Road. Turn left at the first cross street onto Albany Shaker Road. Driving time: 20 minutes.

THE DESMOND ALBANY HOTEL
660 Albany Shaker Road | Albany, NY | 12211
518.448.3500 | http://www.desmondhotelsalbany.com/

Family owned and operated, the Desmond has 322 rooms and suites. Sleep in a king-size four-poster bed, that is a reproduction of a model owned by George Washington. They also feature queen size beds, executive suites, and junior suites. Explore their two indoor courtyards that feature mock storefronts, a koi pond, and beautiful fountains. Enjoy complimentary high speed Wi-Fi, complimentary coffee outside Simpson's from 6:30 a.m. to 9 a.m., use of the indoor pool, hot tub, fitness center, and complimentary parking.

Day Tripping

Historic Eastern Orange County

One-Day Itinerary

Suggested stops

Lawrence Farm Market • Benmarl Winery • Motorcyclepedia •
Washington Headquarters • Newburgh Brewing Company

Suggested Dining

Raccoon Saloon • Newburgh Waterfront

Suggested Lodging

4 Points by Sheraton

*Traveling on the New York State Thruway entering the region at the
Harriman Interchange, Woodbury Toll continue north on I-87 to exit
17 Newburgh. At toll get in the right lane and get on I-84 E. Get off
at the last exit before toll, exit 10 US-9W. Take a left onto US-9W
N. Turn left onto Fostertown Road and left onto Frozen Ridge Road.
Driving time: 10 minutes from toll booth.*

LAWRENCE FARM MARKET

306 Frozen Ridge Road | Newburgh, NY | 12550
845.562.4268 www.lawrencefarmsorchards.com

A family owned fruit and vegetable farm open from Memorial Day
through October. Stop here for pick your own fruit and veggies.
Take a horse-drawn carriage ride around the farm. Don't miss the
homemade cider donuts!

*Continue down Frozen Ridge Road and turn right onto Bingham
Road. Turn left onto Highland Avenue. Driving time: 10 minutes.*

BENMARL WINERY
156 Highland Avenue | Marlboro, NY | 12542
845.236.4265 | www.benmarl.com

Benmarl Winery sits on the oldest continuously planted vineyard in the United States, Slate Hill Vineyard, home to New York's Farm Winery License #1. Located on thirty-seven scenic acres overlooking the Hudson River and Berkshire Mountains with a kickass view for great picture taking. This historic winery was purchased by artist Mark Miller from Andrew J. Caywood, an early American viticulturist in 1957, and in 2006 it was purchased by Victor Spaccarelli who fulfilled his lifelong dream of owning a vineyard. Victor's son Matt is the General Manager and winemaker focusing on producing small batch wines that capture the unique terroir of the vineyard. In addition, Matt and his partner Casey have produced a line of wines, Fjord Vineyards from very small estate grown acre lots and small batches sourced regionally. At the time of writing this, Fjord tasting room was open on sporadic days and times. Ask for directions to their Ridge Road tasting room from the Benmarl staff, and if you visit, make sure to try their award winning Albariño.

Directions: Right onto Highland Avenue, right onto Western Avenue and right onto King Street. Look for parking. Driving time: 5 minutes.

RACCOON SALOON
1330 Route 9W | Marlboro, NY | 12542
845.236.7872 | http://www.raccoonsaloonmarlboro.com/

You will feel like you are entering an old saloon from the Wild West. Ask for a seat by the window overlooking the ravine and waterfalls, which flows into a "sucker hole" and various small pools before ending up in the Hudson River. They have great burgers here served with their homemade ketchup. No outside beverages are allowed, so save that wine for the hotel room.

Directions: US-9W S. Turn right onto North Street. Slight left North

Street becomes Fullerton Avenue. Turn left onto Broadway and right onto Lake Street NY-32). Driving time: 20 minutes.

MOTORCYCLEPEDIA
250 Lake Street | Newburgh, NY | 12550
845.569.9065 | http://www.motorcyclepediamuseum.org/

Motorcyclepedia is a motorcycle enthusiast's paradise with over 450 American motorcycles mainly from the first half of the twentieth century. Gerald A. Doering a motorcycle enthusiast collected Indian motorcycles from 1901-1953. His son Ted also shared in his passion for motorcycles, and in 1971 they began a wholesale motorcycle parts business. With the success of the business they expanded their motorcycle collection. In 2011, they opened Motorcyclepedia "A Family's Attic Full of Motorcycles" featuring more than 400 motorcycles. Along with the motorcycles you will find photographs, posters, memorabilia, machinery, and other items related to bikes.

Northeast on Lake Street and turn right onto S William Street. Right onto Liberty Street. Driving time: 10 minutes.

WASHINGTON HEADQUARTERS
84 Liberty Street | Newburgh, NY | 12550
845.562.1195 | http://snip.ly/d1nyb

Tour the grounds that were General George Washington's Continental Army headquarters during the Revolutionary War. It is at these headquarters that General Washington rejected the idea that he should be king after the war and created the Badge of Military Merit that was the forerunner of the Purple Heart. This site was acquired by the New York State in 1850 and was the first publicly owned and operated historic site in the nation. The home is open for tours Wednesday through Saturday until 4:30 p.m. April through October. Check the website for the winter hours.

Directions: North on Liberty Street and turn right onto Renwick Street. Left onto Colden Street. Driving time: 5 minutes.

NEWBURGH BREWING COMPANY
88 Colden Street | Newburgh, NY | 12550
845.569.2337 | http://www.newburghbrewing.com/

Located in the heart of Newburgh, Paul Halayko, a CPA by trade who got his appetite for beers on a business trip to Germany, partnered with his high school buddy Christopher Basso who previously worked as Brewer at Brooklyn Brewery in 2012. The tap room replicates an indoor German beer hall with long tables and benches with spectacular views of the Hudson River. Their beer focus is lower alcohol beers (but there are a few that are high octane) and have a great flavor profile.

Directions: North on Colden Street and a right onto Washington Street. Left onto Water Street. Turn right onto 4th Street and left onto Front Street. Look for parking. Driving time: 5 minutes.

NEWBURGH WATERFRONT
Front Street | Newburgh, NY | 12550
http://www.ribworks.com/ http://www.blu-pointe.com/
http://cena2000.com/ http://www.therivergrill.com/

Choose from a variety of restaurants and sit on the banks of the Hudson River enjoying the view of Mt. Beacon and watch the boats on the river. Restaurants vary from Billy Joe's Ribworks, Blu-Pointe, The River Grill, Cena 2000, and many more. Take a walk along the water, look at the menus, take in the vibe, and enjoy.

Directions: Get back up to Water Street and take that to RT 9W. Turn right onto 9W and get in the left hand lane to get onto I84-W. Get off at Exit 6 and take a right. Lakeside Drive is on the right at the Diner. Driving time: 10 minutes.

4 POINTS BY SHERATON
AT STEWART AIRPORT
5 Lakeside Road | Newburgh, NY | 12550
845.567.0567 | http://www.starwoodhotels.com/

This property is fairly new and centrally located right off I-84. Rooms are nicely appointed in a contemporary style. There is free wireless internet and each room has a mini refrigerator and a 50-inch flat screen TV. There is a restaurant and bar just off the lobby, and the hotel has a small workout room.

Weekend Rendezvous

Historic Orange County

Three-Day Itinerary

Suggested Stops

Motorcyclepedia • Crows Nest • Jones Farm • Storm King
Arts Center • Brotherhood Winery • Sugar Loaf Art & Craft
Village • Applewood Winery & Naked Flock Cider • Harness
Racing Museum • Museum Village • Palaia Winery • Woodbury
Commons Premium Outlets

Suggested Dining

El Solar Café • Fiddlestix • Jones Farm • Iron Forge Inn • Café
A La Mode • Scalia & Co Craft Kitchen and Bar • Cosimo's Brick
Oven Pizza

Suggested Lodging

4 Points by Sheraton • Chateau Hathorn • Hampton Inn

Friday

*Traveling on the New York State Thruway entering the region at the
Harriman Interchange, Woodbury Toll continue north on I-87 to exit
17 Newburgh. Stay in the right lane as you exit and head towards I-
84 E. Get on I-84 E and get off at exit 8 for NY-52 Walden. Turn right
onto S Plank Road and right onto Dupont Avenue. Dupont Avenue
becomes Wisner. Turn left onto Little Britain Road and right onto
Cerone Place. Turn right onto Lake Drive and right onto Lake Street.
Driving time: 15 minutes.*

MOTORCYCLEPEDIA
250 Lake Street | Newburgh, NY | 12550
845.569.9065 | http://www.motorcyclepediamuseum.org/

Motorcyclepedia is a motorcycle enthusiast's paradise with over 450 American motorcycles mainly from the first half of the twentieth century. Gerald A. Doering a motorcycle enthusiast collected Indian motorcycles from 1901-1953. His son Ted also shared in his passion for motorcycles, and in 1971 they began a wholesale motorcycle parts business. With the success of the business they expanded their motorcycle collection. In 2011, they opened Motorcyclepedia "A Family's Attic Full of Motorcycles" featuring more than 400 motorcycles. Along with the motorcycles you will find photographs, posters, memorabilia, machinery, and other items related to bikes.

Head northeast on Lake Street (NY-32) and right onto Broadway. Driving time: 5 minutes.

EL SOLAR CAFE
346 Broadway | Newburgh, NY | 12550
845.561-3498

Located on Broadway in Newburgh this restaurant is a little gem. You will feel like you are in the Mediterranean with a combination of eclectic Latin and Mediterranean dishes. Jose Hernandez and his wife Gisela Pacheco are passionate about their restaurant and are there to answer all your questions. The food is fresh and delicious and their Sangria will not disappoint. If you bring your own bottle of wine the corkage fee is $10.

Directions: Head west on Broadway (NY-17K) and take it to Lakeside Road. Turn right onto Lakeside Road. Driving time: 15 minutes.

4 POINTS BY SHERATON AT STEWART AIRPORT
5 Lakeside Road | Newburgh, NY | 12550
845.567.0567 | http://www.starwoodhotels.com/

This property is fairly new and centrally located right off I-84. Rooms are nicely appointed in a contemporary style. There is free wireless internet and each room has a mini refrigerator and a 50-

inch flat screen TV. There is a restaurant and bar just off the lobby, and the hotel has a small workout room.

Saturday

Directions: Turn left onto NY-17K E. Turn right onto NY-300. Turn left onto NY-207 E / NY-300 S. Slight right onto NY-32 S. Turn left onto Quaker Avenue. At the traffic circle take the third exit onto Main Street. Driving time: 15 minutes.

FIDDLESTIX
319 Main Street | Cornwall, NY | 12518
845.534.3866 | http://www.fiddlestixcafe.com/index2.html

This is the place for a fresh country breakfast. Exceptional food is served, showcasing the chef's creativity and it is made with seasonal produce from local farms. If you like cheesecake but don't want anyone to see you eating it for breakfast, order the Strawberry Fields Forever, French Toast stuffed with strawberry cheesecake. Torn between breakfast or lunch, The Roots will solve that problem with a 7-inch Belgian waffle topped with chicken fingers, bacon, and Dijon maple dressing. Order their scones before they run out. Don't let the creativity scare you. You can make your own omelet and order some pancakes too!

Directions: Northeast on Main Street and slight right onto Hudson Street. Stay on Hudson Street and turn right onto Mountain Road. Driving time: 10 minutes.

HIKE THE CROW'S NEST
Mountain Road | Intersection of US9W, NY 293 | Cornwall-on-Hudson, NY
http://snip.ly/40ty5

First off, wear sneakers or hiking shoes, no flip flops or heels. You are going to have magnificent views of the Hudson Valley. The Howell Trail (blue trail) is 3.6 miles and involves some intermediate hiking but once you get to the top the effort is well worth it! On the way down you'll go across a small bridge over a stream. If it has rained, be careful as it can be slippery. There are other trails available that are shorter like the Bobcat Trail .4 miles (white trail) or the Bluebird Trail .6 miles. (blue and red trail)

Directions: Head South on Mountain Road and turn right onto US 9W N. Turn right toward Angola Road (follow signs) then left onto Angola Road. Driving time: 5 minutes.

JONES FARM
190 Angola Road | Cornwall, NY | 12518
845.534.4445 | http://www.jonesfarminc.com/

After the hike, you will have worked up an appetite so a stop at Jones Farm is perfect. As you enter the farm, watch out for livestock wandering around. When entering the barn house - bakery & gift shop your mouth will begin to water simply as a result of the delicious smell of the baked goods. The country store is the place to shop for local produce, eggs, honey, gourmet foods, and more. They have daily specials for breakfast and lunch. Then wander over to the old dairy barn that has been converted to a large gift shop. It's a great place to look for a unique gift that you will not find anywhere else. Just when you thought you were done, stop at the Art Gallery where the walls are covered with original oils, pastels and watercolors, unique prints of the Hudson Valley and West Point, and local photography.

Directions: Northeast on Angola Road and turn left onto Cedar Lane. Turn left onto Quaker Lane. Right onto NY-32 N. Left onto Orrs Mills Road and left onto Old Pleasant Hill Road. Left onto Museum Road. Driving time: 5 minutes.

STORM KING ARTS CENTER
1 Museum Road | New Windsor, NY | 12553
845.534.3115 | http://stormking.org/

This outdoor sculpture park and open air museum sits on 500 acres so make sure you wear shoes comfortable for walking. Explore the collection of more than one hundred modern sculptures created by some of the most acclaimed artists of our era. Tours are offered or you can stroll the grounds and look at the art on your own.

Directions: Old Pleasant Road to left onto Orrs Mills Road. Left onto NY-94 W. Right onto Brotherhood Plaza. Driving time: 10 minutes.

BROTHERHOOD
"AMERICA'S OLDEST" WINERY
100 Brotherhood Plaza Drive | Washingtonville NY | 10992
845.496.3661 | http://www.brotherhood-winery.com/

Brotherhood is the oldest continuously operating winery in America, and a visit here is full of history of winemaking in the Hudson Valley and the country. It was started by John Jaques a cobbler who moved to a small town called Little York, which is now Washingtonville, New York in 1810. The first vintage Brotherhood produced was in 1839, the same year construction of the underground cellar began. Today you can tour the underground cellar, which has become a museum, and relive the history of Brotherhood. On display are artifacts dating back to the 1800's along with the history, the people, the vintage labels, and more. You will get a sense of how important Brotherhood was not only to the Hudson Valley, but to wine tourism as an industry. Taste their B Sparkling, a great inexpensive sparkling wine. If you like it sweet, try the Carpe Diem Spumante. One of the favorites around the holiday time is their Holiday Spiced Wine.

Directions: Turn right onto NY -94 W. Turn left onto Glenmere Road and left onto Pine Hill Road. Driving time: 20 minutes.

SUGAR LOAF ART & CRAFT VILLAGE
1371 Kings Hwy | Chester, NY | 10918
http://www.sugarloafnewyork.com/fun/

As I traveled the Shawangunk Wine Trail I always ended up driving through Sugar Loaf and stopped each time, especially during the holidays. This is a small community of independent artists. They have beautiful art galleries, craft and jewelry shops, and more. You might even check the schedule at the Sugar Loaf Performing Arts Center and catch a show or play while in town. Since the stores are all independent the hours vary, but they are all open on the weekends. You must stop as you're driving through!

Directions: Pine Hill Road to right onto Hambletonian Road. Turn right onto Ridge Road E and left onto 4 Corners Road. Driving time: 5 minutes.

APPLEWOOD WINERY & NAKED FLOCK CIDER
82 4 Corners Road | Warwick, NY | 10990
845.988.9292 | http://www.applewoodwinery.com/

Jonathan and Michelle Hull started Applewood Winery in 1993. It sits on a 120-acre farm full of apple trees. Applewood's wines are produced from New York State grapes along with grapes from their own vineyard and fruit from their orchards. Jonathan having always produced a cider decided to take his cider production to the next level and launched "Naked Flock Cider." Their Original Cider is fermented with champagne yeast and sweetened with a touch of local honey. They produce three varieties of cider that are made with Hudson Valley Apples. Keeping on the apple theme, Applewood also produces an apple based gin and vodka. Taste it all in their tasting room. During the Fall you can also pick apples from the orchard.

Directions: West on 4 Corners Road and right onto Kings Highway. Left onto Wisner Road and left onto Lower Wisner Road. Right onto Iron Forge Road. Driving time: 10 minutes.

IRON FORGE INN
38 Iron Forge Road | Warwick NY | 10990
845.986.3411 | http://www.ironforgeinn.com/

Located at the foot of Mount Peter, the Inn is located on the site of an historic forge in a revolutionary era home that was built in

1760. A graduate of the Culinary Institute of America, chef/owner Erik Johansen changes the menu with the seasons and focuses on local ingredients. Feeling good, try their four or seven course tasting menu. Small plates and big ones too are served in the Tap Room. Try Crispy Pork Belly or Crispy Duck Breast with creamy Bleu Spätzle and Zucchini. A $15 corkage fee applies if you choose to bring your own wine.

Directions: Head southwest on Iron Forge Road and turn right onto NY-17A W. Turn left onto NY-94/Oakland Avenue. Follow NY-94 W. Slight right onto Hathorn Road. Driving time: 10 minutes.

CHATEAU HATHORN
33 Hathorn Road | Warwick, NY | 10990
845.986.6099 | http://www.chateauhathorn.com/

An old-world charm Inn with a European flare. Nestled on the grounds of a nature sanctuary, the views and wildlife sightings are tranquil. The interior of the building boasts beautiful dark wood touches creating a romantic vibe. All seven suites have a full bathroom, TV, sitting area, queen size bed, Wi-Fi and some with fireplaces. Breakfast is served each morning with gourmet cheeses from Switzerland, fresh fruits, and croissants.

Sunday

Directions: Head northeast on Hathorn Road. Take a slight left onto NY-94 E. Driving time: 5 minutes.

CAFFE A LA MODE
1 Oakland Avenue | Warwick, NY | 10990
845.986.1223 | http://caffealamode.com/

Begin your day with some serious coffee at Caffe A La Mode. They are known for having a great selection of coffees, both flavored and imported, but their specialty is the Graham Cracker Coffee. Menu items are traditional with omelets, pancakes, French Toast, egg sandwiches, and wraps. Feel free to order dessert too!

Directions: Oakland Avenue to Main Street. Main Street (NY-17A) turns into Maple Avenue (NY-17A) and right turn to Main Street in Goshen. Driving time: 20 minutes.

HARNESS RACING MUSEUM
240 Main Street | Goshen, NY | 10924
845.294.6330 | http://www.harnessmuseum.com/

If you're a harness racing fan this museum is for you. Housed in the Good Time Stable, formerly known as "The Trotting Horse Museum." In 1996 it changed its name to the Harness Racing Museum & Hall of Fame. The museum houses artifacts relating to the greatest steeds, such as Goldsmith's Maid who was the most winning horse in harness racing history. Visit the art gallery where you will view paintings of the famed horses and "The Story of Harness Racing" by Currier & Ives. View informative films and take part in the interactive exhibits. If you ever wanted to be a harness racing jockey, try their 3D simulated ride. The museum overlooks Goshen's Historic Track that was established in 1838 as the oldest working racetrack in the country. The best part is, admission is free.

Directions: Head southwest on Main Street. Left onto Park Place and left onto S Church Street. Turn right onto South Street. Left onto NY-17M W/Harriman Drive. Merge onto NY-17E / US-6E. Take exit 129 for Museum Village Road. Turn left towards NY-17M E, then right towards NY-17M E and left onto NY-17M E. Driving time: 15 minutes.

MUSEUM VILLAGE
1010 State Route 17M | Monroe, NY 10950
845.782.8248 | http://museumvillage.org/

If you are a history buff, you will enjoy the Museum Village. See, hear, touch, and understand life in nineteenth century America in this unique open-air historical museum. This village is the vision of Rosco William Smith who was the founder of Orange and Rockland Electric Company in 1905. He was an avid collector of items from textiles and porcelain to horse-drawn carriages. At times he accepted farm tools as payment for electricity. He began to display these artifacts to educate people, and in 1950 he opened Museum Village to display it all. Visit the different buildings like the Blacksmith to learn about the importance of repairing the equipment and making necessary farming items for the community; the Wagon Shop; the Candle Shop where you can dip your own candle; the School House where you can see what it was like in rural school in the nineteenth century; the Livery area which shows the many different kinds of transportation vehicles that were used. There are many other buildings that house displays and exhibits dating back through American history.

Directions: Head southeast on NY-17M and take a right onto Gilbert Street. Left into shopping center. Driving time: 5 minutes.

SCALIA & CO CRAFT KITCHEN AND BAR
785 State Rt. 17M | Shoprite Plaza | Monroe, NY | 10950
845.395.0906 | http://www.scaliaandco.com/

Located in the heart of Monroe, Scalia's brings grandma's homemade dishes to your table. Dine on a Paninni or Piadini, which is served on a homemade flame grilled flat bread. If you are really hungry choose from the many pasta dishes along with small plates to share. They have lunch specials for $9.95 that include a choice of appetizer and a main dish. They have a nice local beer menu. Their corkage fee is $25 if you want to bring in your own bottle.

Directions: Left onto Gilbert Street. Left onto High Street. Left onto Lakes Road. Continue straight onto Carpenter Place. Left onto Mapes Place. Right onto Spring Street. Turn left onto County Route 105 / Bakertown Road. Left onto NY-32 N and left onto Sweet Clover Road. Driving time: 20 minutes.

PALAIA WINERY
10 Sweet Clover Road | Highland Mills, NY | 10930
845.928.5384 | http://www.palaiavineyards.com/

Take a trip back to the seventies where it was all about peace, love, and rock- n -roll. That is the vibe at Palaia Winery. In the year 2000, Jan and her husband Joe purchased a 200-year-old cow farm "The Seaman Homestead at Sweet Clover Farm" and planted 1500 vines. Built in the early 1800's the homestead now sits on thirty-two acres of what is left from the tract of land purchased from Aaron Burr in 1784. In 1888, the barn was added to the property and today it is home to the winery and tasting room. Their wines range from dry to sweet. They have music every weekend and a kickass outdoor stage venue that rocks in the summer months.

Directions: Take a right onto NY-32 S to Woodbury Commons. Driving time: 10 minutes.

WOODBURY COMMONS PREMIUM OUTLETS
498 Red Apple Courtyards | Central Valley, NY | 10917
845.928.4000 | http://www.premiumoutlets.com/outlet/woodbury-common

Did someone say shopping? No trip to the Hudson Valley is complete until you shop at Woodbury Commons. You name the outlet shop and it's at Woodbury Commons. Plan your attack, park, shop, and leave. Don't be surprised if someone in a car follows you to yours, as they just want your space. Tip: If you are an AAA member, make sure you stop at the information desk for your discount book.

Directions: Head North on NY-32. Driving time: 5 minutes.

COSIMO'S BRICK OVEN – WOODBURY
100 NY-32 | Central Valley, NY | 10917
845.928.8265 | http://cosimosgroup.com/woodbury

At the end of the day, step into Tuscany at Cosimo's. The open floor plan with vaulted ceilings makes it a perfect venue to stop for dinner. Try the wood fired pizzas as they are wonderful. If you aren't in the mood for pizza choose from their wide variety of specialties, such as Blackened Steak Salad, Grilled Chicken Penne, or Wood

Fired Snapper. There is an entree for everyone. The corkage fee is $15 if you bring your own bottle.

Directions: Head southwest on NY-32 S. Continue on Averill Avenue. Turn left onto Centre Drive just after the RT- 17 interchange.

HAMPTON INN – WOODBURY
60 Centre Drive | Central Valley, NY | 10917
845.782.9600 | http://snip.ly/esr45

Relax and unwind in this 136-room hotel. Enjoy views of the mountains, free Wi-Fi, a gym/fitness center and an indoor pool. The hotel is close to major routes and walking distance to Woodbury Commons for your outlet shopping.

Day Tripping

Sites of Dutchess County

One-Day Itinerary

Suggested Stops
Madava Farms | Crown Maple Syrup • Millbrook Vineyards & Winery • Innisfree Gardens • Sprout Creek Farms • Frances Lehman Loeb Arts Center

Suggested dining
Aurelia • Essie's Restaurant

Suggested lodging
Hampton Inn & Suites

Taconic Parkway North to NY-55 E and take a left onto Clove Valley Road. At traffic circle continue straight onto Clove Road. Continue onto Chestnut Ridge Road. Turn right onto Corbin Road and right onto McCourt Road. Driving time: 15 minutes.

MADAVA FARMS | CROWN MAPLE
47 McCourt Road | Dover Plains, NY | 12522
845.877.0640
https://www.crownmaple.com/visit-madava-farms

This is the place to see and learn about the process of making maple syrup. Set on 800 acres, Madava Farms is full of maple and red maple trees. Crown Maple is one of the best maple syrups around. It's the only one I purchase. Take the sixty-minute tour of the sugarhouse where you'll see the journey of the maple sap as it travels from the trees to the barrel in their state-of-the-art facility. The tour concludes with a Crown Maple Syrup tasting. After the tour feel free to hike the property in the designated areas and take in the views

North on McCourt Road to Left onto Corbin Road. Turn right onto Chestnut Ridge Road. Turn left and stay on Chestnut Ridge Road. Turn left onto NY-343 W. Turn right onto Church Street and right onto Franklin Avenue. Driving time: 15 minutes.

AURELIA
3299 Franklin Avenue | Millbrook, NY | 12545
845.677.4720 | http://aureliarestaurant.com

Dine outdoors on the terrace or inside on Mediterranean influenced cuisine. You will find dishes made with meat and poultry sourced from the local Hudson Valley farms. They serve homemade ravioli and gnocchi with fresh soups and seasonal salads. Try their Seared Duck Breast with macerated figs, roasted potatoes, frisée, and truffle salad or their Stuffed Poblano Pepper with quinoa, mustard greens, charred corn, and soffrito. If you bring your own wine the corkage fee is $20.

Head east on Franklin Avenue and turn left onto Sharon Turnpike. Turn right onto Valley Farm Road and right onto Shunpike and left onto Wing Road. Driving time: 10 minutes.

MILLBROOK VINEYARDS & WINERY
26 Wing Road | Millbrook, NY | 12545
845.677.8383 | http://www.millbrookwine.com/

Known as the "Flagship Winery of the Hudson Valley" John Dyson purchased the 130-acre Wing Dairy Farm in 1982, his first vineyard and winemaking venture with his brother-in-law and General Manager David Bova. Winemaker John Graziano has been with them since the beginning crafting amazing award-winning wines. Try their Proprietor's Special Reserve Cabernet Franc, Block Five East Pinot Noir, and their Tocai Friulano. Grab a bite to eat at their Vineyard Café and enjoy a bottle on the grounds or in the new Four Season room overlooking the vineyard. The views are spectacular! The Millbrook portfolio goes beyond the Hudson Valley as they own Williams Selyem in Sonoma, CA, Villa Pillo, Tuscany, Italy, and Pebble Ridge Vineyards in the North Central Coast in CA. Some of these wines are available for purchase in the tasting room.

Directions: Left onto Wing Road and right onto Shunpike. Turn left onto US-44 E. Turn right onto South Road and right onto Tyrrel Road. Driving time: 15 minutes.

INNISFREE GARDENS
362 Tyrrel Road | Millbrook, NY | 12545
845.677.8000 | http://www.innisfreegarden.org/

Noted as one of the world's ten best gardens, this 150-acre Asian inspired garden was once the summer home of Walter and Marion Beck. The gardens consist of streams, waterfalls, terraces, rocks, plants and a 40-acre glacial lake. It is one of the undiscovered treasures in the Hudson Valley. Innisfree is open seasonally from May through mid-October, Wednesday through Friday 10 a.m. to 4 p.m. and weekends from 11 a.m. to 5 p.m. It will take approximately ninety minutes to tour the gardens.

Directions: Turn left onto South Road from Tyrrell and left onto US-44 W. Get on the Taconic State Parkway south. Exit Stringham Road, turn right onto Todd Hill Road and left onto Stringham Road then right onto Noxon Road. Turn right onto Lauer Road. Driving time: 20 minutes.

SPROUT CREEK FARM
34 Lauer Road | Poughkeepsie, NY | 12603
845.485.8438 | https://sproutcreekfarm.org/

Sprout Creek Farm is a working farm and educational center on 200 acres of land surrounding Sprout Creek. Visit and tour the farm. You'll see their free-range cows, sheep, goats, turkeys, chickens, and pigs. Stop into the creamery where the magic happens and view the cheese making. Their cheeses are made from their herd of grass-fed cows and goats, made in the old tradition of European farmstead cheese. Take home a container of their goat cheese (that freezes really well) or their Bogart, Toussaint, Margie to name a few. I haven't met a cheese from Sprout Creek that I didn't like.

Directions: Turn right onto Noxon Road. At light turn left onto Titusville Road. Left onto Red Oaks Mill Road. Right onto New Hackensack Road – NY-376. Right onto Raymond Avenue. Park on Raymond Avenue and walk into Vassar College. Driving time: 15 minutes.

FRANCES LEHMAN LOEB ARTS CENTER
124 Raymond Avenue | Poughkeepsie, NY | 12603
845.437.5237 | http://fllac.vassar.edu/

This art gallery was founded in 1864 and was the first college-university in the country to include an art museum in their original plan. There are over nineteen thousand works to catch a glimpse of in six galleries. You will see impressive paintings, sculptures, drawings, prints, photographs, textiles, glass, and ceramic wares. Memorable items to view are the Warburg Collection of Old Master prints, a group of Hudson River School paintings given by Matthew Vassar at the college's inception. There are many other works of art by major European and American twentieth century painters to view.

Directions: Take Raymond Avenue to 44/55 W. Stay in the right lane. As the road bends behind the Poughkeepsie Grand you go straight onto Mill Street. At the wide intersection stay to the right. Restaurant will be on the right. Driving time: 15 minutes.

ESSIE'S RESTAURANT
14 Mount Carmel Place | Poughkeepsie, NY | 12601
845.452.7181
http://www.essiesrestaurantpk.com/

You are in for a treat at Essie's from Culinary Graduate, Executive Chef/Owner, Brandon Walker, who began cooking with his mother at the age of 15. His cooking is influenced by his grandmother who is from Jamaica and his mother with southern roots. This super casual environment is elegant, yet has a bit of industrial look with the exposed brick. His specialty is taking food that you can identify with to a high level. With relationships with local artisan producers, his dishes are seasonal and based on what is available locally. Try his Chicken and Dumpling, prepared as chicken confit, lascinato kale, celery root, onions, carrots, and a Jamaican spin on the dumpling. His Pasta Bolognese with dates, apricots, almonds, aged goat cheese and preserved orange. You just might end up coming back for Sunday Brunch.

Take US – 9 south. Driving time: 8 minutes.

HAMPTON INN & SUITES
2361 South Road | Poughkeepsie, NY | 12601
845.463.7500 | http://snip.ly/yrymj

Located close to the mall, restaurants, golf, and historic sites this hotel is easy to get to. The hotel offers 129 rooms and it is pet friendly. It has free Wi-Fi, workout center, indoor pool, and complimentary breakfast. The suites are spacious and named after Hudson Valley historic places and people. A true Hudson Valley experience, the hotel is decorated with pictures of the region's historic attractions and sights.

Weekend Rendezvous

Historic Dutchess County

Three-Day Itinerary

Suggested Stops
Innisfree Gardens • Frances Lehman Loeb Arts Center • Sprout
Creek Farm • Walkway Over the Hudson • Locust Grove •
Franklin D. Roosevelt Home National Historic Site • Beacon
Farmers Market • Dia: Beacon • Bannerman's Castle Tour •
Hudson Beach Glass • Denning's Point Distillery • Madam Brett
Homestead • Mount Gulian Historic Site • 2 Way Brewing
Company

Suggested Dining
La Puerta Azul • Julie's Restaurant • Ice House • Crave
Restaurant • Red Line Diner • Poppy's Burger & Fries • Baja 328
Tequila Bar & Southwest Grill

Suggested Lodging
Hampton Inn & Suites • Courtyard by Marriott

Friday

*Directions: Taconic Parkway North to the US-44 exit toward
Poughkeepsie/Millbrook and take a right onto US-44 E. Turn right onto
South Road and right onto Tyrrel Road. Driving time: 5 minutes.*

INNISFREE GARDENS
362 Tyrrel Road | Millbrook, NY | 12545
845.677.8000 | http://www.innisfreegarden.org/

Noted as one of the world's ten best gardens, this150-acre Asian
inspired garden was once the summer home of Walter and Marion

Beck. The gardens consist of streams, waterfalls, terraces, rocks, plants and a 40-acre glacial lake. It is one of the undiscovered treasures in the Hudson Valley. Innisfree is open seasonally from May through mid-October, Wednesday through Friday 10 a.m. to 4 p.m. and weekends from 11 a.m. to 5 p.m. It will take approximately ninety minutes to tour the gardens.

Directions: Tyrell Road to left onto South Road. Left onto US-44 W. Driving time: 5 minutes.

LA PUERTA AZUL
2510 US-44 | Salt Point, NY | 12578
845-677-2985 | http://www.lapuertaazul.com/

Take one step into La Puerta Azul and you will feel like you are in Mexico complete with an indoor waterfall. The Guacamole is prepared at your table and it is delicious. They usually have live music on the weekends, so sit back, relax, and enjoy. Bringing in your own bottle is not permitted.

Directions: Left onto US-44 W. Continue onto Main Street in Poughkeesie and turn left onto Raymond Avenue. Turn right at the end of Raymond Avenue onto Hooker Avenue. At the light turn left onto Wilbur Avenue. At the end turn right onto Spackenkill Road. Go straight and turn left onto US-9 S. Hotel will be on your right. Driving time: 30 minutes.

HAMPTON INN & SUITES
2361 South Road | Poughkeepsie, NY | 12601
845.463.7500 | http://snip.ly/yrymj

Located close to the mall, restaurants, golf, and historic sites this hotel is easy to get to. The hotel offers 129 rooms and it is pet friendly. It has free Wi-Fi, workout center, indoor pool, and complimentary breakfast. The suites are spacious and named after Hudson Valley historic places and people. A true Hudson Valley experience, the hotel is decorated with pictures of the region's historic attractions and sights.

<u>Saturday</u>

Directions: Turn right and go south on US-9 and make a U turn at the next light. Go north on US-9 and take Spackenkill Road- NY-113 exit. Make a left hand turn onto Wilbur Avenue just past Oakwood School. At the end of Wilbur turn right onto Hooker Avenue. At the next light turn left onto Raymond Avenue. Julie's will be on the left after the third traffic circle. Driving time: 10 minutes.

JULIE'S RESTAURANT
49 Raymond Avenue | Poughkeepsie, NY | 12603
845.452.6078

A cozy family restaurant located by Vassar College. For a great home cooked breakfast this is the place to be and great value too. They offer a diverse menu of pancakes, omelets, breakfast wraps, and homemade muffins to get your day started.

Directions: Leave your car parked and walk up to the Frances Lehman Loeb Arts Center.

FRANCES LEHMAN LOEB ARTS CENTER
124 Raymond Avenue | Poughkeepsie, NY | 12603
845.437.5237 | http://fllac.vassar.edu/

After breakfast take a walk across the street to Vassar College. There is a beautiful lake toward the back, and then head over to the Frances Lehman Loeb Arts Center. This art gallery was founded in 1864 and was the first college-university in the country to include an art museum in their original plan. There are over nineteen thousand works to catch a glimpse of in six galleries. You will see impressive paintings, sculptures, drawings, prints, photographs, textiles, glass, and ceramic wares. Memorable items to view are the Warburg Collection of Old Master prints, a group of Hudson River School paintings given by Matthew Vassar at the college's inception. There are many other works of art by major European and American twentieth century painters to view.

Directions: Raymond Avenue to Collegeview Avenue. Left onto Fairmont Avenue. Right onto Manchester Road. Merge onto NY-55 E. Turn right onto Noxon Road just after Page Lumber. Left onto Lauer. Driving time: 15 minutes.

SPROUT CREEK FARM
34 Lauer Road | Poughkeepsie, NY | 12603
845.485.8438 | https://sproutcreekfarm.org/

Sprout Creek Farm is a working farm and educational center on 200 acres of land surrounding Sprout Creek. Visit and tour the farm. You'll see their free-range cows, sheep, goats, turkeys, chickens, and pigs. Stop into the creamery where the magic happens and view the cheese making. Their cheeses are made from their herd of grass-fed cows and goats, made in the old tradition of European farmstead cheese. Take home a container of their goat cheese (that freezes really well) or their Bogart, Toussaint, Margie to name a few. I haven't met a cheese from Sprout Creek that I didn't like.

Directions: Right onto Noxon Road to NY-55W. Turn right onto Main Street behind Civic Center. You can park in the circle or take a right onto N. Water Street as you come down Main. Just past the train station, take a left and the Ice House is on the left. There is parking just past the boat ramp as well as back up on the hill. Driving time: 20 minutes.

ICE HOUSE
1 Main Street | Poughkeepsie, NY | 12601
845.232.5783 | http://poughkeepsieicehouse.com/

Back in the day ice was harvested from the Hudson River and stored in icehouses such as the Poughkeepsie Ice House, which today is a restaurant. The exposed bricks and stamped concrete floors are reminiscent of the era before. Dine inside or out on the banks of the Hudson River and watch the sunset. Start your meal with "Le Cast" Mac n Cheese made with local cheese, or their Seafood Mac & Cheese. Choose your entreé from options such as Sesame Crusted Ahi Tuna or choose from their daily specials and sip on local brews and wine. If you bring your own bottle of wine the corkage fee is $15.

Directions: Main Street to left onto Davies Place. Right onto Mill Street. Straight onto Verazzano Blvd. Left onto Washington Street and right onto Parker Avenue. Driving time: 5 minutes. (You can also walk to the walkway from the Ice House and take the elevator to the top).

WALKWAY OVER THE HUDSON
61 Parker Avenue | Poughkeepsie, NY | 12601
https://walkway.org/

Walk off lunch on the Walkway. Once a railroad bridge at 212 ft. above the Hudson River and 1.25 miles across, it is now the longest pedestrian bridge in the world. It crosses the Hudson River from Poughkeepsie to Highland with rail trails going as far east as East Fishkill and west to New Paltz. Signage gives a brief history of the bridge, and the views are magnificent so don't forget your camera.

Directions: Parker Street to left onto Washington Street. Continue to US-9 S. At traffic light Locust Grove will be on your right. Driving time: 10 minutes.

LOCUST GROVE
2683 South Road (Rt 9) | Poughkeepsie, NY | 12601
845.454.4500 | http://www.lgny.org/

Take in some history and Morse code at the home of Samuel Morse. In 1895, William and Martha Young purchased the mansion, redecorated it, and added gardens. Today the grounds are beautiful, with gardens and hiking trails that will bring you down to the river. Take a tour of the mansion and see the Young's family collection of Hudson River School paintings and early nineteenth century American furniture. Tour the Museum Pavilion where you will see the exhibit that explores Samuel Morse's two careers, an artist first and inventor of the telegraph and Morse Code.

Directions: Take a left onto US-9 N. Driving time: 15 minutes.

FRANKLIN D. ROOSEVELT HOME
NATIONAL HISTORIC SITE
4097 Albany Post Road | Hyde Park, NY | 12538
845.229.9115 | http://snip.ly/czcui

Home to his Springwood Estate, President Franklin D. Roosevelt lived here from his birth in 1882 to 1945. Tour the property that includes grave sites, rose gardens, hiking trails, and the many places from which the President addressed the nation during his four terms as President. Roosevelt's life from the early years through his presidency, from the Great Depression to the New Deal era and World War II, are all presented here. It is also home to the first US Presidential Library.

Directions: Take a right onto US-9 S. Turn left onto Washington Street NY-9G N at Marist College. Crave is right under the Walkway. Driving time: 10 minutes.

CRAVE RESTAURANT & LOUNGE
129 Washington Street | Poughkeepsie, NY | 12601
845.452.3501 | http://www.craverestaurantandlounge.com/

Tucked under the "Walkway Over the Hudson," reservations are a must at this small quaint, fine dining restaurant that brings Manhattan to Poughkeepsie. Gracious hospitality and incredible food will have you wanting to come back. Edward Kowalski, owner, executive chef, and graduate of the Culinary Institute of America uses the freshest ingredients in a New American menu that is built around seasonal produce. Small plates make it easy to try a few different items and the regular entrees are well portioned. There is a corkage fee of $15 if you bring your own bottle. Insider's tip: if you share a taste of the wine the fee is usually waived!

Directions: Head south on Washington Street and turn right onto Verazzano Blvd. Go straight at light onto Mill Street. Left onto Davies Place and right onto Main Street. Left onto US-9 S to Fishkill. Driving time: 25 minutes.

COURTYARD BY MARRIOTT
17 Westage Drive (Rt 9 & I84) | Fishkill, NY | 12524
845.897.2400 http://snip.ly/o1k06

Located at the crossroad of the East – the intersection of Interstate 84 and Route 9 – this hotel is close to it all. You'll be greeted by a nice friendly staff and you will enjoy free Wi-Fi, fitness center, and indoor pool. They offer standard guest rooms with King, two Queens or two Doubles, and one-bedroom suites with a King and sofa bed or two Doubles and a sofa bed. Rooms are equipped with hair dryers, iron, and complementary coffee/tea.

Sunday

Directions: Just across the street. Head north on US-9.

RED LINE DINER
588 U.S. 9 | Fishkill, NY | 12524
845.765.8401 | http://dineatredline.com/

Red Line Diner is your typical but not so typical diner. You'll find your usual breakfast entreés and then some. If you like Portobello mushrooms, try their Portobello Powerhouse, mushroom cap stuffed with fresh spinach, egg whites, mozzarella cheese, and a touch of house made tomato sauce, or dine on one of their breakfast wraps or quesadillas. Don't forget to have a cup of coffee, as it's the best cup you'll have for the entire stay of your trip.

Directions: Go south on US-9 and get on I-84 W. Take exit 11 NY-9D/Wappingers Falls. Take a left off the exit onto NY 9D S. Turn right onto Beekman Street. Bear right onto Beekman Street N and continue to Long Dock Road. Take a slight right onto Red Flynn Drive. Driving time: 10 minutes.

BEACON FARMERS MARKET
Red Flynn Drive | Beacon, NY | 12580
http://www.beaconfarmersmarket.org/

Stop here to get some local produce and other items to bring home. You'll find farm fresh veggies, grass-fed beef, local cheeses, flowers, soap, wine tasting, and other culinary specialties. The market is open every Sunday from 10 a.m. to 3 p.m. from May 15 into late fall.

Directions: South on Red Flynn Drive to Long Dock Road to Beekman Street N. Turn right onto Beekman Street. It's a 2-minute car drive and a 5-minute walk.

DIA: BEACON
3 Beekman Street | Beacon, NY 12508
845.440-0100 | http://www.diaart.org/sites/main/beacon

This museum opened in the renovated Nabisco box factory on the banks of the Hudson River. Spend some time viewing contemporary art collections from the 1960's to the present. You'll see some amazing and quirky art. See works by such artists as Joseph Beuys, John Chamberlain, and Robert Irwin. The Warhol exhibit is worth the trip in itself.

Directions: Go back to the Farmers Market. Tours leave from the waterfront. Reservations are essential.

BANNERMAN'S CASTLE TOUR
http://www.bannermancastle.org/

This tour leaves from the Beacon Waterfront. As kids, we frequently passed Bannerman's Castle on the train into New York City. It remained a mystery until recently. Frank Bannerman built this fortress in the old style of Scottish castles. This island was primarily used for storing war weapons and explosives. On this thirty-minute boat ride you will learn about the history of Bannerman Castle and Pollepel Island. Once on the island a guided walking tour will take you to the castle ruins and gardens. The tours operate seasonally and must be booked in advance. Check the website for details.

Directions: Long dock Road to Beekman Street N to right onto

Beekman Street. Turn left onto Wolcott Avenue and right onto Main Street. Driving time: 5 minutes.

POPPY'S BURGER & FRIES
184 Main Street | Beacon, NY | 12508
845.765.2121 | http://www.poppyburger.com/

Get ready to bite into a juicy, grass-fed burger! Poppy's is dedicated to bringing high quality local ingredients to you at affordable prices. Chef/owner Paul Yeaple won the Food Network Show Chopped. If you are a vegetarian, no worries, as their homemade crispy bean patty with slaw, cheese, diced onions, and aioli is also delicious. If you are gluten and wheat free, your burger will be served on top of local greens. Don't forget to try their hand-cut fries or sweet potato chips. If you want a beer to go with your burger they serve New York State beer along with local wine and cider.

Directions: Keep your parking space and walk down to Hudson Beach Glass. Also check out the antique shops.

HUDSON BEACH GLASS
162 Main Street | Beacon, NY 12508
845. 440.0068 | http://www.hudsonbeachglass.com/

Located in a restored firehouse on the west end of Main Street enjoy a gallery of beautiful crafted hand blown glass pieces. If you are lucky and you are there on the day they are blowing glass you can watch them create their pieces. There is also a small art gallery upstairs with locally inspired works of art.

Directions: Head southeast on Main Street and turn left onto N. Chestnut Street. Parking is on the right. Driving time: 5 minutes.

DENNING'S POINT DISTILLERY
10 N. Chestnut Street | Beacon, NY | 12508
845.230.7905 | http://www.denningspointdistillery.com/

With the gentrification of Beacon, New York, what was once my car mechanic's garage is now Denning's Point Distillery. There are no remnants of the once garage except for the large garage door which now houses the only urban distillery in the Hudson Valley. Taste through their selection of gin, vodka, and whiskey, and on the weekend there is live music in front of the still.

Directions: If you wish, you can walk this. If not, go southwest on N Chestnut and cross Main Street. Take a left onto Henry Street and a left onto Teller Avenue. Turn right onto Van Nydeck Avenue.

MADAM BRETT HOMESTEAD
50 Van Nydeck Avenue
Beacon, NY 12508
845.831.6533 http://melzingah.awardspace.com/id5.htm

Madam Brett Homestead is the oldest house in Dutchess County, built in 1709 and listed on the National Register of Historic Places since 1976. It's a Dutch style house built for Roger and Catheryna Brett, their children and slaves when they emigrated from New York to Dutchess County. It remained in the family until 1954 and today it is maintained by the Daughters of the American Revolution. You'll find the original scalloped shingles and Dutch doors. The home's seventeen rooms are decorated with original Georgian, Empire, and Victorian furniture. Allow 45 minutes to tour the property.

Directions: Van Nydeck Avenue to Teller. Right onto Teller. Left onto Verplanck Avenue. Right onto NY-9D N. Left onto Lamplight Street. Lamplight Street becomes Sterling Street. Driving time: 10 minutes.

MOUNT GULIAN HISTORIC SITE
145 Sterling Street | Beacon, NY | 12508
845.831.8172 | http://www.mountgulian.org/

A reconstructed eighteenth century Dutch manor house, the original home served as the headquarters of Major General Friedrich Wilhelm von Steuben during the American Revolutionary War. The land where the house stands was purchased from the Wappingers

Native Americans in 1683. The original mansion was destroyed by fire in 1931. In 1966, a descendant of the Verplank family founded Mount Gulian to restore it and it was completed in 1975. Inside you will find artifacts related to the Verplank family. It is open from April through October.

Directions: Head back on Sterling Street to Lamplight Street. Take a right onto NY-9D S. Right onto Beekman Street and left onto W Main Street. Driving time: 5 minutes.

2 WAY BREWING COMPANY
18 W Main Street | Beacon, NY | 12508
845.202.7334 | http://www.2waybrewingcompany.com/

Located overlooking the Hudson River this micro craft brewery opened its doors in September 2014 when 30-year-old Michael O'Herron came home from Colorado to follow his passion. 2 Way is named after the Hudson River, as it is a two-way river, a river that flows both ways. Their specialty beer is Confusion, made from proprietary blend of yeast Michael cultivated from his parents' farm. The tasting room is rustic and you are encouraged to sign the bar… just ask for a sharpie.

East on W Main Street towards Beekman Street. Left onto Beekman Street and right onto NY-9D S. Left onto Main Street. Driving time: 5 minutes.

BAJA 328 TEQUILA BAR & SOUTHWEST GRILL
328 Main Street | Beacon NY | 12508
845.838.2252 | http://www.baja328.com/

Since you spent the day in Beacon, it's only fitting that you end it there. From the minute you walk into Baja the vibe is chic New York City style and upbeat. Order a margarita and choose your tequila from over one hundred varieties, or perhaps a tequila flight. Dine on fresh authentic Southwestern cuisine that will have you wanting more. Bringing your own wine will cost you a $20 corkage fee.

Directions: Head west on Main Street. Take a right onto NY-9D. Get on I-84 E. Go down two exits and get off on NY-9 N. Turn at light at Westage Business Center. Driving time: 10 minutes.

COURTYARD BY MARRIOTT
17 Westage Drive (Rt 9 & I84) | Fishkill, NY | 12524
845.897.2400 http://snip.ly/o1k06

Located at the crossroad of the East – the intersection of Interstate 84 and Route 9 – this hotel is close to it all. You'll be greeted by a nice friendly staff and you will enjoy free Wi-Fi, fitness center, and indoor pool. They offer standard guest rooms with King, two Queens or two Doubles, and one-bedroom suites with a King and sofa bed or two Doubles and a sofa bed. Rooms are equipped with hair dryers, iron, and complementary coffee/tea.

TASTING NOTES

Date:_____ Tasting With:_____ Tasting Location:_____

Wine Name:_____ Winery (Producer):_____

Country:_____ Region:_____Varietals:_____

Color Depth

Watery
Pale
Medium
Dark

Notes:_____

Color Hue

White Wine: *Greenish | Yellow | Straw Yellow | Pale Yellow | Gold | Amber*
Red Wine: *Purplish | Ruby | Red | Garnet | Brick | Brown*
Rosé Wine: *Light Pink | Pink | Salmon |Orangish | Copper*

Clarity

Clear | Slight Haze | Cloudy | Floaters

Notes:_____

Aroma Intensity

Low | Moderate | Aromatic |Strong

Notes:_____

Aromas

Notes:_____

_____

Sweetness

Dry | Semi Dry | Semi Sweet | Sweet

Notes:_____

Body

Light | medium | medium to full
| full bodied | heavy

Notes:_____

Acidity

Tart | Crisp | Fresh | Smooth | Flabby

Notes:_____

_____

Tannins

Low | Medium | Lots

Notes:_____

Type of Tannins

Soft | rounded feeling | dry

Balance

Good | Fair | Unbalanced

Flavor Intensity

Weak | Moderate | Tasty | Powerful

Finish

Short | Medium | Long | Lingering

Flavors

Notes:_____

_____

_____

Overall Tasting Impression

Notes:_____

_____

_____

TASTING NOTES

Date:_____ Tasting With:_____ Tasting Location:_____

Wine Name:_____ Winery (Producer):_____

Country:_____ Region:_____Varietals:_____

Color Depth   ## Color Hue

Watery   White Wine: *Greenish | Yellow | Straw Yellow | Pale Yellow | Gold | Amber*
Pale   Red Wine: *Purplish | Ruby | Red | Garnet | Brick | Brown*
Medium   Rosé Wine: *Light Pink | Pink | Salmon |Orangish | Copper*
Dark

Notes:_____

Clarity   ## Aroma Intensity

Clear | Slight Haze | Cloudy | Floaters   *Low | Moderate | Aromatic |Strong*

Notes:_____   Notes:_____

Aromas   ## Sweetness

Notes:_____

_____   *Dry | Semi Dry | Semi Sweet | Sweet*

Notes:_____

Body   ## Acidity

Light | medium | medium to full   *Tart | Crisp | Fresh | Smooth | Flabby*

| full bodied | heavy   Notes:_____

Notes:_____   _____

Tannins   ## Type of Tannins   ## Balance

Low | Medium | Lots   *Soft | rounded feeling | dry*   *Good | Fair | Unbalanced*

Notes:_____

Flavor Intensity   ## Flavors

Weak | Moderate | Tasty | Powerful   Notes:_____

Finish

Short | Medium | Long | Lingering   _____

Overall Tasting Impression

Notes:_____

_____

_____

TASTING NOTES

Date:_____ Tasting With:_____ Tasting Location:_____

Wine Name:_____ Winery (Producer):_____

Country:_____ Region:_____ Varietals:_____

Color Depth

Watery
Pale
Medium
Dark
Notes:_____

Color Hue

White Wine: *Greenish | Yellow | Straw Yellow | Pale Yellow | Gold | Amber*
Red Wine: *Purplish | Ruby | Red | Garnet | Brick | Brown*
Rosé Wine: *Light Pink | Pink | Salmon |Orangish | Copper*

Clarity

Clear | Slight Haze | Cloudy | Floaters
Notes:_____

Aroma Intensity

Low | Moderate | Aromatic |Strong
Notes:_____

Aromas

Notes:_____
_____

Sweetness

Dry | Semi Dry | Semi Sweet | Sweet
Notes:_____

Body

Light | medium | medium to full
| full bodied | heavy
Notes:_____

Acidity

Tart | Crisp | Fresh | Smooth | Flabby
Notes:_____
_____

Tannins

Low | Medium | Lots

Type of Tannins

Soft | rounded feeling | dry

Balance

Good | Fair | Unbalanced

Notes:_____

Flavor Intensity

Weak | Moderate | Tasty | Powerful

Finish

Short | Medium | Long | Lingering

Flavors

Notes:_____
_____
_____

Overall Tasting Impression

Notes:_____
_____
_____

A Note From Debbie

I hope you enjoy your travels through the Hudson Valley. On your travels if you find a cute restaurant, new winery, brewery, distillery or cidery, please let me know and I will include them in the next edition. If you find any establishment in this book to be closed or inaccurate, please let me know. I welcome your feedback.

Debbie

Debbie Gioquindo, CTC, CSW, WLS
debbie@hudsonvalleywinegoddess.com

www.HudsonValleyWineGoddess.com

Made in the USA
Middletown, DE
18 May 2017